Gay Culture in America

GAY CULTURE IN AMERICA

Essays from the Field

Edited by Gilbert Herdt

BEACON PRESS

Boston

Beacon Press
25 Beacon Street
Boston, Massachusetts 02108

Beacon Press books
are published under the auspices of
the Unitarian Universalist Association of Congregations.

99 98 97 96 95 94 93 92   8 7 6 5 4 3 2 1

Text design by Diane Levy

Library of Congress Cataloging-in-Publication Data
Gay culture in America: essays from the field / edited by Gilbert
  Herdt.
        p. cm.
    Includes bibliographical references.
    ISBN 0-8070-7914-6 (cloth)
    1. Gay men—United States. 2. Subculture. I. Herdt, Gilbert H.,
        1949– .
HQ76.2.U5G37 1991
306′.1—dc20   91-12819
                                                          CIP

*To the gay men and lesbians
of American intellectual life
whose vision is changing our society*

Contents

Preface

This book was inspired by my colleagues in anthropology and sociology, to whom I am indebted. Three years ago I chaired a symposium on gay culture at the annual meeting of the American Anthropological Association. (At the same meeting a parallel session on lesbian culture was held, but the results of that session are not published here.) The participants pointed out the gap that existed in anthologies since Martin Levine's collection *Gay Men* was published in 1979. Little more than a decade has passed, but how much has changed since then. Now we might say that a gay and lesbian culture has come into being.

Our efforts to integrate studies of gay culture, identities, and self-concepts critically examine the meanings and themes of "gay" in American society. We touch on debates regarding what is believed to be "essential" or "socially constructed" in gay men's cultural organization and psychosocial development. Our interest here lies in the legitimacy of the gay experience and the authenticity of gay culture, in both its public and its personal dimensions. We write from the perspectives of cultural anthropology, sociology, and developmental psychology. Thus, our dual concerns with culture and gay men's lives create different questions and interests than those of the arts and literature.

During the past few years, there has been a greatly expanded interest in lesbian identities and communities, both as they are distinct from and as they relate to gay men. While these issues are beyond the scope of the present volume, we hope that this contribution will lead to new avenues of inquiry and understanding.

I have been fortunate to receive the help and advice of several colleagues, among whom I wish especially to thank my friends Marty Levine and Andy Boxer. I am also grateful to Michael Kimmel, Stephen O. Murray, and Richard Herrell for their comments on this book and to John Gagnon for his insights. JoAnne Wykoff first interested us in Beacon Press, and Deborah Chasman has been our faithful editor. We are grateful to them.

Whatever contribution this volume makes is possible only because of those gay and lesbian intellectuals who have come out of the closet and helped in the building of our own cultural traditions, and to them this book is dedicated. They will know that our efforts will be eclipsed one day by a new generation of younger scholars whose work will surpass our own.

Gilbert Herdt
Chicago
February 1991

Introduction: Culture, History, and Life Course of Gay Men

Gilbert Herdt and Andrew Boxer

Nineteen ninety-two marks the twenty-third anniversary of the famous Stonewall riot in New York, which sparked a cultural revolution that transformed gay lives. Since that time, the focus of the study of homosexuality has shifted from the secretive bar to the far more elaborate gay and lesbian communities of major cities around the world. Stonewall was certainly not the only political reaction of gay men to social oppression, but it was a watershed in the political activism that had been growing from the late 1950s onward.[1] The many commentaries on pre- and post-Stonewall events presage the present work, which seeks to examine key roles, images, events, and symbolic processes in the culture of American gay men.

Since the 1960s, the growth and development of both gay and lesbian culture and individuals' identities as gays or lesbians has proved an especially dynamic coevolution in American society. We might think of this as a slow waltz during which the dancers change steps and costumes as their very essence alters in the eyes of their partners. Thus, American society and the gay movement have formed an uneasy partnership. Even while we have been moving toward stabilization, however, the specter of AIDS has appeared on the scene, destabilizing gay culture as the disease attacks individuals and the enemies of homosexuality renew their attack on gays because of the disease.[2]

A generation ago, the issues raised by the presence of gays and lesbians were dismissed by the diagnosis "homosexuality," the negative connotations of which included psychopathology and the stigma of

1

disease discourse in psychiatry. The prejudice hidden in that diagnosis was ignored.[3] But then the concept of "homophobia" did not exist because the gay and lesbian movement itself barely did. Following the declassification of homosexuality as a disease by the American Psychiatric Association in 1972—a deeply political and contentious process—the gay movement proceeded to move ahead on several fronts.[4] The rise of the women's movement and the Gay Liberation Front in the 1960s spurred changes in civil rights and social values that were to have far-reaching consequences, not only for the shape of American society, but also for the meaning of gay selfhood, social roles, and organization. Many inquiries into the category "gay" emerged in Western countries. In sociology, these inquiries concerned the roles, institutions, and networks of gay men. In psychology, they required the study of a new cohort—gays and lesbians—with distinctive developmental pathways and new cognitions, goals, and mental health outcomes. In anthropology, they suggested the shared elements of the gay and lesbian experience, including such new social relationships as that between one's gay lover and one's parents (see chapter 6). Today, these studies lead us to recognize that even adolescents aspire to a gay cultural system and that these aspirations are realized through gay support groups.[5] It is true that these adolescents' lives are tainted by the dread and sorrow of AIDS. However, the disease has also created such new and extraordinary cultural symbols as the AIDS "quilt," which commemorates those who have died and attests the collective community.

Two fundamental issues vex the study of gay men in contemporary American society. First, is there a distinct and legitimate gay culture, and, if there is, what shape has it taken? To answer this, we assume the prior existence of various mainstream cultural motifs in many domains of gay lives that transcend the sexual.[6] Some observers have seen only the sexual or else what is purely peripheral to American culture. Instead of a gay culture, they find only a gay "enclave," "life-style," or "subgroup," that is, only spurious conceptions of gay and lesbian relationships and lives.[7] Is it legitimate, by contrast, to speak of a "women's culture" or an "Afro-American culture" in America? Both the legitimacy and the authenticity of gay lives are thereby called into question. Second, if a distinct and legitimate gay culture does exist or is at least emerging, how has it created a new life course for the individual gay man over the past twenty years? Are there generational differences—a "generation gap"—between younger and older gay men?[8] If there are, our second question is of necessity linked to our first.

Thus, when we ask whether gay men are born and not made, we must simultaneously wonder whether gay culture has, paradoxically, been made and not born. Are these twin developments—gay identity development and the emergence of a gay culture—"natural," inevitable, and authentic? How shall we measure the authenticity of a new identity and its symbolic foundation in a newly born culture?[9] When is a cultured pearl denied its precious status by virtue of artificial design? These questions lead us to agree with many scholars who feel increasingly dissatisfied with intellectual frameworks that polarize gay identities as either socially shaped or biologically determined.

The "Homosexual" and "Gay" Categories in Culture

It is never easy to define any cultural group in our highly pluralistic society. Such criteria as race, class, gender, geographic region, socioeconomic position, and political beliefs are often hard to reconcile—or even to identify as representative of a particular group. Compounding the problem of defining a legitimate gay culture, urban and rural variations in sexual expression have, over the past three centuries, been associated with competing sexual ideologies, especially those of "reproduction" and "pleasure."[10] The historical cultural categories "homosexual" and "gay" in particular must be taken into account in understanding the formation of gay culture. We shall argue for the existence of a gay *cultural system,* with a distinct identity and distinct institutions and social supports in particular times and places. We see this as a major battleground for social change in America into the twenty-first century.

"Authenticity" as a criterion of gay culture is meant to indicate here what is genuine as opposed to what is spurious in gay men's worldviews and relationships. Relevant to this issue is Edward Sapir's discussion of the anthropological problem of what makes a culture great or feeble, balanced or unstable, satisfying or frustrating to its natives.[11] We do not presume to hold God's truth in such matters, and we are aware that many will feel uneasy in raising the question. However, a critical inquiry into the nature of this rapidly changing cultural community is necessary if we are to see the development of human lives in a system of continuing oppression,[12] one that is fascinated by its own hedonism and liberal democratic conception of human nature.[13] To ask, What is authentic in gay men's lives? is to question what is optimal, valuable, and life cherishing. Ultimately, gay culture is a perspective on human nature and the world, not just on sexuality and consumerism.[14] The search for authenticity thus leads to an understanding of meaning and purpose in adults alive today and to a consideration of the institutions and opportunities for socialization that will be available to the gay youths of tomorrow.[15]

For more than a century, "homosexuality" reigned supreme, until, riding a wave of social activism, "gay" began to overtake it. Today they are competing identities in every sense.[16] The term "homosexual," coined in 1869 by Benkert, found its way into the medical and historical literature, where homosexuality was viewed pathologically, as a disease—especially the disease of effeminacy.[17] Its victims were largely male; female homosexuals were to remain invisible.[18] The early sexologists, uniting with the turn-of-the-century homosexual liberation proponents (such as Karl Ulrichs and Magnus Hirschfield), tried to humanize the pathology and stigma, but not ultimately to challenge it.[19] Their effort was based less on a reclassification of homosexuality than on human rights arguments accepting homosexuality as the intractable nature of the invert.[20] Even the 1972 reclassification of homosexuality as a life-style rather than as a disease, while socially progressive, was ultimately ambivalent regarding the life-style argument.[21]

"Gay" as a category is not prominent in popular discourse until the late 1950s and early 1960s (though gay novelists such as Edmund White make it seem prevalent earlier). By the 1970s, it was increasingly common; by the 1980s, it was canonical in the gay cultural system, though still not in American culture writ large. For instance, the *New York Times* did not allow the word "gay" to appear in its pages until the mid-1980s. However, the use of the word "gay" is less important than, its pragmatic consequences secondary, this new cultural system "gay"—which increasingly marks a full spectrum of social life: not only same-sex desires but gay selves, gay neighbors, and gay social practices that are distinctive of our affluent, postindustrial society.

It seems ideologically significant that a hundred years of research on homosexuality, marking its beginnings with Karl Ulrichs's twelve-volume study in the nineteenth century, have so very often been concerned with the causes rather than the outcomes of "homosexuality."

To ask, for instance, why people desire the same sex is very different from asking whether they are happy, or successful, or competent. Particularly in medical research and disease discourse, the issue has been fixated on individual development more than on the formation of a gay cultural community.[22] Gradually, however, the focus of such studies—and the source of these studies as well—has shifted. Scholars of "homosexuality" are more and more gays or lesbians themselves, and they are concerned, not with the etiology of a "disease," but with the cultural history of lesbians and gays, with elucidating the early outlines of "homosexuality." They have thus revealed that a more heterogeneous collection of people and institutions is gathered under the rubric "homosexuality" than even Kinsey and his colleagues had discovered.[23] The shadowy and secret lives of a whole generation of older homosexuals no longer reflect the social reality experienced by gays today.[24] A hundred homosexuals do not, say we, a gay make.

"Gay" today is perceived—more in urban centers, and more frequently among younger cohorts—as a distinct cultural category. Its signs and symbols are no longer the stigmatized homosexual secrets of James Baldwin's "Giovanni's Room," and its images are not those of such movies as the 1960s *The Boys in the Band*. Gay culture is now characterized by shared institutions and by such positive images as the fiction of Edmund White and David Leavitt and the film *Long Time Companion*. The Gay Pride Day Parade more than anything symbolizes this change, permitting the greatest opportunities for full community participation (see chapter 9). "Gay," in other words, represents more than a sexual act, as "homosexual" once did—more even than "clone" (see chapter 2). It signifies identity and role, of course, but also a distinctive system of rules, norms, attitudes, and, yes, beliefs from which the culture of gay men is made, a culture that sustains the social relations of same-sex desire.[25]

It is commonly agreed that homosexuality and heterosexuality are distinctive prototypes of sexuality,[26] but the difference between homosexual and gay is still largely ignored. Bell and Weinberg could speak of "homosexualities" in the plural, for example, without distinguishing "gay" from "homosexual" life-styles or gay as a new pathway of social development that involved "coming out" and social activism. Even Kinsey's controversial emphasis on behavior obscured the differences between homosexual and gay: he reduced cultural meaning and social action to sex acts, thus obviating people's particular desires in an imposed framework.[27] Such work belongs to a historical period that precedes gay activism. What we still have to face is the confusion between the concepts homosexual and gay, compounded by a confusion between folk and analytic categories still present in research.

Much of the prevailing confusion comes from our American preoccupation with the causes of homosexuality. Seldom, for instance, do we ask about the causes of heterosexuality—owing, no doubt, to the influence of the "disease model" of homosexuality.[28] Freud, searching for biological bisexuality, assumed heterosexuality to be the norm.[29] Cross-cultural researchers continue to argue that absent fathers and dominant mothers "cause" homosexuality when the evidence for such a model is in some societies ambiguous and in others nonexistent.[30] Nearly every form of mental illness, including schizophrenia, has in the past been associated with homosexuality.[31] Psychiatry and psychoanalysis have recently, and unfortunately, reified the disease model, although there are important signs of change in this regard.[32] Now more than ever, a cultural model is needed to free up the historical consciousness.

Ironically, by stressing the causes of *individual* examples of homosexuality, American cultural discourse has obscured and ignored the causes of collective "homosexual" roles and "gay" culture, thus rejecting the legitimacy of any inquiry into the origins and authenticity of the gay community. As the debate emerged in the 1960s, a different strategy placed homosexuality culturally and spatially either within the domain of "deviance" and "deviant subgroups" or within that of the management of stigma and disfigured identity.[33] The development of homophile movements in the 1950s and 1960s challenged this imagery, leading to the gay liberation movement[34] and to the rewriting of history and society so much in evidence today. Anthropologists— building on the insights of gender researchers—have stressed important differences between sexual behavior and cultural identity.[35] Stigma remains, of course—for the general public and even many specialists, "homosexual" is still interchangeable with "gay," and any attempt to assert "gay" identity must contest the claim of stigma, in self and social action.

Confusion between homosexual and gay also taints our understanding of the coming-out process, in spite of the fact that much headway has been made. Some stage model theories among psychologists and sociologists, though sensitive to successive same-sex desires in experience, attention, recognition, and declaration of the person's identity and meanings, are perplexingly vague in differentiating gay and homosexual as distinct cultural systems and life-course trajectories.[36] Kenneth Plummer, for instance, mentions several sorts of "potential sources for homosexual identification," including sexual experience with people of one's own sex, strong emotional attachments to or daydreaming about the same sex, attachments to cultural objects (e.g., football boots!), feeling gender confused, feeling different, and participating in social or cultural events or activities that result in being labeled gay by others.[37] Yet Plummer, as are anthropologists, is sensitive to new stages and degrees of acculturation and to commitment to the gay and lesbian cultural system.[38] Here, the fact of being gay is not the same thing as living one's life openly as a gay person and a member of the gay community;[39] the ultimate arrival point, however, depends on social status and culture.

We are not concerned with ideal, Platonic definitions of homosexual or gay desire.[40] We have in mind a higher-order issue about how tightly bound—that is, how rule bound, inclusive, and cohesive in their shared signs and symbols—the "homosexual" and "gay" cultural systems are.[41] Take, for example, the issue of "declaration." If we ask, Has this individual "come out" to many (or most) significant others? and the answer is no, that person still operates under the "homosexual" system. But if we ask, Who has this person come out to? Why has he or she come out? What job has he or she taken? etc., the potential answers present a wide range of social relationships, cultural activities, and personal intentions that challenge the preconceptions about and the accepted ontology of homosexuality. In fact, the answers may indicate that we have a "gay" person on our hands. This point illustrates that "coming out" can be a lifelong process: people go through identity stages at different rates and with different experiences.[42] Yet we are still left with the central cultural problem, What does a person come out *to be?* What are his or her educational and career goals, his or her expectations regarding family relationships and sexual or romantic partnerships?

As Herdt has shown from the literature on adolescent homosexuality, four ontological preconceptions still profoundly color an understanding—both among the youths concerned and those researchers who have studied them (especially outsiders who are not gay)—of the developmental processes of becoming "gay."[43] These are as follows.

First, people assume that the youths are heterosexual: everyone should be straight growing up. Second, adolescent homosexuals privately experience isolation; they feel stigmatized (internal homophobia) because they desire the same sex. Third, to express their desires erotically, homosexuals must act or dress like the opposite sex, being gender reversed in self-identity and behavior. Finally, anyone who has homo-erotic desires must be like everyone else who has them, thus conforming to the stereotyped symbolic images of "homosexuality" in the social imagination of the hegemonic culture that oppresses homosexuals. The mythology of the "homosexual" has been imprisoned by these preconceptions of homosexuals as queers, faggots, and fairies—but not completely.

From the Homosexual Bar to the
Gay Pride Day Parade

In the Stonewall Riot of 1969, to vulgarize it, was consummated the anger and frustration of a small group of homosexual "queens," who fought back against police harassment, their fight leading them from the oppressive, secretive bar to the streets. Most everyone knows that story, but fewer are aware of the political activism that led up to the riot.[44] This moment in American history, this shedding of secrecy, serves as a symbol of the many major changes that followed and the less significant ones that came before. Secrecy had spawned what Eve Sedgwick calls the "epistemology of the closet," the fabric of gay culture.[45] But the "out-of-the-closets-and-into-the-streets" rhetoric did not in itself change the general perception that "homosexual" life-styles embrace "unorthodox sexuality."[46] Neither did it soon change the individualized nature of coming out as a declaration to others of a different sexual orientation. Nor did it immediately challenge the "camp" sensibility that celebrated the old homosexuality—the "camp" aesthetic of speech and dress more easily lent itself to subversive attack than to direct cultural or personal transformation.[47]

Here is the problem facing gay sensibility: its roots are in cultural and personal histories that largely predate gay culture as we now know it—the symbolic expressions of Gay Pride Day parades, pink triangles, or the macho gay clone, complete with leather boots. It is indeed telling that the event that we associate most with the founding of gay culture in the popular imagination originated in a spatial/metaphoric change—from an old closet bar to the streets of New York. It remains laden with the power politics and the implosion/explosion of self-secrecy in which that riot involved all participants. The fact that the New York gay community had a difficult time getting the mayor to place a plaque at the site of the riot further suggests that the explosion has thus far been contained. In the long term, however, gay culture has developed mainly through cultural and social movements and events, of which we highlight two: the consolidation of gay urban neighborhoods and the increasing national recognition given to the Gay Pride Day Parade.

How precisely did the gay neighborhood contribute to the forging of a distinctive gay and lesbian cultural system? Two lines of inquiry provide answers to this question. The first concerns the recruitment and immigration patterns of such major gay urban centers as New York, San Francisco, Chicago, and Los Angeles (see chapter 4). Manuel Castell's impressive analysis suggests that the demographic density of San Francisco's Castro district heightened gay sociality by dense interaction and political strength in numbers.[48] A self-recruitment factor led to gay men desiring—rather than being forced—to reside there. The concept "ghetto" does not apply to the Castro for this reason. In chapter 4, Steven Murray writes that gays came to the Castro or Greenwich Village in search of more freedom and acceptance and for the *communitas* of belonging, one meaning of culture. The rhetoric of the prior generation advised, "Go to the cities." How much times have changed since the folk hero Howard Brown wrote, "When the homosexual flees his small safe home town for the big, strange city, he cannot count on finding either a populace more enlightened or legal protection more humane than what he has left behind. He finds, if he is lucky, anonymity and others like himself—a subculture within whose purlieus and preserves he can find friends."[49] Contrast that sad image to Martin Levine's self-confident conclusions of a decade ago, when he spoke of the self-conscious formation of a "homosexual culture" in New York, Los Angeles, and San Francisco, leading to great openness in life-style, and, possibly, a concomitant "heterosexual flight" into the suburbs.[50]

We might argue that a new trend in gay culture has emerged. In his study of the gay "satellite communities" of Los Angeles, Michael Gorman suggests that the existence of gay culture no longer requires a dense gay population (see chapter 3). A generalized level of social tolerance makes living in such situations possible today. There is also room in the suburbs for gay life-styles, but, as Frederick Lynch shows, such life-styles are more akin to the older "homosexual" than the newer "gay" cultural system.

The second line of inquiry that we might pursue concerns the kind of sociality this urban culture promotes among gay men. How are their social relationships conducive to a more inclusive gay worldview? By "sociality" we mean here a system of rules and norms that structures social being and moral relationships. The processes of *coming out* and then *coming to* gay neighborhoods culturally condition the ideas and feelings of gays. Greater social acceptance enables these men to find the passion and intense male bonding denied them elsewhere. Such *communitas* has facilitated a new level of cultural identification with the social community in the lives of gay men (see chapter 2).

If the gay neighborhood is not a ghetto, then certainly it is less an asylum. Its citizens are not inmates, not physically confined. Yet the nature of the issues that Goffman explores in his classic essay on mental patients and other marginals affords a perspective for contrasting homosexual and gay as categories of American social life. "Homosexuality" in an earlier era meant the stigma and suffering of discredited selfhood. The stigma was so contagious that its "disease" could contaminate even family, coworkers, and straight friends simply by association. The emergence of the homosexual ghetto helped change all this. Like the asylum, the ghetto neighborhood set up a barrier between the homosexual and the world at large, hence a "curtailment of self" with negative effects that became part of the coming-out processes. The ghetto neighborhood, in other words, ultimately compelled the formation of a new cultural order, complete with retraining and resocialization (see chapter 1). The moral career of the closeted homosexual man who went to San Francisco or New York and became an openly gay man represented a reaction against homophobia. By glorifying in the "intense contamination" that straights felt in their presence, such men converted that contamination into the social practices, politics, and sexuality of the "gay"—a cleansing of gay culture resulting in a new persona. Gay neighborhoods thus built a sociality contrary to that of their heterosexist surrounds. Much as Goffman describes the asylum as a "milieu of personal failures in which one's fall from grace is continuously pressed home," the new gay neighborhoods symbolically reversed the situation, in the folkways and gay humor that ultimately paved the way for the success stories of business and social life that came from embracing gay-segregated living.[51]

The stigma of homosexuality thus paved the way for a gay cultural system built on its crumbling foundations, at least in the big cities. Attitudes about "gay" increasingly suggest a fundamental transformation in perspective. Stonewall meant that gays no longer had to hover in secret bars to pass the time or hide from local authorities or the next-door neighbors; it symbolized the beginning of the end of closet homosexuality. In the gay neighborhoods of San Francisco, New York, and Los Angeles, the neighbors are usually gay or at least sympathetic, and the authorities are gay or mindful of gay political power.

This transition from homosexual (secret) to gay (public) also signifies a transformation of gay social and cultural concerns to a larger, even global arena. The social investment of gays in their communities is more intense now, though some see AIDS as undermining this.[52] A new cultural consciousness is emerging: social networks of gay and lesbian friends and friends of friends crisscross our country. A larger national scene expands not only mobility but social reality.

Tonnies's well-known contrast between *Gemeinschaft* and *Gesellschaft* is useful to understanding gay culture here.[53] As sociopolitical changes have supported the existence of more urban communities of gay social interest—a more decided identification as gay and thus a greater degree of *communitas,* whether in Dallas or Seattle—a larger national urban culture (*Gesellschaft*) was not only possible but inevitable. For this reason, gay is no longer merely an enclave or a life-style;[54] personal commitment to a new order of public good now prevails in the meccas of the Castro and Greenwich Village. Aside from national gay newspapers and periodicals, organizations such as the Lamda Legal Defense and Education Fund, the National Gay and Lesbian Task Force, and more recently the "Names Project" (to commemorate those who have died from AIDS) have crystallized a new moral order of gay prosocial attitudes and political activism across the country.

This shift from *Gemeinschaft* to *Gesellschaft,* from gay community to gay culture nationally, has been symbolized as much as anything by our national liberation day: the Gay Pride Day Parade, held in late June, to commemorate the Stonewall riot. Richard Herrell's path-breaking analysis of the parade in Chicago reveals the emergence of community pride and commitment (see chapter 8). Yet he also provides a means of understanding how the simultaneous holding of the parade throughout towns and cities across the United States consolidates in this symbolic process an emerging *Gesellschaft*, a more inclusive gay culture vis-à-vis other pluralistic cultural systems within our society.

What makes Chicago's Newtown neighborhood a gay *Gemeinschaft*, Herrell asks? It is a "place to be gay"—constructed out of a diverse neighborhood history, pre-Stonewall—and a gay place in that its inhabitants and visitors are safe from abuse, can meet friends and attend gay functions, and patronize gay businesses. Both Murray's account of the gay community in San Francisco (see chapter 4) and Levine's of the "clone" culture of Greenwich Village (see chapter 2) compare favorably to this urban sociality. These urban centers meet Herrell's criterion of a place that is safe from abuse. We must not underestimate this boundary criterion for the authenticity of a gay culture. Gorman finds in Los Angeles a more diffuse collection of "gay satellite communities" spread out across a wide area, but distinctive of that city's ethos (see chapter 3). A thriving gay cultural system emerges from the patchwork. Lynch's study of southern California suburban gays is a nice example of such a satellite community, though it shows as well the incomplete transition from the homosexual to the gay cultural models (see chapter 6).

Without protection from the violence of homophobia and the promise—however utopian at the moment—of protection from discrimination, no social community can long endure or marshall the energy and resources necessary to construct a culture. Gerstell and her colleagues write of coming out in Chicago's Newtown neighborhood as a process of widening circles of declaration of gay identity.[55] The process may developmentally mirror gay culture formation today: anchored in the more secure circle of Chicago's gay neighborhood, youthful gays expand their selfhood along with their social networks (see chapter 1). Gay men's identities derive from self-interests, Herrell says, not from parents and peers in childhood, as is the case with straights. This is more true of Anglo youths than of other ethnic groups, as Carrier suggests in his portrait of a gay Mexican-American man (see chapter 8). John Peterson explores how the dual pressures of racism and homophobia affect black gay men's same-sex behaviors (see chapter 6). The discovery and confirmation of gay selfhood proceeds through social relationships. First in sex, then in love, Herrell says, selfhood instantiates gay culture. Herrell, Murray, and others argue that AIDS has deemphasized sex among gay men.[56] "Less sex is more," Murray quips. Because being gay is spatially and metaphorically identified with urban cores, as is AIDS, the repression of sexuality is an understandable expression of contemporary popular culture. Being safe now means contingent sex, negotiated sexuality.[57] AIDS has hence obliterated any easy account, constructionist or essentialist, of the safety and danger of sex in urban gay culture while it has politically activated local communities in unprecedented ways no less controversial in gay sociality.[58] The gay organization Act Up vitally illustrates this point throughout major cities in America.

Perhaps the deeper point is that sexuality is more basic to gay men's views of their being and nature. Gagnon suggests that what made the development of gay culture in the 1960s and 1970s possible is also what made it distinctive in our country: "An openness of sexual expression and a new cult of manliness."[59] For instance, adolescent females in a New York high school find the gay circle the only open discourse arena for expressing desires and discussing sexual experiences.[60] With sexuality so pivotal in gay experience, anal sex (among other sexual forms) increased.[61] And AIDS risk increased. Bisexuality became more common. These implications of AIDS are ever present throughout the chapters of this book. Yet there is more. Eroticism is not only easier in the gay culture; it is more a part of gay men's view of human nature. Freud's "polymorphous perverse" idea of the erotic has found a congenial home in gay culture.[62] When coupled with the new masculinity—Levine referred to it as "clone culture"—the transformation from gay enclave or life-style to distinctive culture was made complete.[63] Because of AIDS and other sociopolitical changes, it is not surprising that clone masculinity has died, Levine now says (see chapter 2). Its death, like that of the decline of homosexuality as a cultural system, has hastened the rise of a more vital gay culture, testifying to the complex symbolic transformations taking place in America.

Gay Self and Life Course

These historical and political changes suggest that gay culture is now simultaneously creating a new life course for the gay man in America. This "cultural life course" (to use Robert LeVine's concept) embodies same-sex desire and what many refer to as "life-style" goals and social networks.[64] "The truth of the matter," said Martin Levine, "is that gay life-styles are a far cry from stereotyped images" and vary to the same extent as those of heterosexuals."[65]

As sociopolitical changes have hastened the visibility of the gay and lesbian movement in national forums and media—and here the AIDS epidemic has been pivotal—the gay life course anticipates coming out as its most significant developmental event.[66] This cultural notion—coming out—is seen more as a sequence of steps rather than as a single happening. The stage models of (mostly) gay and lesbian psychologists increasingly recognize this series of life events.[67] They reproduce the folk model of gays themselves in this regard. Herdt views coming out as a "rite of passage," the vitality and sacred character of which varies across generations and cultures.[68] Murray relates remarkable changes in the San Francisco community that have contributed to the meanings of coming out there among diverse ethnic groups (see chapter 4). We sense increasingly, however, that other milestones and features of the gay life course need more recognition now—alongside the highly clustered experiences of coming out in the teens and twenties for most, though certainly not all, gay men.

While the old specter of the stigma and disease model of homosexuality is still a negation of the gay life course, the many published critiques of this model are now so well known and integrated into our folklore that they form a stable mythology of what *homosexuality* was before *gay* came to be. Gay fiction—from such writers as David Leavitt and Edmund White—gives a human voice to this mythology, further consolidating the shared meanings of gay culture.

Science is another matter, as Henry Minton has shown.[69] Compassion and progressive attitudes do not automatically translate into scientific understanding or the acceptance of homosexuality, as, for instance, in Terman's famous longitudinal study of exceptional people, including some who were homosexual.[70] In spite of his humanism, their fate was interpreted in the negative images of disease.

According to Minton, Terman himself was not to blame; the bias "lies in his professional identity"—the old view that same-sex desire made homosexuality pathological.[71] (For instance, Terman felt that his subjects were too concerned—that is, pathologically concerned—with sex. Of course, they were in all probability, closeted and their lives therefore severely constrained.) The situation has not *fundamentally* altered. Homophobia is accepted in science and society even when other forms of bigotry are not, at least not openly.[72] Indeed, mainstream science still remains erotophobic, uncomfortable claiming the erotic as a part of human nature.[73] A newer science, not just a new gay mythology, is being reformulated by mostly (but not exclusively) gay and lesbian scholars who refuse to be "servants of power" and who seek instead "alternative guidelines in their studies of minorities."[74]

Homosexuality—not gay—has been the subject of much developmental analysis but little prospective longitudinal research, particularly across age groups or life stages.[75] Such gaps have also been noted in the study of sexuality in general. To the extent that the findings of developmental research have had an effect on either social theory or clinical practice, they have served primarily to provide what is believed to be scientific verification of the preconceptions mentioned earlier regarding the origins of homosexual behavior in early childhood. Such a misuse of developmental research results from combining longitudinal and retrospective findings, rendering the developmental perspective a problematic "history of confusion" and a confusion of "histories."[76] Investigators employing a developmental paradigm have focused principally on linking various derivatives of early experience (e.g., maternal and paternal identification), including aspects of infancy and early childhood, to adult homosexual behavior—but *not* to being gay. This line of inquiry thus represents a concern with causality and delineation of continuities through functions and mechanisms presumed to give rise to adult forms of homosexuality. This concern with origins and causes necessarily neglects life course development after childhood—especially gay life course development.

Causal inferences made from retrospective data are highly problematic since adults' self-representations and understandings are infused with current cultural constructs and ideologies.[77] Additionally, recent findings in family research suggest that influences within families are bidirectional.[78] Causal inferences typically consider only the ways parents influence their children. Children, however, influence parents in as many—albeit different—ways as parents influence children.[79] A growing body of research suggests that across the family life cycle parents are actively socialized by their children, from infancy throughout adulthood, in diverse ways, from discipline strategies to political values.[80]

Still, the early development of gay men receives excessive attention. (There is little comparable research on lesbians, by contrast, and existing studies raise questions about parallel factors operating in women.)[81] On the basis of newer and more refined studies of adults, gay men's early development is now being reinterpreted by employing an implicit concept of reciprocal socialization. For example, Richard Green's longitudinal study of the "causes" of homosexuality follows an earlier line of developmental research and attempts to link aspects of childhood sex-role interests and identifications to adult gender roles and sexual orientation.[82] Developmental hypotheses elaborated by Green are concerned with whether and how gender identity precedes the emergence and development of sexual orientation, albeit in a clinically constituted sample. Green's work is not concerned with gay or lesbian identity development and the life course of youths after adolescence.[83]

Despite the recent conclusions of a number of developmental and personality researchers on the lack of continuity across the life course,[84] most developmental research on homosexuality has focused on examining continuities related to sexual orientation. In contrast, there is a lack of accumulated information regarding the course of individual change and the effect of life events across the life course and subsequent to an initial coming out. With concern fixed on childhood, too little attention has been devoted to studying either adolescence or adulthood as other than an *outcome* of childhood or experiences *across* the life course.

A major problem concerns the concept "life cycle" itself. Over the past fifty years, it had been compelling for developmental psychologists to talk about the life cycle, even though that concept—Erik Erikson and Daniel Levinson not withstanding—is now seen to be less useful or precise.[85] This is because it no longer captures the social reality it was meant to represent or explain, and the reasons why are illuminating for understanding gay culture. Nearly three decades of research on adult development and aging have demonstrated that patterns of growth and change in adulthood are never the same for any given group, generation, or historical cohort.[86] Historical and cultural changes constantly alter patterns of growth, development, and life course. Development in adulthood is thus not nearly as ordered or predictable as some had previously assumed, including those who believed that homosexuality was always a sign of disease.[87]

Consensus regarding the expectable course of life among persons of particular ages provides the basis of age stratification.[88] It has been suggested that age functions similarly to the way in which the differential allocation of valued resources and rewards occurs—including prestige, honor, and remuneration (based on occupational attainment). Confusion continues regarding the distinction between *age stratification,* which is based on differential access to resources/rewards (often leading to "agism" or age discrimination), and *age categorization,* a consensual understanding of regularized and expectable actions and intents that endure over time and are characteristic of particular ages within particular cohorts of individuals.

Age is now assuming a decreasing significance in shaping the lives of adult Americans. It is no longer surprising to hear about a thirty-two-year-old college president, or a seventy-year-old new father, nor a fifty-five-year-old man who just decided to come out.[89] Age as a chronological marker is of little significance for the study of lives today, except as represented by the socially shared meanings attached to particular ages across the life cycle. Without such knowledge of the social meanings attached to historical time, age itself becomes an "empty" variable.[90] It now seems evident that the life course experience of any one person cannot be understood apart from the cultural order that structures and provides meaning for that experience. It is precisely this social definition of life that transforms the study of the life span into the study of the life course.[91] This latter concept provides a bridge between cultural systems and individual lives. "Life course," then, which is culturally structured, must be differentiated from such terms as "life cycle" or "life span," which refer only to change over time without consideration of the cultural meanings required to make sense of such change. The life course approach can help elucidate the current experiences of gay men in a unique historical context.

The concept of cohort (or generational unit) is central to understanding how members of a generation respond to their cultural circumstances;[92] the significance of this larger historical context has long been recognized as an important defining characteristic of particular life patterns. But a major problem has been the definition of the cohort to be studied.[93] While two groups of persons born as little as one year apart may be considered as separate cohorts, the definition of cohort used in a particular study has depended largely on the investigator's concept of that notion rather than on the life experiences of the individuals concerned—and the definitions that people have of their own lives may be of greater importance.[94]

Stonewall and the advent of AIDS are cohort-defining events for multiple generations of men. It remains an open question as to how exactly the concepts of cohort and generation function among communities of gay and lesbian individuals over the life course. Chapter 1 elucidates some of the mechanisms of intergenerational transmission of gay cultural values from older generations to youths through the institutionalized gay and lesbian youth group of the gay community in Chicago.

Are there generational or—in developmental terms—historical co-hort differences in the experience of coming out? Most psychologists and sociologists concerned with gay identity formation have ignored the question.[95] Herdt suggests that, in Chicago, there have been four fuzzily bounded cohorts since 1900. Murray, however, argues for more microscopic, crosscutting variations bounded by cohort rather than by setting and personal history. Surely, the diverse nature of the San Francisco gay population, drawn to the city as Mecca, is a critical post-1960s factor here. Stability of urban populations may thus influ-ence how gay culture is age and cohort stratified. Is such a view differ-ent from the nature of cohort changes in the wider population[96] or, say, in the Japanese-American culture? To the extent that no hiding or passing is involved in other populations, yes. The gay culture is sin-gularly remarkable for the quick rise in its visibility. This confounds cohort differences over the past twenty years because so much change in situations, roles, and identities has occurred so quickly, eclipsing in certain regards other features of age, class, and ethnic stratification within gay culture. To highlight the cultural changes in gay and lesbian life course trajectories, we may ask, Is coming out in 1987 as a sixteen-year-old adolescent in Chicago the same process as coming out in 1970 as a forty-year-old in San Francisco? Obviously, the psychological is-sues and social consequences are different. A middle-aged man must reconcile the time that has passed with the limited time ahead of him.[97] An adolescent, on the other hand, is reckoning with the future in a new way and must deal with the personal and social meanings of time and time mastery, looking toward the life that has yet to be lived.[98]

Too often we have presumed that creating a positive self-representation is the same for a middle-aged man or woman as for an adolescent or young adult.[99] Yet we also know that there are significant differences in the coming-out experiences of urban, suburban, and ru-ral groups within the same historical period.[100] More frequently over-looked is the question of how the individual's identity and life course have evolved after the initial coming-out process.

To illustrate the effect of historical and cultural changes on the gay life course, a case in point is the example of contemporary gay and lesbian youths in Chicago (see chapter 1). While the opportunities for constructing a positive gay or lesbian identity have been rapidly changing over the last decades, adolescents coming out today are the youngest beneficiaries of these changes in our society. Historically, of course, there were fewer opportunities for the open community socializing and socialization than are available to today's urban youths. Until relatively recently, pressures for assimilation as "straight" were very great. This aspect of the life course, then, self-identification as gay or lesbian during adolescence, is a unique developmental process found only in current cohorts of some youths and thus carries different consequences for the life course.[101] Where earlier generations of same-sex-attracted persons remained hidden—"closeted"—and had to "pass" for fear of discredited identity—the former homosexual closet—today's gay youths are able to strive for and achieve unprecedented life goals and open social relationships. Adolescents currently coming out have the unprecedented opportunity to integrate their homoerotic desires with other components of their developing identities, including social roles, life-style choices, and transitions into gay cultural communities.

Lesbian and gay youths today are also faced with unique developmental challenges. In addition to the normal developmental tasks of adolescence, young gays and lesbians must both overcome the cultural stereotypes of homosexuality and give up previously internalized heterosocial life goals. (This identity change may involve some "grief work" and mourning as previously held expectations for marriage, heterosexual parenthood, etc. are replaced with new expectations, ideals, and ambitions.) While previous generations have faced these or similar problems, youths today have begun the coming-out process in the cultural and historical context of AIDS. Gay and lesbian adolescents must make decisions regarding the meaning, management, and expression of their sexuality. Without meaningful and socially shared precedents on which to model their own decision making—precedents provided by gay institutions and role models—gay and lesbian youths may be led to increasingly divergent social constructions of the life course.[102] The problem of life course construction itself may be a unique developmental task for gays and lesbians. The first generation of post-AIDS youths is likely to have some of the longest lifetime histories of gay or lesbian identity.

While it is popular to hear of the graying of America, it must be realized that gay men and lesbians also grow old. Gay middle adulthood, new patterns of aging, and life course development in the second half of life are emergent themes in research today (see chapters 3 and 6). While cohort-defining events such as AIDS create new dangers in the expression of sexuality, they also create new opportunities to consolidate and strengthen gay identity. Michael Gorman (chapter 3) mentions a new reckoning with death and spirituality among some of his informants. A new level of self-awareness—a second coming out— can also emerge. This is not surprising since the initial coming-out process, while providing important gains, brings grief and loss (of images and expectations of which shall not be lived out). The experience of AIDS may reactivate the experience of grief and provide a new opportunity—a new context—for dealing with it. Older gay men may have a new resilience in dealing with adversity. There are also now new, emergent patterns, of love and caretaking, available to them in gay culture alongside new forms of sexual behavior: a "new set of rules for the game," Gorman says, part of the new gay life course. All these changes parallel new definitions of what constitutes family in our society as well as "official" recognition of same-sex partnerships in some urban centers.

In the following chapters, the reader will find gay culture represented in a variety of forms and through multiple lenses. Informants live across the country and have reached varying positions in the life course. What they have in common is that being gay—and the reproduction of this cultural identity—no longer depends on sex per se. What one can do and be as a gay or lesbian is now reflected in a rich literature and more elaborate set of social roles than ever before. The horizon of gay culture, though more clearly bounded than a generation ago, has also been greatly expanded and will in time become even more diffuse, with new potentialities available for the self and the community of the future.

Notes

1. See John D'Emilio, *Sexual Politics, Sexual Communities* (Chicago: University of Chicago Press, 1983); Kenneth Plummer, *Sexual Stigma* (Boston: Routledge & Kegan Paul, 1975); Jeffrey Weeks, *Sexuality and Its Discontents* (London: Routledge & Kegan Paul, 1985); Martin Levine, "Gay Ghetto," in *Gay Men*, ed. M. Levine (New York: Harper & Row, 1979).
2. See Darrell Yates Rist, "AIDS as Apocalypse," *Christopher Street*, no. 132 (1989): 11–14.
3. See Robert J. Stoller, "Psychoanalytic 'Research' on Homosexuality: The Rules

of the Game," in *Observing the Erotic Imagination,* by R. J. Stoller (New Haven, Conn.: Yale University Press, 1985), pp. 167–83.

4. On homosexuality as a disease, see R. Bayer, *Homosexuality and American Psychiatry* (New Brunswick, N.J.: Rutgers University Press, 1981). On the growth of the gay movement, see Barry D. Adam, *The Rise of a Gay and Lesbian Movement* (Boston: Twayne, 1987); D'Emilio, *Sexual Politics;* Levine, "Gay Ghetto"; Stephen Murray, *Social Theory, Homosexual Realities* (New York: Gai Saber Monographs, 1984); Kenneth Plummer, *The Making of the Modern Homosexual* (London: Hutchinson, 1981), and "Going Gay: Identities, Life Cycles, and Lifestyles in the Male Gay World," in *The Theory and Practice of Homosexuality,* ed. J. Hart and D. Richardson (Boston: Routledge & Kegan Paul, 1981), pp. 93–110. Study of this new social formation has largely been the province of sociologists and social historians. See Barry D. Adam, *The Survival of Domination* (New York: Elsevier, 1978); John H. Gagnon and William Simon, *Sexual Conduct* (Chicago: Aldine, 1973); David Greenberg, *The History of Homosexuality* (Chicago: University of Chicago Press, 1988); Murray, *Social Theory, Homosexual Realities;* Plummer, *Sexual Stigma;* Richard R. Troiden, "The Formation of Homosexual Identities," in *Adolescence and Homosexuality,* ed. Gilbert Herdt (New York: Haworth, 1989). The anthropology of this "variable and multileveled culture" is in its infancy, which helps explain the preeminence of psychological/deviance study of "coming out" events and processes up to the present.

5. See Gilbert Herdt, "Introduction: Gay and Lesbian Youth, Emergent Identities, and Cultural Scenes at Home and Abroad," *Journal of Homosexuality* 17 (1989): 1–42.

6. John H. Gagnon, "The Creation of the Sexual in Early Adolescence," in *Twelve to Sixteen: Early Adolescence,* ed. J. Kagan and R. Coles (New York: Norton, 1971).

7. Reviewed in Murray, *Social Theory, Homosexual Realities;* and chapter 4.

8. Andrew Boxer and B. J. Cohler, "The Life Course of Gay and Lesbian Youth: An Immodest Proposal for the Study of Lives," in *Gay and Lesbian Youth,* ed. Gilbert Herdt (New York: Harrington Park, 1989), pp. 315–35.

9. Eve Sedgwick, *Epistemology of the Closet* (Berkeley and Los Angeles: University of California Press, 1990).

10. John D'Emilio and Estelle Freedman, *Intimate Matters: A History of Sexuality in America* (New York: Harper & Row, 1988).

11. Edward Sapir, "Culture Genuine and Spurious" (1924), in *Selected Writings of Edward Sapir in Language, Culture, and Personality,* ed. D. G. Mandelbaum (Berkeley: University of California Press, 1949).

12. Adam, *The Rise of a Gay and Lesbian Movement.*

13. Susan Sontag, "Notes on Camp," in *A Susan Sontag Reader* (Harmondsworth: Penguin, 1982).

14. Dennis Altman, *The Homosexualization of America, the Americanization of the Homosexual* (New York: St. Martin's, 1982).

15. Herdt, "Introduction: Gay and Lesbian Youth."

16. Lee M. Kochems, "Meanings and Health Implications of Gay Men's Sexuality" (paper presented at the annual meeting of the American Anthropological Association, Chicago, November 1987), and "Creating Gay Culture: Redefining American Gender Ideology" (n.d.); Weeks, *Sexuality and Its Discontents;* Greenberg, *The History of Homosexuality.*

17. See, e.g., Sigmund Freud, *Three Essays on the Theory of Sexuality* (1905), in *The Standard Edition of the Complete Psychological Works of Sigmund Freud*, ed. J. Strachey (London: Hogarth, 1953–74), 18:125–245.
18. Monika Kehoe, "Lesbians over 65: A Triply Invisible Minority," *Journal of Homosexuality* 12 (1986): 139–52.
19. Adam, *The Rise of a Gay and Lesbian Movement;* Weeks, *Sexuality and Its Discontents.*
20. See Freud's famous "Letter to an American Mother" (1935), reprinted in Ronald Bayer, *Homosexuality and American Psychiatry* (Princeton, N.J.: Princeton University Press, 1987), p. 27.
21. See Bayer, *Homosexuality and American Psychiatry.*
22. Karl Heinrich Ulrichs's monumental study is *Forschungen über das Ratsel der Mann Mannlichen Liebe* (1898), 12 vols. in 1 (New York: Arno, 1975). On psychoanalysis and disease discourse, see Irving Bieber, *Homosexuality: A Psychoanalytic Study* (New York: Basic, 1961). On individual development, see Boxer and Cohler, "The Life Course of Gay and Lesbian Youth."
23. See, e.g., Donald Webster Cory, ed., *Homosexuality: A Cross-cultural Approach* (New York: Burton & Westermark, 1956); Michel Foucault, *The History of Sexuality,* trans. Robert Hurley (New York: Vintage, 1980); Jonathan Katz, *Gay American History: Lesbians and Gay Men in the USA* (New York: Crowell, 1976); D'Emilio, *Sexual Politics;* D'Emilio and Freedman, *Intimate Matters.* A. Kinsey, W. Pomeroy, and C. Martin, *Sexual Behavior in the Human Male* (Philadelphia: Saunders, 1948).
24. Carol Warren and Barbara Laslett, "Privacy and Secrecy: A Conceptual Comparison," in *Secrecy: A Cross-cultural Perspective,* ed. Stanton K. Tefft (New York: Human Sciences Press, 1980).
25. See Kochems, "Meanings and Health Implications," "Creating Gay Culture"; Levine, "Gay Ghetto."
26. Gagnon and Simon, *Sexual Conduct.*
27. A. P. Bell, M. S. Weinberg, and S. Hammersmith, *Sexual Preference* (Bloomington: Indiana University Press, 1981). Kinsey, Pomeroy, and Martin, *Sexual Behavior in the Human Male.* On Kinsey's behavioral orientation, see Gilbert Herdt, "Developmental Discontinuities and Sexual Orientation across Cultures," in *Heterosexuality/Homosexuality,* ed. June Reinisch et al. (Oxford: Oxford University Press, 1990), pp. 208–36.
28. Boxer and Cohler, "The Life Course of Gay and Lesbian Youth"; Gagnon and Simon, *Sexual Conduct;* Stoller, "Psychoanalytic 'Research' on Homosexuality."
29. Freud, *Three Essays on the Theory of Sexuality.* See also Richard Isay, *Homosexual Development* (New York: Farrar, Straus, Giroux, 1988); Weeks, *Sexuality and Its Discontents.*
30. Herdt, "Introduction: Gay and Lesbian Youth."
31. Stoller, *Observing the Erotic Imagination.*
32. Bayer, *Homosexuality and American Psychiatry;* Gilbert Herdt, "Cross-cultural Forms of Homosexuality and the Concept 'Gay,'" *Psychiatric Annals* 18 (1988): 37–39; Terry S. Stein and Carol J. Cohen, "Psychotherapy with Gay Men and Lesbians: An Examination of Homophobia, Coming Out, and Identity," in *Psychotherapy with Homosexuals,* ed. E. S. Hetrick and T. S. Stein (Washington, D.C.: American Psychiatric Press, 1984), pp. 59–74.

33. On deviance, see Howard Becker, *Outsiders* (New York: Free Press, 1963); Erik Erikson, *Childhood and Society* (New York: Norton, 1968). On stigma, see Erving Goffman, *Stigma* (Englewood Cliffs, N.J.: Prentice-Hall, 1963).

34. Dennis Altman, *Homosexual* (New York: Avon, 1973).

35. For gender research, see John Money and A. Ehrhardt, *Man, Woman, Boy and Girl* (Baltimore: Johns Hopkins University Press, 1972); Stoller, "Psychoanalytic 'Research' on Homosexuality." For the anthropological approach, see J. Carrier, "Homosexual Behavior in Cross-cultural Perspective," in *Homosexual Behavior: A Modern Reappraisal*, ed. J. Marmor (New York: Basic, 1980), pp. 100–122; K. Read, *Other Voices* (Novato: Chandler & Sharpe, 1980); Carole S. Vance, ed., *Pleasure and Danger: Exploring Female Sexuality* (Boston: Routledge & Kegan Paul, 1984); C. Warren, *Identity and Community in the Gay World* (New York: Wilcox, 1974); D. Wolf, *The Lesbian Community* (Berkeley and Los Angeles: University of California Press, 1979). Wolf's *Lesbian Community* is reviewed in Gilbert Herdt and Robert J. Stoller, *Intimate Communications* (New York: Columbia University Press, 1990).

36. See E. Coleman, "Developmental Stages in the Coming Out Process," *Journal of Homosexuality* 7 (1982): 31–43; V. C. Cass, "Homosexual Identity Formation: Testing a Theoretical Model," *Journal of Sex Research* 20 (1984): 143–67; Plummer, *Sexual Stigma;* R. R. Troiden, "The Formation of Homosexual Identities," *Journal of Homosexuality* 17 (1988): 43–73.

37. Plummer, *Sexual Stigma,* pp. 135–36. See also Karla Jay and Alan Young, *The Gay Report* (New York: Summit, 1977); Thomas S. Weinberg, *Gay Men, Gay Selves* (New York: Irvington, 1983); Weinberg's *Gay Men* is reviewed in Herdt, "Introduction: Gay and Lesbian Youth."

38. Kenneth Plummer, "Lesbian and Gay Youth in England," in Herdt, ed., *Gay and Lesbian Youth,* pp. 195–224. For an anthropologist's point of view, see J. Carrier, "Sexual Behavior and the Spread of AIDS in Mexico," in *The AIDS Pandemic: A Global Emergency,* ed. R. Bolton (New York: Gordon & Breach, 1989).

39. John A. Lee, "Going Public: A Study in the Sociology of Homosexual Liberation," *Journal of Homosexuality* 3 (1977): 49–78.

40. Roger Scruton, *Sexual Desire: A Moral Philosophy of the Erotic* (New York: Free Press, 1986).

41. Clifford Geertz, *Local Knowledge* (New York: Basic, 1983).

42. Boxer and Cohler, "The Life Course of Gay and Lesbian Youth."

43. Herdt, "Introduction: Gay and Lesbian Youth." On ontological preconceptions, see H. G. Gadamer, *Truth and Method* (New York: Crossroad, 1965).

44. For background, see Adam, *The Rise of a Gay and Lesbian Movement;* D'Emilio, *Sexual Politics.*

45. Sedgwick, *Epistemology of the Closet.*

46. Altman, *Homosexual: Oppression and Liberation* (New York: Avon, 1973).

47. See Sontag, "Notes on Camp"; Vito Russo, "Camp," in Levine, ed., *Gay Men,* pp. 205–10.

48. M. Castells, "Cultural Identity, Sexual Liberation and Urban Structure: The Gay Community in San Francisco," in *The City and the Grass Roots: A Cross-cultural Theory of Urban Social Movements* (London: Edward Arnold, 1983).

49. Howard Brown, *Familiar Faces, Hidden Lives* (New York: Harcourt Brace Jovanovich, 1976), p. 89.

50. Levine, "Gay Ghetto," p. 201.
51. Erving Goffman, *Asylums* (Garden City, N.Y.: Anchor, 1961), p. 67.
52. Rist, "AIDS as Apocalypse."
53. F. Tonnies, *Gemeinschaft und Gesellschaft* (Leipzig, 1887), trans. C. P. Loomis as *Community and Society* (New York: Harper Torchbooks, 1963). See also Max Weber, *The Theory of Social and Economic Organization,* trans. A. M. Henderson and T. Parsons (New York: Free Press, 1947).
54. Robert N. Bellah, R. Madsen, W. M. Sullivan, A. Swidler, and S. M. Tipton, *Habits of the Heart: Individualism and Commitment in American Life* (Berkeley and Los Angeles: University of California Press, 1985).
55. C. Gerstell, D. Feraios, and G. Herdt, "Widening Circles: An Ethnographic Profile of a Youth Group," in Herdt, ed., *Adolescence and Homosexuality,* pp. 211–28.
56. J. H. Gagnon, "Disease and Desire," *Daedalus* 118, no. 3 (1989): 47–77; R. Stall, T. Coates, and C. Hoff, "Behavioral Risk Reduction for HIV Infection among Gay and Bisexual Men: A Review of the Results from the United States," *American Psychologist* 43 (1988): 878–85.
57. The AIDS epidemic, associated with the "golden age" of fast and dirty sex that Randy Shilts seemed so angry about in *And the Band Played On: Politics, People, and the AIDS Epidemic* (New York: St. Martin's, 1987), is a plague not only on gay sexuality but on gay sociality too.
58. On the danger of sex, see Susan Sontag, *AIDS and Its Metaphors* (New York: Farrar, Straus, & Giroux, 1988).
59. Gagnon, "Disease and Desire," p. 53.
60. Michelle Fine, "Sexuality, Schooling and Adolescent Females: The Missing Discourse of Desire," *Harvard Educational Review* 58 (1988): 29–53.
61. Gagnon, "Disease and Desire."
62. Freud, *Three Essays on the Theory of Sexuality.*
63. Levine, "Gay Ghetto"; Altman, *The Homosexualization of America.*
64. Robert LeVine, "Adulthood among the Gusii of Africa," in *Themes of Work and Love in Adulthood,* ed. Neil J. Smelser and Erik H. Erikson (Cambridge, Mass.: Harvard University Press, 1980), pp. 77–104.
65. Levine, "Gay Ghetto."
66. On visibility, see Dennis Altman, *Coming Out in the Seventies* (Boston: Alyson, 1981). On AIDS and visibility, see Shilts, *And the Band Played On.*
67. Although these stage models appear to be developed as "maturational models," see T. S. Weinberg, "Biology, Ideology, and the Reification of Developmental Stages in the Study of Homosexual Identities," *Journal of Homosexuality* 10 (1984): 77–84. See also Boxer and Cohler, "The Life Course of Gay and Lesbian Youth"; Troiden, "The Formation of Homosexual Identities."
68. Herdt, "Introduction: Gay and Lesbian Youth"; see also chapter 1.
69. Henry L. Minton, "Femininity in Men and Masculinity in Women: American Psychiatry and Psychology Portray Homosexuality in the 1930s," *Journal of Homosexuality* 13 (1986): 1–22, 12–13.
70. L. M. Terman and C. C. Miles, *Sex and Personality: Studies in Masculinity and Femininity* (New York: McGraw-Hill, 1936).
71. Minton, "Femininity in Men," p. 13.
72. John P. DeCecco, "Sex and More Sex: A Critique of the Kinsey Conception of Sexuality," in *Homosexuality/Heterosexuality: Concepts of Sexual Orientation,* ed. Da-

vid M. McWhirter et al. (New York: Oxford University Press, 1990), pp. 367–86.

73. Margaret Nicholls, "Lesbian Relationships: Implications for the Study of Sexuality and Gender," in ibid., pp. 358–64.

74. Minton, "Femininity in Men," p. 13.

75. S. F. Morin, "Heterosexual Bias in Psychological Research on Lesbianism and Male Homosexuality," *American Psychologist* 32 (1977): 629–37; see also A. T. Watters, "Heterosexual Bias in Psychological Research on Lesbianism and Male Homosexuality (1979–1983), Utilizing the Bibliographic and Taxonomic System of Morin," *Journal of Homosexuality* 13 (1986): 35–58.

76. Retrospective and prospective data may render quite different life histories. The origin of this confusion is commonly attributed to Freud, although he himself pointed out, "So long as we trace the development from its final outcome backwards, the chain of events appears continuous, and we feel we have gained an insight which is completely satisfactory or even exhaustive. But if we proceed the reverse way, if we start from the premises inferred from the analysis and try to follow these up to the final result, then we no longer get the impression of an inevitable sequence of events which could not have been otherwise determined. We notice at once that there might have been another result, and that we might have been just as well able to understand and explain the latter" (Sigmund Freud, "The Psychogenesis of a Case of Homosexuality in a Woman" [1920], in Strachey, ed., *Standard Edition*, 18:15–172).

77. It is not surprising to learn that culturally defined attributes of behaviors such as sex-role definitions are so important in organizing adult personality since internalization of the situation is a major determinant of personal expression, as recognized by symbolic interactionist perspectives in social science (C. Cooley, *Human Nature and the Social Order* [New York: Scribner's, 1902]; M. Janowitz, ed., *W. I. Thomas on Social Organization and Social Personality* [Chicago: University of Chicago Press, 1966]; A. Strauss, ed., *George Herbert Mead: On Social Psychology* [Chicago: University of Chicago Press, 1964]).

78. R. Q. Bell and L. V. Harper, *Child Effects on Adults* (New York: Wiley, 1977); Andrew M. Boxer and Anne C. Petersen, "Pubertal Change in a Family Context," in *Adolescence in Families,* ed. G. K. Leigh and G. W. Petersen (Cincinnati: South-Western, 1986), pp. 73–103; Bertram J. Cohler, "Personal Narrative and Life Course," in *Life-Span Development and Behavior,* vol. 4, ed. Paul Baltes and Orville G. Brim (New York: Academic, 1982), pp. 205–41; B. J. Cohler and E. S. Geyer, "Psychological Autonomy and Interdependence within the Family," in *Normal Family Process,* ed. F. Walsh (New York: Guilford, 1982); J. A. Cook and B. J. Cohler, "Reciprocal Socialization and the Care of Offspring with Cancer and with Schizophrenia," in *Life-Span Developmental Psychology: Intergenerational Relations,* ed. N. Datan, A. L. Greene, and H. W. Reese (Hillsdale, N.J.: Erlbaum, 1986), pp. 223–43; G. O. Hagestad, "Problems and Promises in the Social Psychology of Intergenerational Relations," in *Stability and Change in the Family,* ed. R. W. Fogel, E. Hatfield, S. B. Kiesler, and E. Shanas (New York: Academic, 1981), pp. 11–46.

79. Cook and Cohler, "Reciprocal Socialization."

80. Daphne Blunt Bugental and William A. Shennum, "'Difficult' Children as Elicitors and Targets of Adult Communication Patterns: An Attributional-Behavioral

Transactional Analysis," *Monographs of the Society for Research in Child Development,* serial no. 205 (Chicago: University of Chicago Press, 1984); Cook and Cohler, "Reciprocal Socialization"; R. E. Dawson and K. Prewitt, *Political Socialization* (Boston: Little, Brown, 1969); Lillian Troll and Vern L. Bengtson, "Intergenerational Relations throughout the Life Span," in *Handbook of Developmental Psychology,* ed. B. Wolman (Englewood Cliffs, N.J.: Prentice-Hall, 1982).

81. See, e.g., M. Schneider, "Sappho Was a Right-on Adolescent: Growing Up Lesbian," *Journal of Homosexuality* 17 (1989): 111–30; *Lesbian Psychologies: Explorations and Challenges,* ed. Boston Lesbian Psychologies Collective (Urbana: University of Illinois Press, 1987), pp. 177–94; J. Sophie, "A Critical Examination of Stage Theories of Lesbian Identity Development," *Journal of Homosexuality* 12 (1985/86): 39–51.

82. See, e.g., Isay, *Homosexual Development;* Charles Silverstein, *Man to Man: Gay Couples in America* (New York: Morrow, 1981). These and other authors suggest the nonlinearity of development. Since their interpretive focus is partially on early childhood, a type of essentialist position results from their conclusions that gay children are born and respond to their fathers in particular and sometimes erotic ways; in consequence, fathers may withdraw or reject their sons, as in Isay's model of how gay men experience the oedipal crisis or somewhat similarly in Silverstein's Laius complex.

83. Richard Green, *The "Sissy Boy" Syndrome* (New Haven, Conn.: Yale University Press, 1987).

84. O. G. Brim, Jr., and J. Kagan, "Constancy and Change: A View of the Issues," in *Constancy and Change in Human Development,* ed. O. G. Brim, Jr., and J. Kagan (Cambridge, Mass.: Harvard University Press, 1980); K. Gergen, *Toward Transformation in Social Knowledge* (New York: Springer, 1982); B. J. Cohler, "Adult Developmental Psychology and Reconstruction in Psychoanalysis," in *The Course of Life,* vol. 3, *Adulthood and Aging,* ed. S. I. Greenspan and G. H. Pollock (Washington, D.C.: U.S. Government Printing Office, 1981); Bernice L. Neugarten, "Personality and Aging," in *Handbook of the Psychology of Aging,* ed. J. E. Birren and K. W. Schaie (New York: Van Nostrand-Reinhold, 1977), pp. 626–49, and "Time, Age, and the Life Cycle," *American Journal of Psychiatry* 136 (1979): 887–94.

85. E. H. Erikson, *The Life Cycle Completed: A Review* (New York: Norton, 1982); D. Levinson, C. Darrow, E. Klein, M. Levinson, and G. McKee, *The Seasons of a Man's Life* (New York: Knopf, 1978).

86. G. H. Elder, Jr., "Adolescence in Historical Perspective," in *Handbook of Adolescent Psychology,* ed. J. Adelson (New York: Wiley, 1980), pp. 3–46; see also Hagestad, "Problems and Promises."

87. L. Kohlberg, D. Ricks, and J. Snarey, "Child Development as a Predictor of Adaptation in Adulthood," *Genetic Psychology Monographs* 110 (1984): 91–173; Richard Isay, "The Development of Sexual Identity in Homosexual Men," *Psychoanalytic Study of the Child* 41 (1986): 467–89.

88. G. H. Elder, Jr., "Age Differentiation and the Life Course," in *Annual Review of Sociology* (Palo Alto, Calif.: Annual Reviews, 1975); P. Ragan and J. Wales, "Age Stratification and the Life Course," in *Handbook of Mental Health and Aging,* ed. J. Birren and R. B. Sloane (Englewood Cliffs, N.J.: Prentice-Hall, 1980), pp. 377–99; see also Troll and Bengtson, "Intergenerational Relations."

89. Gunhild Hagestad and Bernice Neugarten, "Age and the Life Course," in *Handbook of Aging and the Social Sciences,* ed. E. Shanas and R. Binstock, 2d ed. (New York: Van Nostrand–Reinhold, 1984). See also Neugarten, "Time, Age, and the Life Cycle."

90. Bernice L. Neugarten and N. Datan, "Sociological Perspectives on the Life Cycle," in *Life-Span Developmental Psychology,* ed. P. Baltes and K. Werner Schaie (New York: Academic, 1973).

91. See Bertram J. Cohler and Andrew M. Boxer, "Settling into the World—Person, Time and Context," in *Normality and the Life Cycle,* ed. D. Offer and M. Sabshin (New York: Basic, 1984), pp. 145–203.

92. Karl Mannheim, "The Problem of Generations" (1928), in *Essays on the Sociology of Knowledge,* trans. P. Kecskemeti (New York: Oxford University Press, 1952), pp. 276–322; David I. Kertzer, "Generation as a Sociological Problem," *Annual Review of Sociology* 9 (1983): 125–49.

93. Kertzer, "Generation as a Sociological Problem"; C. Nydegger, "Multiple Cohort Membership" (paper presented at the annual meeting of the Gerontological Society, San Francisco, November 1977); N. B. Ryder, "The Cohort as a Concept in the Study of Social Change," *American Sociological Review* 30 (1965): 843–61; Irving Rosow, "What Is Cohort and Why?" *Human Development* 21 (1978): 65–75.

94. G. H. Elder, Jr., *Children of the Great Depression* (Chicago: University of Chicago Press, 1974), "Age Differentiation and the Life Course," and "Adolescence in Historical Perspective."

95. Boxer and Cohler, "The Life Course of Gay and Lesbian Youth"; Herdt, "Introduction: Gay and Lesbian Youth."

96. Elder, "Age Differentiation and the Life Course," and "Adolescence in Historical Perspective."

97. See Bernice L. Neugarten, "The Awareness of Middle Age," in *Middle Age,* ed. R. Owen (London: British Broadcasting Co., 1967).

98. A. L. Greene, "Future Time Perspective in Adolescence: The Present of Things Future Revisited," *Journal of Youth and Adolescence* 15 (1986): 99–113. Certainly the AIDS epidemic figures centrally as a cohort-defining event; it also alters individuals' expectations regarding their future life course, particularly those living with HIV infection. See Rose Weitz, "Uncertainty and the Lives of Persons with AIDS," *Journal of Health and Social Behavior* 30 (1989): 270–81.

99. See, e.g., Plummer, "Going Gay." For analyses that examine older generations, see D. C. Kimmel's studies of middle-aged and aging homosexual men, which examine developmental issues related to coming out as well as the individual's position in the life cycle in the context of cultural and historical influences ("Adult Development and Aging: A Gay Perspective," *Journal of Social Issues* 34 [1978]: 113–30, and "Life History Interviews of Aging Gay Men," *International Journal of Aging and Human Development* 10 [1980]: 239–48). See also Raymond Berger, *Gay and Gray: The Older Homosexual Man* (Urbana: University of Illinois Press, 1982); Kehoe, "Lesbians over 65"; John A. Lee, "What Can Homosexual Aging Studies Contribute to Theories of Aging," *Journal of Homosexuality* 13 (1987): 43–71; Mina K. Robinson, "The Older Lesbian" (master's thesis, California State University, Dominguez Hills, 1979). For other developmental models, see V. Cass, "Homosexual Identity Formation: A Theoretical Model," *Journal*

of Homosexuality 4 (1979): 219–35, and "Homosexual Identity Formation: Testing a Theoretical Model," *Journal of Sex Research* 20 (1984): 143–67.

100. Reviewed in Herdt, "Introduction: Gay and Lesbian Youth"; see also chapter 6; and Murray, *Social Theory, Homosexual Realities;* Troiden, "The Formation of Homosexual Identities."

101. Examined further in Andrew M. Boxer, "Life Course Transitions of Gay and Lesbian Youth: Sexual Identity Development and Parent-Child Relationships" (Ph.D. diss., University of Chicago, 1990).

102. Ibid.

ONE

"Coming Out" as a Rite of Passage: A Chicago Study

Gilbert Herdt

The emergence of a gay and lesbian movement in the West-ern world over the past two decades is regarded by social theorists as a major feature of culture change in the latter twentieth century. Among the structural forces thought to have contributed to this change are the human rights movements, greater sexual equality for women, the shift from an industrial to a service-sector economy, and alterations in the family. Current historical trends thus suggest the background for a major psychosocial formation in our time: the con-struction of a gay and lesbian cultural system and the concomitant emergence of a process of identity development related to this, which goes by the name "the coming out." This chapter explores the anthro-pology of this process in a teenage group in Chicago.

The American folk idiom "coming out" has emerged to refer to many psychocultural processes and social events. On a global level, the idiom refers to a single act whereby someone declares his or her iden-tity as "homosexual" or "gay" or "lesbian" to family, friends, or co-workers who assumed the person to be "straight" or "heterosexual." The declaration may occur in public, private, or secret contexts, and its emphasis is on a single attribute: being "homosexual."[1] On the level of cultural ideology as well, "coming out" as a folk category suggests si-multaneous alterations in sexual orientation, gender identity, and be-havior: amplification of same-sex desire as the key structural principle

29

organizing the gay man or lesbian's conceptions of person, selfhood, time, and sociopolitical conduct.[2] Although the "coming-out" concept conveys a single event pinpointed in time and space, many writers today recognize a multiplicity of events, stretching over years, as the phenomena of coming out. This transformational *process* is adopted here as a major symbol of person and gender change typifying and legitimizing the culture of gay manhood.

Much of the work on coming out has come not from anthropology but from psychology. The developmental social psychology of coming out has made substantial gains, but it has also muddled the cultural issues. The main problem has been its failure to examine the cultural system and contexts surrounding gay/lesbian identity formation.[3] This gap is due in part to its lack of ethnographic perspective. Dank's classic study, for instance, revealed differences in the context of coming out, but it was restricted to cognitive category change—from "heterosexual" to "homosexual"—and it never addressed the wider sociocultural foundation of these categories and contexts in the social values and institutions of American culture, treating them instead as individual difference phenomena.[4] Two issues seem to explain this perspective. One concerns the continued emphasis on the act of coming out as a single decontextualized event of the lone individual. The other concerns an exaggeration of individual stage models over cultural process, which unreflectingly use "sex" as their focus of change regardless of the cultural meanings rather than the study of identity and relationship components, of whole persons.

The anthropological problem with these ethnopsychology folk models is revealed most clearly in the continued equivalence of "homosexual" with "gay/lesbian" self-image categories.[5] Not only is the distinctiveness of the cultural meanings surrounding "gay" and "lesbian" obscured, but there remains a surprisingly strong tendency, even among gay and lesbian researchers, to use the cultural constructs interchangeably.[6] The conceptual lumping has obscured gender, class, ethnic, age, and cross-cultural differences in the meanings of "homosexuality."[7] Nowhere is this more evident than in those quasi-experimental studies that overrepresent the white middle-class college student.[8] We are now aware of the gendered bias in these models, which equates male and female experience and underrates the distinctiveness of women's lives and relationships in conceptions of "gay" culture.[9]

Because of its distinctiveness, popularity, and symbolic elaboration in Western culture, coming out is best interpreted today as a life-crisis event that resembles the rites of passage that anthropologists have studied around the world. Since the time of Van Gennep, the understanding of life-crisis events has revealed recurrent structural factors that shape identity and status changes of the kind implied by the term "coming out." At minimum, we must now distinguish individual "puberty" rites from collective initiations into broader social units, such as secret societies and fraternities.[10] The contrast illuminates not only the coming-out process but historical changes in gay culture in urban America.

Coming out is not only the key ritual of gay culture: it is a particularly powerful cultural domain in which to refine the study of *rites de passage* in complex societies. Fieldwork in Papua New Guinea, where initiation rites among the Sambia emphasize the role of institutionalized male homosexual relations from childhood to young adulthood in transforming sexuality and social relations, has, in turn, led me to the study of gay coming-out processes.[11] I see these as an arena of compelling possibilities for viewing powerful identity transformations among Chicago youths. Central to this work is Van Gennep's idea of the "relearning process" in ritual.[12] That is, through ritual, people unlearn major ideas and feelings vital for their subsequent social roles and development. Because coming-out transformations illustrate the "unlearning" necessary for transitions into gay/lesbian roles/statuses, I was not surprised to find coming out referred to as a rite of passage in popular lesbian and gay literature.[13] Yet I was dismayed that so few of its cultural meanings had been described.

Historically, the secret world of the gay bar and covert social networks made homosexuality an individualized sort of puberty rite into a secret oppressed society.[14] There was no manifest gay culture at the time. Today, the political power of the gay and lesbian community suggests that coming out is more of a collective initiation rite, a public coming-of-age status-adjustment transition into the adult gay community. The media accounts in *Time* magazine, for example, have trivialized coming out as an act of political protest, whereas social surveys have depersonalized it as a bundle of diffuse traits and states, the result of which is homosexual "preference."[15] Both these accounts do not fully grasp the contemporary context of gay culture. Humanistic and fictional accounts tend toward the opposite direction; they personalize the events as a self-affirmation of the person's desire to find the new identity.[16] The emergence of coming-out groups in American and other Western cities today embodies coming out in real-life "experience near"[17] situations, affording unprecedented opportunity for ethnographic study.

The questions of what changes in the person and what changes in his or her social relationships are both involved in conceptualizing coming out as a rite of passage. A key to understanding is that these alternative moral worlds—here we can use Carol Gilligan's language[18]—require profound changes in thought and discourse regarding social relationships and in the self, changes that require unlearning and deconstruction of cultural ideas as much as "learning" of new roles. Such transformations in gendered worlds are far more profound, involving much more of the whole person—body, soul, and mind— than previously implied by the stage-model accounts of, for example, individual difference psychology, which have not appreciated that the new culture requires restructuring of personhood and social surround, not just changes in cognitive category or self-identity.[19]

The most recent and dramatic form of such emergent organizations is the adolescent coming-out group. Such groups meet regularly in major urban centers of the United States, including Chicago, New York, the San Francisco Bay Area, Minneapolis, and Seattle. Thus far, none have been intensively studied ethnographically, though an exploratory profile of the Chicago youth group begins to address the need for ethnography of coming out in the contexts of a gay community.[20]

This chapter examines these issues in the study of the Horizons coming-out group in Northside Chicago. Our interdisciplinary investigation of two hundred gay and lesbian adolescents (aged fourteen to twenty) is concerned with the construction of social reality and psychosocial adjustment not only in sexual orientation and behavior but also in gender, selfhood, and social relations in the gay and lesbian community. These youths' confrontation with stigma, discrimination, and self-hatred is a heroic feature of their "unlearning" in American urban settings. Coming out once meant entry into a secret club of a hidden world, with socialization into its "homosexual" cultural system, and the tavern was a pivotal social context.[21] Today, Horizons permits adolescent entry first into a self-affirming semisecret group, then by collective socialization into a "gay" cultural system, with new and open social relationships. To understand this change requires in turn a reconceptualization of "homosexual" and "gay" cultural systems.

Chicago: The Historical Setting

Coming out must be placed in a particular historical and social field. Study of cultural change in the lesbian and gay movement reveals generational differences in coming-out experiences, despite the unfortunate tendency in the psychological literature to treat coming out as a uniform, ahistorical, stage-driven process.[22] Our work in Chicago has pointed up the existence of four overlapping but distinct historical cohorts who have constructed coming out in different pathways of adjustment across cultural epochs.[23]

The first cohort dates from the turn of the century to the 1930s. These persons, now in their late sixties and older, grew into adulthood and discovered their same-sex desires without typically ever having come out. Most of them remain largely invisible.[24]

The second cohort can be bounded roughly from World War II to 1969, the year of the famous Stonewall riot in New York. The members of this cohort, in their forties and older, recall the *communitas* of having been brought together under the turbulent circumstances of World War II, recognizing or fulfilling same-sex desires for the first time while serving in the armed services. As John D'Emilio has written, "For men and women conscious of a strong attraction to their own sex but constrained by their milieu from acting upon it, the war years eased the coming out processes and facilitated entry into the gay world."[25] Postwar changes, such as the founding of the Mattachine Society, gave way to heightened social dis-ease and activism in the late 1960s. Especially critical was the emergence of the gay tavern: "The bars were seedbeds for a collective consciousness that might one day flower politically", a prophecy borne out.[26] K. Vacha reports many positive recollections among members of this generation.[27] These Chicagoans still experienced their homosexuality in largely negative terms, however; many remain closeted to avoid harassment, legal sanctions, and violence. Their coming out was late in life and difficult if it occurred at all.[28] Many remain closeted today.

The third cohort came out in great numbers amid the activism of the "sexual revolution" and the Gay Liberation Front, which saw the Stonewall riot as its watershed. The gay rights movement paralleled earlier civil rights movements[29] and found the most support among children of affluent middle-class families. For lesbians and gays now in their thirties and older who became gay identified after Stonewall, this riot is a symbolic marker: it marks the point at which the cloak of oppression was thrust off. The riots, in fact, are celebrated annually throughout the United States in late June as a cultural event—known as the Gay Pride Day Parade. What seems increasingly clear is that the males in this cohort inaugurated a gender role change as well, a new cult of manliness that rejected gender-inversion images of the past.[30] Now people could live more openly as lesbian- or gay-identified adults, and they did so particularly in such urban gay "ghettos" as Greenwich Village in New York or the Castro District in San Francisco.[31] Social liberation, "free love" bathhouse sexual intercourse, and its lusty male etiquette are highly associated with this "golden age" of the third co-hort.[32] Social networks facilitated mass coming out. Nevertheless, these persons came out as individuals, their experience reflecting less the influence of self-affirming groups and more the vagaries of partic-ular places and times. In Chicago, they did not generally have support-ive coming-out groups, though by the mid- to late 1970s these became visible.

The fourth cohort dates from 1982 and the advent of the AIDS epidemic.[33] By the early 1980s, the major urban centers of America witnessed the onslaught of AIDS and the beginning of radical changes in sexual values and life-styles among gay men. Not only did this alter the sexual revolution of the previous cohort—with its "rhetoric of the old gay movement"[34]—but it also ushered in a new epoch of coming out for teenagers and young adults, the youths of our Chicago study. For the first time, an institutionalized process of initiating and social-izing youths emerged.

Historical changes in the social field of Chicago reveal the limita-tions of prior psychological and sociological study. Virtually all work on adolescent coming out has been conducted through retrospective surveys of adults who remembered their teenage years—who did not come out in self-affirming groups.[35] These studies are also based on culturally and ethnically limited samples—such as those of Bell, Wein-berg, and Hammersmith—with small middle-class minority represen-tation.[36] Such historical cohort analysis problems are compounded by the changing symbolic meanings of the coming-out process across these cohorts.

It is difficult to do justice to the historical and cultural change that has occurred in Chicago. Older gays and lesbians may exaggerate or glorify it in memory, but other accounts independently testify to the change. For example, a report from 1967—the period immediately prior to Stonewall—tells how the Kinsey Institute for Sex Research conducted a pilot study of five hundred white homosexual men in Chicago. The researcher's description highlights the tremendous historical change that has ensued:

> In Chicago, termed a "bad scene" by its homosexual inhabitants, most homosexuals had to remain under cover. Except for gay bars, which were run by absentee owners and frequently closed at the whim of the police, homosexual men and women had few places in which to gather. Persons seeking sexual contact were often subjected to police extortion or arrest. The climate of suspicion, the markedly low level of cohesion among the city's homosexual population, and the homosexuals' despair over their social circumstances made it extremely difficult for the Institute to obtain a large and diverse sample in Chicago.[37]

By contrast, youths in Chicago today face a unique cultural opportunity. First, they experience a city more open than ever before, an openness distilled in the social institution that facilitates their identity and role development, the Horizons agency gay and lesbian youth group. This group is situated in between their mainstream heterosexual parents and friends, on the one hand, and gay and lesbian adult advisers, role models, and their friends, on the other. Second, they are growing up in the historical context of AIDS and other sexually transmitted diseases, and their conduct—like that of their heterosexual peers—shows heightened awareness of the epidemic.[38] AIDS has plagued the gay and lesbian community, inserting its presence into many social events and intimate encounters, so that the cultural knowledge of being and acting gay today can no more be disentangled from the reaction to AIDS than, say, the effect of the eugenics movement on the acculturative experience of newly arriving immigrants in early twentieth-century Chicago.[39] Where early cohorts lived closeted and in fear, suffering such huge psychosocial costs as the alcohol abuse associated with the bar culture of that generation, and where the third cohort is now besieged frontally with the death and grief of AIDS, today's youths—witness to these preceding life-styles—are in response developing an alternative cultural reality and future life course.[40] Many Horizons' youths, for instance, now assume the possibility of achieving unprecedented gay life goals and open social relationships at home, school, and work.[41]

Ethnographic research on the gay community in Chicago began in early 1987 and has focused on the Newtown neighborhood. Historical and social change in this gay neighborhood since 1970 has been the subject of intense ethnographic study.[42] The neighborhood is being gentrified; the former heterogeneous ethnic and class composition is rapidly changing.[43] This area borders what Nelson Algren called the "city's enormous heart," compared to the "spiritual Sahara" of its suburbs.[44] Here, we have worked in the main social support organization of gays and lesbians in Chicago—Horizons Community Services, our field site and interview center.[45] Horizons began in the early 1970s as a small, storefront operation, supported by meager donations. Today, it has expanded and has a paid, full-time staff and hundreds of volunteers. Among its services are psychological counseling, AIDS support groups, women's rap groups, and legal and professional assistance.

Its well-known youth group, begun in 1978, has today an extraordinarily diverse population drawn from throughout the metropolitan Chicago area. Organized as an informal "drop-in" rap group, youths meet regularly on Saturday afternoons in the Horizons building. The group is the largest in the entire Midwest area for gay adolescents, which explains why a few young people attend from distant suburbs and as far away as Michigan or Indiana.

The group limits membership by age, from fourteen to just under twenty-one. On turning twenty-one, members must leave the group, which is a source of considerable turmoil to the "graduates." The mean age of our interview subjects is about eighteen. Blacks make up 30 percent and whites 43 percent of our sample, with 12 percent Hispanic, 2 percent Asian, and 13 percent of mixed ethnic background. Three-fourths of these youths attend high school or some other kind of school. More than half of them live at home. Yet the majority of our youths have not come out to their parents. Interviews reveal that the average age of disclosure of their homosexuality to others as 16 for females and 16.75 for males. Two-thirds first come out to peers in school or to friends. We ask adolescents to define what coming out means to them; most identify this as revealing same-sex desires or gay experiences either to a friend or to themselves. Eighty percent of our sample tell us that they have come out (as they define it) to someone; simply attending the group is not enough to define oneself as gay or lesbian. The class composition is about evenly divided between working and middle class. Catholicism and Protestantism are prominent religious orientations.

As stated above, most of these adolescents live at home. They are not runaways, prostitutes, drug addicts, or psychiatric patients. To the passerby, they appear much like other teenagers; only the diverse ethnicity of the group makes it so visible in Chicago, with its marked neighborhood boundaries.

Furthermore, many Horizons' youths "gender blend"—a new concept—their fashions and conduct, emphasizing a new kind of androgynous sexuality. They poke fun at their parents and society for being so conventional. Their unisex hairstyles, sometimes alienating those youths in the group who are more typically masculine or feminine, express the symbolic protest of a gay culture that is mainstreaming and assimilating. Gender, that is, is up "for grabs," a negotiated territory of new ways of being young and gay.

The historical emergence of the gay and lesbian community in Chicago has thus eventuated in the Horizons youth group, which is widely recognized as distinctive of the pioneering nature of the community. A cultural system of normative gay and lesbian beliefs, concepts, and goals is expressed in local gay newspapers, churches, and shopping areas and through Horizons itself. The Annual Gay Pride Day Parade in Chicago is likewise a key symbolic event whereby the community represents to itself and to other interest and minority groups its "independence day" and political power (see chapter 8). It is interesting to note that it is the Horizons gay youth group that always leads this parade. The gay community, in other words, provides an alternative socialization regime—cultural reality and social practices—to that of the youths' mainstream heterosexual homes. Many adolescents in Chicago who feel themselves to be gay or lesbian do not come to Horizons, of course, but the great expansion of the youth group over the years testifies to its increasing visibility in the city and its surrounds.

Preliminal Events

Van Gennep's concerns with the explicitly sexual nature of puberty rites and the removal of the initiate from secular to liminal contexts are helpful guides for understanding coming-out events as a ritual process.[46] Obvious points of conflict between gays and straights emerge here with shifts in fundamental categories: person, time, space, and action. Van Gennep's classic model has three transition phases—separation from secular and everyday relationships; the transitional phase following this, referred to as the liminal period (after *limin*, "threshold"); and the reaggregation outcome, whereby the ritual agent, having achieved a new status and new cultural knowledge, is returned to secular relationships. These processes create competitive spheres of influence and prestige between the gay youth group and relevant mainstream peer groups. Here one sees the testing of moral norms and the reconstitution of the heterosexual self—a process of stripping of identity, the sociologist Erving Goffman has argued—particularly in the wholesale treatment of a cohort as a "batch."[47] These are clues for understanding why some in the gay community refer to the coming-out process as a rite of passage.

In the structure of coming-out transitions, the phase of separation begins when the adolescent feels and then acknowledges feeling somehow different from parents and peers. Many adolescent informants say that they felt "unique" or "different" from an early age, the sensibility they associate with same-sex attractions or experiences in late childhood. For instance, one teenager recalled watching, at the age of ten, Captain Kirk (of the television show "Star Trek") peel off his shirt and being titillated: "Somehow I knew it wasn't something to talk about. . . . I pretended that nothing happened." Homoerotic fantasies or attachments begun in this period are usually hidden; around puberty, they become intense. A few youths feel themselves to be homosexual or gay even before puberty, and others also experience heterosexual interest or sexual experimentation between late childhood and mid-adolescence.[48] Several youths sense (without being able to label) themselves as "bisexual" for a time. The majority of males feel themselves always to have been exclusively attracted to the same sex. Some have participated in heterosexual dating, and others have not. Some gay male youths experience little interest in contact sports, whereas some young lesbians express a strong interest in sports, especially team sports, which they feel sets them apart from their heterosexual peers. Hence, secrecy regarding inner desires emerges fully around puberty: youths may sense that one parent (usually the mother) has some awareness of their same-sex interest, but disclosure of such feelings rarely occurs until well after puberty. These events characterize what Van Gennep would call the preliminal stage, wherein the "self-suspicion"[49] of feeling "different" leads to introspection, withdrawal, and often alienation from peers and family.

Threshold Symbolism

For the youths who attend Horizons, the transitional event that signals a desire for external change comes when they first approach Horizons' door. Such approaches are typically ambivalent and are, more properly, approach and avoidance tactics. The search for self-understanding at this stage is fraught with strong emotions: extreme fear, guilt, self-hatred, and despair. What at an earlier time some psychiatrists labeled "homosexual panic"—sudden fear that one could be homosexual, usually by situational homoerotic recognition—is different from these fears of Horizons' youths. Theirs are existential identity claims. Who am I? Am I unique? How can I fit in? Such questions underlie their approach to Horizons. Some come in desperation, finally so much in need of another "home" that they overcome their own trepidations and pass through the door. Others hear of Horizons on radio or television talk shows, or they may overhear high school friends discussing how "fags" hang out there. Most youths say that they pondered and worried for months before they mustered the courage to enter Horizons' doors.

Here we have quintessential signs of threshold symbolism: the door represents a porthole into a "magical circle," Van Gennep would have said, its attractions and dangers the frontier of a sacred territory. "Sacred" here means powerful and untouchable. Youths express wild and fantastic ideas about what they imagined awaited inside. Secrecy is a torment at this point because most youths have never had to face a life crisis or make dramatic decisions of this kind alone, without the counsel of family and friends. Their images of the inner sanctum suggest the never-never land of all that is bizarre, crazy, powerful, evil, and potentially good, exciting, and fulfilling, the sacred of contagious and sympathetic magic. Teens report how they feared being confronted inside the door with drag queens, child molesters, junkies, prostitutes, and even crazies.

Initiation into New People's Group

Surprise is a primary sentiment in many teenagers' narratives of what they experience once they enter Horizons because the setting is so un-

expectedly ordinary. The storefront of the one-story building is bland
and its interior plain, much like the lobby of a small business office: a
few chairs, a desk, a sweep of windows, bulletin boards, a Coke machine. Around noon, on Saturdays, however, there is a press of people:
the typical flurry of activity as youths jam into the lobby, hugging and
chattering, the older initiates boisterous, showy, and joking. A bulletin
board of gay and lesbian news and community events stands out, proclaiming the territory gay. The "old-timers" from the youth group are
full of life, mostly proud of themselves, and they show it. They wear
the brightest colors, sport the most diverse range of fashions—from
army fatigues to high camp—their hair ranging in color from black
and blond to green and unnaturally maroon. The adult advisers, in
their twenties and thirties, are around too, but they are more adult and
citizen-like. Youths are friendly with them, and the overall scene projects the energy, intensity, and moment-by-moment spontaneity of a
high school: this is, after all, Saturday afternoon, a special "free time"
for most American adolescents.

The adolescent newcomer's reception is also unexpectedly warm, remarkably praising and positive, for advisers make every effort to acknowledge the courage of "new people" in joining the group. The
youth group meets in a large room filled with old sofas, metal folding
chairs, and the tattered hand-me-down posters of rock concerts.
People form a circle of chairs, and the youth group advisers summon
attention. The first order of business is to ask who is new to the group;
the show of hands is followed by asking the new youths their first
names. Each person is loudly applauded; most look shy and embarrassed by the attention. The format of meetings is semiformal, with no
necessary commitment to come again; thus, the group is organized as
a spontaneous "drop in." In fact, however, a core of "regulars"—fifteen
or twenty or so—come every Saturday. Hundreds throughout the year
come and pass on. A few new faces become regulars; the others show
a few times and disappear. But no one discusses this transience, so
noticeable to an ethnographer: a sign that the "core" (regular) adults
and youths, new and old, are interchangeable actors in a ritual drama
that transcends their particularity.

The format of the meetings is simple. The group collects for two
hours, divided into two segments broken by a fifteen-minute break.
Advisers and youths preselect a topic for discussion. There may be a
presentation or video related to coming out, gay community activities,
and, nowadays, AIDS. This focuses the main group "rap." However,

all "new people," those who have come for four Saturdays or less, are ushered into a smaller separate room, where they huddle with one or two advisers as an isolate.

The rule that newcomers cycle through this incoming secluded rap group is strict. This month of seclusion has special features. Its discourse is not raucous but subdued, and much of its content is inductive and often tense. Many new youths seem scared: they are just coming out, and their emotional intensity and fear, the heightened teaching about AIDS, and the special feeling of isolation all contribute to the impression of this being an ordeal of initiation par excellence. Many resent being singled out and separated from the larger group like an anonymous batch. Some leave and never return. Will they ever return, advisers wonder?

The code of solidarity, a special etiquette surrounding the interaction of the youth group, is the most intangible and subtle of ritual signs hidden to an outsider. A primary value underlying this code is the equality of status among new youths. To act superior is to be frowned on, regardless of someone's race, sex, or class. Hierarchy is foreign; likewise, to act aloof, to hold oneself distant, denies the group a strongly sought solidarity. The body contact at Horizons expresses this value physically. One is struck by the touching, by males sitting in the laps of females, by frequent kisses and hugs—which "feel" not erotic but rather friendly to the ethnographer—by the matching and borrowing of clothes, by the loaning of money to each other, by the constant shared confidences among these remarkably diverse adolescents.

The code of solidarity extends to a value never to judge other youths in the group. In Chicago, with its pronounced ethnic traditions, continuing racism, and intergroup tensions, this cohesion among multicultural adolescents is remarkable.[50] Someone may have green hair, wear leather, and act bizarre, but this is to be accepted. As one white male told me, "You can't make judgments in this environment because everyone else [on the outside] is making them. We come here to escape that. I mean, most people's parents give 'em hell if they know [they are gay], and, you know, it's just not right to judge them." This does not meant that judgments (and strong ones at that!) are not directed by youths toward parents and "society." There are disparaging remarks made about straights—"breeders"—who are prejudiced or "gay bashers." Strong negative sentiment is voiced against homophobia and gays who remain closeted. But this code is tacit and absorbed only slowly. Group values and norms permeate the discourse throughout, but the values of equality, solidarity, and acceptance of diverse life-styles are pivotal.

What do teenagers in the new people's group say about coming to Horizons? Joyce, a nineteen-year-old white female with a punk hairdo and jeans, came to the group several years ago. She has a steady "girlfriend" and now holds a job. For her, coming out meant "being honest with people about your sexuality." She has become a veteran group member and, increasingly, an activist in local gay culture, indicating that for some of Horizons' youths, the group serves as a springboard into the adult community.

Kurt is a studious-looking youth who has returned temporarily to Chicago after attending college elsewhere. He came out this year at school. Recently, he has also come out to his family. He feels "very accepted" by the friends to whom he has come out. His father's attitude, he tells the group, is that he can "do as he wishes," even though his father believes that homosexuality is "immoral." He came to Horizons for a different "voice," he says. Kurt tells the group that they provide him critical supportive "contact" with other gay people, so important to him right now.

Kevin is a nineteen-year-old white Italian American, a junior in high school. He is outgoing, energetic, and known for his good sense of humor. He is clean cut and is teased by others for having the "all-American boy" look. He says that he is "very popular" in school, which is important to him because of his career aspirations. He is on the Student Council and is a leader in extracurricular activities at school. He has never come out at school, however, and he loses his humor when he tells why: a rumor had gotten around shortly before his coming to Horizons that he was gay, and it "cost" him several of his friends. This shook him up. "Reality" is costly, he tells the new people. He argues that, if he came out in school, his popularity would plummet. Since then, he says, he has had to date the "pom-pom" girls (an idiom for suburban heterosexual females) to keep up his straight image. The youth group allows him to be "himself," he says, an irony because his fright and attempt to "pass" as straight led him to Horizons and thus to coming out in its seclusionary group.

Two forms of name taboo indicate the liminal nature of the new person's semisecret status in the youth group. First, there is the use of pseudonyms by some youths in the group. These are the adolescents who are most secretive and fear being identified. Most Horizons' youths use their true first names, though it is rare for surnames ever to be mentioned at Horizons. An analogous practice is that a few youths assume nicknames in the group, liminal tokens not used outside the circle of Horizons. One prominent member, for instance, goes by the name "Bowie," after David Bowie, the popular androgynous punk-rock movie star. Second, there is a taboo that provides a boundary mechanism vis-à-vis mainstream social relationships: never to speak the name of a group member on the "outside" for fear of betraying the youth's secret identity. This taboo parallels a rule established by advisers—not to approach gay youth group members on the streets in the city, lest they lose their "cover" and be discovered as gay by accompanying parents or friends—to whom they are not yet "out." These rules establish a boundary of secrecy to protect new youth group members from the outside world.

The imprint of homophobia and violence are never far from the secrecy discourse of Horizons newcomers. A vivid incident provides a reminder of it. We were completing interviews on a Saturday afternoon in mid-March 1987 when a bloodied man burst through the doors seeking help. He had been assaulted next door in the local gay newspaper offices by two men wielding baseball bats. The assailants fled. The police never caught them, but their sirens and a crowd of spectators who gathered jolted the youths. Some from the new people's group had observed the wounded man seek our help and the ensuing police search. They were horrified and felt helpless as the adults pushed by and took charge: a grim and dramatic reminder to them that the safety attendant on the youth group ends at its front doors. Indeed, the youths themselves refer to this idea as their "vulnerability syndrome" outside Horizons: a further sign of secrecy and of "passing" as straight. The magical boundaries that exclude the oppressive world must not be taken for granted in coming out. This assault was also a sign of ever-present violence against gays, as portrayed in the media and adult discourse.[51]

The secrecy of living a "double life" constantly crops up in the new people's group. "It's better with gays now," said Roy, a black twenty-year-old. "It's more real. My straight friends never discussed sex. It's a taboo. [They don't discuss] religion either. Gays are just more open than straights," he said. Roy tells how he had to invent a "girlfriend" in high school, where he was closeted, to keep his peers "off his back." "They kept bugging me, and I felt bad about it [inventing a girlfriend]. . . . You can't come out and survive where I went to school," he told me.

Roy had a hard time in high school, and his hiding illustrates the double life of homophobia in the schools. Educated in a private, lower-middle-class religious school in Chicago, Roy was bright, articulate, and reflective with me, yet he was in dismay over his school history. He relates that he was not only "closeted" in high school but that he "even helped to get rid of an openly gay kid," who was too "flamboyant." The boy was teased and bullied. "It was rough on him until he left. . . . I did know that there were other quiet gays around," but Roy avoided them. That is why he had to invent the fiction of a girlfriend, he says. Recently, after entering Horizons, Roy came out to his parents, "who are not handling my gayness very well." They will not take telephone messages for him at home, where he still lives, apparently because they feel that to do so would promote his gay lifestyle.

In short, the new people's group secludes and protects the youths, furthering their initiation. They can discuss why they came and how they feel before entering the larger group, which socializes them further into the cultural system of the gay community.

The Larger Group: Liminal Space

The weekly meetings of the Horizons youth group have an atmosphere resembling an extracurricular teenage happening, in all its emotional intensity, fun with friends, and adult-supervised learning through conversations. The "old-timers" enjoy the group immensely, and most of them say they would not miss it for anything. They are completely engaged: group stands out as a bright light to end their week. Their seclusion past, they enter the larger Horizons' group as public initiates.

This liminal phase more fully incorporates youths into Horizons. Now they feel that they can pour their hearts out to their friends and not be judged. Their feeling of belonging makes the heterosexual conventions they must obey at home, school, or work seem unreal, as if they belong to another time and place. Here begins a widening circle of coming out beyond Horizons. The youths invest their selfhood in the group and find reflected back to themselves the new desires and necessities of their lives, which they feel can be discussed fully here and only here.[52]

The content of formal group discussions is far reaching. "Sex" is a constant theme—not sex acts per se but how to be "gay" and what to do about homoerotic feelings and relationships. How does one begin dating others of the same sex? How does one initiate sex? Love is another constant theme, though its signs are expressed in topics beyond romance, as are coming out to straight friends, being called names at school, trying to understand parents' reactions and fears, and learning how to make same-sex relationships and contacts "work" in the climate of the AIDS epidemic. Parents are a constant source of exasperation and amusement. Complaints about harassment and discrimination occur regularly. "Spirituality" is a strongly evocative theme that resonates in the inner worlds and families of the youths, a number of whom are religious and feel condemned or dirty for "sinning" and "doing the devil's work" by coming out. These and other signs of the cultural system ("homosexuality") of earlier cohorts emerge in the concerns of the youths regarding gay sex and love.

A constant stream of gossip, tales of missed romance and intrigues, and "anxiety attacks" about being suspected of gay leanings make up the stream-of-consciousness discourse in which these teenagers delight. Only here—a world apart from mainstream Chicago—can youths find a context wherein the gay and lesbian content of their lives is not only permitted but institutionalized. The themes of their talk are liberating because they suggest that by coming out their social life can expand and become meaningfully "gay." This discourse makes of the youths participants in a cultural system of "gay identity." An example will illustrate the point.

"Gay humor" is an important historical mediator of Horizons' youth group sociality, and it contrasts sharply the early "homosexual" and the present "gay" cultural systems. As a form of ethnic humor, gay argot, puns, jokes, and the moods through which they are conveyed seem highly particularistic. Turning stereotypic labels back on someone humorously—such as calling someone "fag" or "dyke"—is common. "Faggot," for instance, can be a cute endearment to a close friend. "Queer" is not. "Queer" seems to hit too close to the youths, who see it as a smear. They cannot sufficiently convert its antisocial "homosexual" meanings into positive feelings that "minstrelize" (the term is Troiden's) the gender conventions of society.[53] The symbolic use of the term "gay" is conversely related to this difficulty with "queer" because theater and its "gay life" are seen as the very antithesis of the pitiful old Hollywood stereotype of the "queer."[54] Obviously,

breaking down "homosexual" stereotypes from an earlier historical period is a hidden text here. Clichés such as gay men being child molesters, sex crazed, and woman haters or lesbians being weight lifters and
man haters are frequent targets of jokes and stories. Group solidarity
is cemented by joining in these spontaneous one-liners, for the jokes
represent the self's declaration of coming out as requisite for being
newly included in the category "gay." Not only does gay humor thus
subjectively mark the "ethnic" boundaries of the youth group. But it
also symbolically objectifies the "homosexual" and "gay" cultural systems of Horizons' youths and young adult gays, who struggle with the
issue of discrimination in the face of many "closeted" homosexual persons who continue to pass as straight in a society that discredits and
would isolate them.[55]

The content of the larger Horizons group discourse and its cultural
meanings can only be sketched here, but several key themes have already emerged. First, and perhaps foremost, is the unlearning of a fundamental assumption that all people in all times and places are heterosexual. The brunt of this discourse is that being different, being gay or
lesbian, does not mean that one is crazy or sex crazed. Almost all Horizons' youths are gay identified. Yet no one denies that someone else
in the group may have had "straight" or "bisexual" experiences. There
is instead a keen attention to overcoming what Evelyn Hooker once
called society's own "heterosexual ethnocentricity."[56] Indeed, coming
out to *oneself* speaks frontally to this issue: the reluctance to place oneself into the new category—"gay"—is a sign of resistance to further
transitions into gay social relationships that extend beyond Horizons
into adult lesbian and gay community contexts. The transition process
may abort; those afraid of further assimilation into gay culture take
their leave rapidly from the group and may not return. Others, however, continue a journey that involves giving up the conception of the
self as a heterosexual in the new-found Horizons activities and ties.

Second is the adolescents' confrontation with the preconception of
gender inversion. This feeling of the new initiates concerns the common stereotype that the homosexual is gender inverted, a male in a
female's body, a woman who desires a woman who must therefore act
like a man. This old homosexual structure of cultural fantasies and
gender ideas is symbolically "tested" at Horizons, where youths find
adult gays and lesbians who seem ordinary—not necessarily conventional, but not gender reversed either. A few male youths at first wear

makeup and cross-dress; some female youths also take on male-like appearances. Class and color codes influence these ritualized personae. New stereotypes enter. "Lipstick lesbians," for example, are those who appear feminine and wear make-up. The old homosexual preconception is soon unlearned, however: the youths discover that they can dress and act—and be—"themselves" and still be gay. However, they usually uphold an individual's right to dress and act as he or she likes. Indeed, the youths themselves talk about "gender blending" as a stage of coming out that alters with time but is a new cultural feature of being gay.[57] Their changing self and personhood are incorporated into new social relationships that "naturalize" these feelings and appearances, their preferred code of gender role norms deriving increasingly from the gay cultural system.

Third is the theme of stigma and oppression, which goes by the name "homophobia." Adolescents have been victims, even perpetrators, of prejudice and bigotry in their jokes or jabs at "queers" and "dykes" in school, as we have seen. Before Horizons, fear turned its back on the secret self—closet homosexuality—by reacting negatively to others who had come out or embraced gay personhood. Many Horizons youths have been on the receiving end of this stigma and fear in high school. Fear of AIDS has heightened it. Learning to decode and recognize homophobia as a problem of oppression in society rather than as a deficit in the self is the focus of many group discussions on homophobia. Ultimately, the youths learn the attitude that it is self-homophobia that is most destructive of all, as commonly represented, for example, in a teenager saying to a peer, "You are just being self-homophobic."

These discourse themes thus suggest that, by coming out, youths should end secrecy and the "homosexual" giving up or denial of self-strivings in favor of the formation of gay- and lesbian-identified cultural goals and strategies for a new personhood in future relationships.

The Role of Adult Advisers

The culture and the community provide important role models, aiding the formation and expression of gay identity. Van Gennep's notion of "indirect" rites, which "set in motion" certain "repercussions" in subsequent thought, language, and action, is useful here.[58] The adult advisers at Horizons exemplify what to be and not to be, as lesbians and gays. Their role cannot be underestimated because many youths—in search of acceptance while hiding their sexuality at home and school—have no other adult figures on whom they can model themselves in their coming-out transition.

Youth group advisers are selected by agency personnel to reflect positive features of lesbian and gay life-styles. (Occasionally, heterosexual parents serve as advisers too.) The ostensible function of the unpaid adviser is to facilitate youth group meetings. No therapy is conducted: youths who express such a need are referred to separate psychological counseling services. Even the "advising" of advisers is usually implicit and minimal. Much of the socialization of being and acting gay in the group is by observation rather than by instruction, a doing "gay" model embedded in the social makeup of the group ritual process. Attitudes, beliefs, and the folklore of gay culture are transmitted in the course of social interaction. Advisers range in age from twenty-three to the late forties. Most are service-providing people, including some mental health professionals and interns who volunteer their time. Their motives for taking on the role vary, but they share a commitment to community development and—as my interviews with them have revealed, in a less conscious way—to the furtherance of their own adult coming-out status through volunteer work at Horizons.

The agency's leaders in general, and the youth advisers in particular, represent a broad cross section of Chicago life, though a rather bourgeois one at that. Most adults are indistinguishable in clothes, demeanor, haircuts, makeup, and gestures from mainstream Chicagoans. This "appearance of normality" is in fact both genuine and artificial, in that most advisers are of middle-class origins and are assimilated into mainstream workplaces, including jobs where some of them cannot be openly lesbian or gay.[59] Others, however, are activist and "politically conscious" about self-identifying as gay wherever they are. The fact that adults identified as bisexual are completely absent among advisers says, I think, that bisexuals are outside the mainstream of both American middle-class culture and the gay community.[60]

One taboo above all others stands out at Horizons: advisers having sex with youth group members. This strong moral norm is explicitly conveyed to new adviser recruits when they first undergo intensive training. Likewise, it is taught to youths on their first entering the new people's group. Coded into the morality of this taboo is the image of the parent/child relationship as a vessel of caretaking in the adviser/

youth dyad. Some teenagers may try to fraternize with an adviser outside the group, asking for a telephone number or the chance to have lunch, but these overtures are frowned on. In fact, such youths cannot know that in the private discourse of advisers' meetings all such overtures are considered "inappropriate" and must never be reciprocated. Old stories from previous years tell of the suicide of a youth and expulsion of an adviser through the violation of this taboo, and their contemporary reflections seem both culturally apocryphal and psychologically salient in the minds of advisers. Private interviews with advisers have also confirmed that nothing is regarded as more inviolate than this magical "age-structured" sexual taboo.[61]

The cultural force of the taboo on sex with advisers issues from the folk psychology of contagious-sympathetic magic surrounding homosexuality in American ideology. It is still widely believed that someone can "catch" homosexuality simply by associating with someone else who is gay or lesbian.[62] Some parents of gays whom we have interviewed in Chicago believe that being in the youth group is a "passing" phase of "homosexual" interest that will "go away" if they discourage it. For example, Roy—the black male mentioned above—said that his mother tolerates his going to Horizons but that she will not permit him to take telephone calls or receive visitors at home. Some youths have been ordered to undergo psychiatric treatment by their parents, who hope to change them. Others in our society believe that adults can influence the sexual orientation of children: consider, for example, instances of gay or lesbian teachers being removed from the classroom because some parents fear their gayness would "rub off" on their children. Thus, where the old discourse of the "homosexual" cultural system reigns, it is still believed that the "disease" of homosexuality can subvert the young and seduce them sexually into the "homosexual lifestyle."[63]

One area of active teaching by advisers that does occur concerns AIDS. This instructional enculturation is not felt to violate the ideology of nonintervention because of the epidemic need to protect youths from HIV infection. Education for "safe sex" and the elimination of sexual risk-taking behavior is a top priority of the Horizons agency.[64] Films, booklets, outside speakers, and group discussions actively teach about AIDS and other sexually transmitted diseases, creating a pedagogical link between the adolescent and adult generations who share in the gay cultural system.

Sometimes teaching is more subtle, as when rhetoric turns to concepts such as "love" and "relationships" in the group. Here, there is the inevitable interjection of culturally pluralistic values and standards on the part of adult advisers. At one of the advisers' meetings, for instance, a young man suggested that many youths were unschooled on how to initiate a "date" with someone of the same sex.[65] The advisers themselves were uncertain. Should they teach about dating? Another young adviser shifted the tension by joking, however: "Yes, many youths have never been out on a date. . . . But I wonder if they know that many of their advisers haven't either!" Reflections of the latter-day emergent coming out of advisers themselves are apparent here; they suggest the uncertainty regarding the emerging norms for "love" and "sex" in the gay cultural system.

There is no doubt that advisers are self-selected for and self-consciously concerned with the building of gay solidarity. The clearest example came shortly before the Gay Pride Day Parade in 1987. The youth group was preparing to play its leadership role in the parade festivities. One somewhat older male adviser was in charge of the group that day, and he announced the sale of gay "Rainbow" flags (a nearly universal symbol of the gay and lesbian movement) to raise money for the charitable activities of Horizons. He appealed to the group to purchase and sell the flags to their friends for a modest fee, remarking on how "neat" it would be for them to hang a flag on the wall of their bedroom. "This is helpful for making a gay culture," he said, with such sincerity that no one could possibly have questioned his commitment to the parade.

After Hours: Informal Events in Chicago

Most Horizons youths socialize informally outside Horizons with others from the group. In our individual interviews, we ask all teenagers to name their three best friends, and, typically, one or two of these are from the group. They hold parties at the homes of those where such socializing is possible. "Bowie," a prominent leader in the group, does so. He lives with his same-aged lover in an apartment in the neighborhood, and their place has hosted many impromptu socials. At one time, some young lesbians from the group roomed with them, and other group members often "crash" at their apartment on weekends. The group also sponsors occasional picnics and outings to movies. In the summer, there is beach going a few blocks away at Lake Michigan. Youths sun at a section of the beach not exclusively "gay" but known to be frequented by gays and lesbians, where Horizons holds summer socials as well. Charitable work is encouraged as well, such as helping in clinics that assist persons with AIDS. Advisers are peripheral to the planning of these extracurricular events, and they are never present at the private ones.

After the youth group meeting, a large group of the youths regularly lunch at a nearby fast-food restaurant. The teenagers are not warmly accepted at this straight-owned "hangout." Youths reported, for instance, that they were never allowed to use the washroom, which was confirmed by a member of our research team, who was told that the toilet was "out of order" when she accompanied the youths several times.[66] Nonetheless, outings are happy occasions for the youths. They are "on their own"—the adults are gone—and gossip and stories of the week's events create an atmosphere of gay space and time outside the group. One youth referred to this outing, for instance, as critical for his "mental health" because he knows that he can always "let down his hair" and discuss the week's problems with his friends after the group. Money is shared, and clothes are traded, too, for gender blending involves swapping unisex clothes as well as "trashing" as boring the "costumes of straight people." This after-hours' lunching establishes a warm cohesion of secular boundedness fitting to an initiation age set in the absence of adults.

Going out to cocktail taverns or "juice bars" (where only nonalcoholic beverages are served) is an important entry point into the adult gay community. Though taverns do not have the salience they once did in gay acculturation, they remain a surprisingly prominent feature of the coming-out process for many Chicago youths, especially males. As one former youth group member (a black man in his twenties) said, "It is a very big deal to go to the bars for the first time." The juice bars cater to an underage crowd. The one near Horizons is actually age segregated: persons over eighteen are prohibited before 11:00 P.M., and those under twenty-one are prohibited thereafter, when alcohol is served. Most of the thirty-seven gay and lesbian bars in the Newtown area (in 1987) prohibit underage youths from entering, though in fact some group members frequent a discotheque that is lenient. Here again gender differences enter in. Aside from an all-women's coffeehouse in the neighborhood, it is harder for young lesbians to enter taverns, and only two of the thirty-seven gay bars are exclusively female (eighteen are exclusively male). The youths do use alcohol, but it has a different recreational function and lower social value than among past cohorts. "Cruising" (sexual solicitation) is not prominent among the youths either. Where, in previous cohorts, tavern culture sexualized much contact, especially between males, the values of the prevailing gay cultural system and the fears of AIDS have changed this.[67] "The norm," one nineteen-year-old male told me, "is for safe sex," even though he acknowledged that unsafe sex occurs.

Youths thus learn, in time, of other social settings through which to meet as gays and lesbians, and gender differences become increasingly important as they do. Their widening network of new social relationships and cultural activities demonstrates that transition into community social life through the youth group is becoming an alternative pathway to that of the tavern culture of former cohorts.

The Annual Gay Youth Prom

A major culminating event in adolescent coming out is the Annual Gay Youth Prom sponsored by Horizons and the youth group, which occurs each year concurrently with high school proms throughout Chicago, toward the end of May. The prom is a point of symbolic opposition to mainstream culture, participation in which further erodes the secrecy of the former life-style, highlighting coming out in another arena. In 1987, the prom was held in the large open banquet room of a nearby restaurant, which is a popular meeting place for gays and for heterosexual wedding receptions and similar functions. The restaurant is a strong supporter of Horizons; many of its patrons reciprocate the charitable support of the restaurant by hosting gay functions there. Anchored in a prominent meeting place of the neighborhood, the prom thus provides the youths with a formal and dramatic transition into the gay cultural scenes of mainstream Chicago.

About eighty persons attended the prom in 1987. Most of these were "regulars" from the group, including advisers who also attended to monitor the prom. Adults remarked to me that, compared to previous years, few youths cross-dressed, which they see as a positive sign of the politically "changing times" (reflecting, again, the unlearning of prior stigmatized "homosexual" conceptions). Two youths cross-dressed, however, one of them as a high-fashion female model. They were well accepted.

The overall atmosphere of the prom seemed at first glance indistinguishable from similar cultural scenes in Chicago high school settings. The key difference was that the couples dancing were virtually all composed of same-sex partners. Rarely, a male-female couple danced. The energy and enthusiasm of the youths was quintessentially American adolescent. To all appearances, nothing "special" was going on—until one noticed the same-sex dancing. One liminal reversal relative to the Saturday youth group meeting, however, was that a few advisers agreed to dance with some youths, lowering the taboo on physical contact with them. Gender blending was a prominent theme throughout: hair and clothes blended the sexes, with most males and females donning tuxedos.

Another reversal was a symbolic inversion of the "king" and "queen" positions. A popular young lesbian in the group was elected "king" of the prom and the popular youth "Bowie" its "queen." Thus, the royalty figures minstrelized normative gender conventions, effectively suggesting that gay and lesbian youths are not bound by old-fashioned societal expectations.

Many youths said that they like the idea of hosting a gay alternative to high school proms. In fact, the prom's organization was on the whole typical of mainstream events. A banquet began the festivities, followed by short announcements. A local lesbian celebrity served as "disc jockey," however. She selected music known to be thematic of gay lives from such groups as Bronski Beat and the Communards, popular gay-identified rock groups. Soda was readily available, but alcohol was strictly prohibited. Many of the youths came with dates, some but not all from the youth group. The advisers, too, brought same-sex dates. They remarked later that, compared to conventional "straight" proms, gender-blended Horizons youths are not "captives" to custom, although they are still well behaved.

Judging from the youth group discussion the following week, the prom was felt to be a great success. The youth group adviser (a younger lesbian) that day commented, "You were all—this isn't the right word—well behaved at the prom." The group whistled and applauded. Then, quick as a dart, a fourteen-year-old lesbian remarked, "That's the advantage of not being straight!" Laughter followed. Then another member chimed in, "Yeah, see what happens when you don't repress your sexuality! Things go better [i.e., than if you are closeted]." "It was great" to have the prom, another youth, Jeffery, said. "It's a real advantage to being gay," he said, because "coming out" cements friendships, allowing youths to share in their true feelings with "real" people more than was ever possible before.

The Annual Gay Pride Parade

Marching in the parade that celebrates the anniversary of the Stonewall riots is a popular demonstration of public participation in the youth group. No other event at Horizons is as well planned and universally participated in, both by adults and by youths involved in the three days' festivities. In 1987, the parade attracted about 100,000 people in Chicago, lasted hours, and was capped by a short speech by his honor the mayor, the late Harold Washington. Floats and banners are prepared; all manner of groups, churches, and businesses send delegations. The youth group has led the parade in Chicago for years; a small coterie of male and female youths carried the Horizons banner at the head of the parade. These are the most "out" and socially active gay youths, the ones who are not afraid to be photographed or shown on the evening television news leading the entire parade. One young lesbian, for instance, told me that she could not march because she had to get a job soon; she was afraid to be seen for fear that this would ruin her chances of gaining employment. Another eighteen-year-old male was seen carrying the banner on television by his mother, who hid the fact from her husband. Later, she became supportive of the boy's coming out. While publicity is an issue and fear of coming out so publicly remains, nevertheless, culmination of initiation into the gay youth group means marching in the parade.

Many youths describe the parade as a "peak experience" of the Horizons youth group and, indeed, of their entire adolescent coming-out process. It is "shocking" and "amazing" for them, they say, to see so many gay and lesbian people crowded in the streets, open to public view—so defiantly at odds with the youths' own fearful approach to Horizons at the start. Being part of this social body is eye opening, and their stories reveal its nature as a true liminal experience for them. Their sentiments would have warmed the Durkheim of *The Elementary Forms of the Religious Life* (1915), who saw, in the massing of group festivals, a phenomenological foundation of crowd psychology on which the collective consciousness of culture is constructed. The parade is indeed often referred to by body metaphors and deep emotions, as if the isolated self were drawn out of its secret recesses in the private body into a new and public sociality. The youths talk, in fact, as if they feel renewed and reborn, a liminal feeling that supports the often-heard sentiment, "I am not alone or unique; I have found many others like me." The parade thus mirrors the collective initiation of youths who speak metaphorically as if they were reborn with a new self and social role in the parade experience.

Richard Herrell (see chapter 8) has well documented the meanings of the parade in the polity of Chicago. His work suggests that the social communication of political power and the press for recognition of the diversity of lesbian and gay life-styles are integral to the cultural meaning of Gay Pride Day. But there is an enigma of solidarity in the Lesbian and Gay Parade, composed as it is of many cohorts, the two genders, and diverse interest groups. "Gay solidarity" is everywhere manifest in high rhetoric, yet the diversity and even conflict between pluralistic life-styles emerges pragmatically in the multitude of floats by gay businesses, churches, Alcoholics Anonymous, persons with AIDS, gays in drag, lesbians on motorcycles, Parents and Friends of Lesbians and Gays (PFLAG), and other factions that signify the extraordinary range of persons ("from all walks of life") who represent the gay and lesbian movement. Other cities in the Midwest also send delegations—pilgrimages—to the parade; floats and banners arrive from Indiana, Michigan, and Wisconsin. None are turned away.

"Cultural diversity" as a theme in the gay cultural system thus communicates to the youths that they do not have to deny their gender or ethnic origins, their religion or class status, to take a place in the emerging gay cultural system. In this symbolic message we find a final theme of unlearning the older "homosexual" preconceptions: all gays are *not* alike. The reduction of the gay or lesbian person to one sex act in folklore and the media is thus challenged on a grand scale. The symbolic learning of this conception of multicultural diversity represents a final transformation in identity prior to youthful entry into the widening circle of adult relationships and institutions.

Leave Taking and Reincorporation

At age twenty-one, youths must take their leave from the group. This "graduation" is traumatic for some who may not yet have found their way. We have observed individual youths become tearful and despondent over their leave taking. Because some youths come to the group as late as age twenty, they still are in the throes of coming out at their twenty-first birthday. In fact, a few youths actually hide their true age at Horizons in order to remain in the group beyond their twenty-first birthday. Others who have participated in the group since their earlier adolescent years have an easier time of it. One of our interviewers was angered and puzzled by this strict rule of exclusion at age twenty-one, and all of us have wondered about the absence of a formal "postgroup" coming-out group.[68] However, from the perspective of the ritual process of the youth group, this boundary rule is not mysterious. Every rite of passage has its beginning and must have its end. Age twenty-one is in most respects entry into American adulthood. These symbolic markers raise with more finality the question of symbolic death and rebirth images in the passage beyond Horizons.

Van Gennep wrote that the ritual novice is often considered "dead" by the community, once he or she passes into the liminal stage.[69] He or she exists in a timeless ritual space outside normative society. The many cultural forms of symbolic death and rebirth in transition rites the world over seem to signify the mysteries and revelations of the control over social reproduction that is exercised by the hegemony of a secret society or elite.[70] The social structural goal of initiation is status change; the personal identity change is what Victor Turner made famous as an existential "stage of reflection," wherein initiates are "divested of their previous habits of thought, feeling, and action."[71] Both personal and societal are components of the process of coming out: of nurturing a new self born at Horizons and demonstrating this with a new social status in the parade. Yet the emotional sense of being regarded as "dead" by significant others who react negatively to youthful coming out is also suggestive of the deeper symbolic and psychological theme.

"My parents couldn't deal with it," a nineteen-year-old youth said recently to the youth group, of his coming out: "My mother said, 'You are dead to me. How can you be queer?' She said there would be no family name (I am her only son). . . . And why did it have to be *me*? 'You are my only son. . . . It cannot be.' She kicked me out [of the house]. She refuses to talk to me. I had to go and live with my lover. This was a year ago. She still acts like I don't exist." The day on which this story was revealed, the youth group was at once indignant. They have heard the sentiment before. But each new story reinforces their feeling that straights "do not understand" them. Paradoxically, though, a few youths defended the parents. "You have to give them time" to accept "it," two youths argued. Another young women, an eighteen-year-old who has been out for two years, disagreed. "You have to live your own life. . . . Decide what you want. They can't live your life for you." She said that at first her parents thought that she "was going through a stage, that I was confused." After a year, they stopped saying that, especially when they were introduced to her girlfriend. After two years, they said, "We don't know you anymore." "It" was no longer a stage, they felt: "You have to go to a shrink." She saw a psychiatrist for a time. Her parents, she hinted, no longer recognize her because of the new lesbian person she has become. Notice that the "it" in two of these narratives is unmarked and open ended: it signifies not only being gay but one's very existence as a person.

Although these self-reports of gay and lesbian youths being "dead" may seem extreme—indeed, some parents do accept their children as gay more readily—they mirror a process that is independently re-ported from the narratives of the parents of gays themselves. Many parents say that they felt that their children were dead or gone to them on hearing of their coming out. Ann Muller documented this reaction among Chicago parents, which pertains, in part, to the feeling of loss that parents experience in relation to their lifelong aspirations for grandchildren or identification with the life goals of their offspring.[72] Our own study of the parents of gays suggests that it takes years for many of them to reconcile their perceptions of their children with those children's gay identities after coming out.[73] On the other hand, the most positive parents join a local chapter of the national organiza-tion Parents and Friends of Lesbians and Gays. PFLAG is probably the most widely applauded parade group. Parents themselves speak of a reciprocal status change process of "coming out," only here their idiom refers to revealing to their own relatives and friends—and per-haps even to the nation—that they have a gay or lesbian child.[74] The ever-present prejudice in society still hems in these progressive parents, too. For instance, an older father, a leader of the Chicago PFLAG group, was interviewed by the newspapers. He told with pride his story of his sons' coming out. But then, at the completion of the inter-view, the reporter cautioned him, "I can't use your real name in the story because your business might be affected. . . . Some of your cus-tomers might boycott you." Thus, we see the positive and negative signs of contagious/sympathetic status change reflected on and tainting the families of gay youths. This finding of secrecy, stigma, and "coming out" in the status changes of parents of gays provides an important clue for interpreting the final phase of assimilation after coming out.

Graduation from Horizons at age twenty-one suggests full entry into the gay and lesbian community. The semisecrecy of the youth group is left behind. Coming out at this point is not of course a uniform process for many youths. Some of them, for a variety of reasons, remain secretive or continue to hide and "pass" as heterosexual. For the others, however, exit from Horizons is entry into a far wider world of public gay-identified social relationships.

To understand this statement requires a recognition that there are two different meaning systems operating within our society: the "homosexual" cultural system and the "gay" (lesbian) cultural system. The "homosexual" represents the historically older disease/stigma discourse that kept these persons closeted. The "gay" cultural system, however, incorporates new meanings that are still disparaged in the mainstream heterosexual society but that are lauded in lesbian and gay discourse.

What began with magical thinking—that a youth could be heterosexual by avoiding homosexual feelings or that one could magically become gay, contagiously picking up the role and identity merely by entering the doors of Horizons—has not transpired. Does not the self come to know that its own unique course in life is not settled so easily or definitively? Like the survivors of older "homosexual" cohorts, youths vary considerably in acceptance of the desires and necessities of their gay identities. The problems of being gay and black differ from those of being gay and white since racism must be handled. The issues of gender differentiate because adjustment into adult life creates gender-specific problems for males and females—with the ever-present sexism, and how women face the issue of having children, as time passes. The religious turmoil of devout Catholic gay youths is unknown to the agnostic teen. The middle-class slant of Horizons raises the specter of classism. In general, however, compared to earlier historical cohorts, it is more probable than before that youths will eventually come out across the full range of contexts in which they situate themselves: school, home, work, and friendships. What mediates their sociocultural declaration of a gay or lesbian identity in these domains are three factors: gender, ethnicity, and class. Space does not permit me to review these issues.[75] Generally, however, the literature suggests that white middle-class males come out earliest and more fully in all domains, white females somewhat later and less fully, and working-class and underprivileged blacks and Hispanics more slowly and in-completely—if at all. Obviously, stigma and oppression remain struc-tural barriers here and will continue to do so for years.[76] The meanings of coming out are therefore culturally variable across the spectrum of lesbians and gays, a tautology necessary for interpreting the final tran-sition into adult gay and lesbian lives.

Being openly gay or lesbian in all social situations is a category change of the most profound sort in self and other representations and relationships. This transition requires more than the mediation or un-learning of secrecy. It means repudiation and symbolic transformation of the stigmata of homosexuality—in psyche and in the world. Secrecy in tribal initiation rites is commonly associated with the revelation of sacred and related esoteric knowledge to novitiates.[77] Usually, the ex-istence of a secret structure empowers initiates vis-à-vis those who are structurally excluded.[78] In previous cohorts, the "secret gay world" ex-isted to avoid stigma—that is, to empower gays more—by enabling them to live secretly as gay and publicly as straight.[79]

Horizons is a way station on the road to a new and different cultural empowerment. It is not the end but rather the means to the achieve-ment of gay and lesbian personhood in public life. What began as a semisecret initiation into a seclusion group concludes as a delayed so-cial puberty rite of status entitlement in the emerging gay and lesbian community. It is precisely the unlearning of secrecy and the integration of same-sex erotism into psyche and society that are at stake here.

The revelation of complete initiation into Horizons, including marching in the parade, is that the world is populated by many for-merly secret homosexuals who have come out as lesbian and gay. Their presumed heterosexuality is now a moot point. It is rather the power of the older, dominant conception of homosexuality that remains problematic, for there are still many secretive homosexuals in our so-ciety whose identities cannot be understood except by attention to the covert signs and symbols of a "homosexual cultural system." Some of them have proved to be a significant roadblock to fighting the AIDS epidemic, for example, because they fear that using their position will mean their exposure as homosexuals.[80] In the coming-out process of adolescents today, it is thus the homosexual, not only the heterosexual, that is a roadblock. Both the closet homosexual and the before-coming-out heterosexual conception of the self exercise a pull back into the closet. Giving up this secrecy of the homosexual self is tanta-mount to repudiating the profane nature of one's prior existence. Tak-ing on a lesbian or gay status in all social arenas extends in an unprec-edented way the reach of a gay cultural system into multiplex relationships that challenge the morality of that profane existence. It challenges gender and erotic conventions, posing dangers of defile-ment and pollution to stable heterosexual and secret "homosexual" sta-tus hierarchies throughout our society: to youths, their parents, and the gay community.[81]

Van Gennep believed that the privilege of all novitiates in transition rites was to learn how "to manipulate sacra without regard of fear of danger from the supernatural."[82] His concepts "sacra" and "supernat-ural" are of course problematic in complex societies, for he had in mind esoteric religious icons. Yet, by seeing the meaning of "secret homosexual" as profane, and by attending to the many signs of sym-pathetic/contagious magical belief in and about gay youths and their significant others, we can identify and interpret the local means of "sacra" and "supernatural" in the emergent cultural system of gays and lesbians.

What is most feared by the Horizons youths is not merely being discredited, as "homosexual," in their former lives: it is the obliteration of self and personhood that would remove from them their feelings of being alive and real at all. In their transition to gay and lesbian identi-ties and statuses, they come to hold being gay as the supreme value, the ultimate good, on which they have staked their existence. There-fore, gay identity writ large becomes for them sacred, and its antithesis becomes the secret homosexual. The construction of gay psyche in re-lationships throughout society requires the ability to express and rep-resent this sacra—gay identity—without fear of self-obliteration and the loss of all that is good in themselves and in society to them. This represents the kind of achievement of rebirth to which Van Gennep alluded. Not only does this repudiate the old homosexuality dis-course—of failed heterosexuality, gender inversion, self-stigma, and the homogeneity of being gay—but the cultural system of gay fore-shadows a utopian world wherein sexual secrecy and coming out will no longer be necessary, the expression of same-sex desires being automatically accorded the credit of personhood formerly denied.

Conclusion

Social and political changes in our society have transformed the meanings of "homosexuality." Various investigators have argued whether "homosexuality" and "gay" should be identified as communities or cultures, ghettos, or life-styles.[83] On the psychological side, theorists have regarded the phenomena in terms of "identity" and "sexual orientation" stages. The problems related to the coming-out process among contemporary adolescents cannot easily be mapped onto these concepts. Perhaps in earlier cohorts they could have been; however, a sharper definition of the contemporary meanings of the gay and lesbian cultural system provides a different conceptual perspective.[84] "Homosexuality" is an older cultural system that overlaps with but is separate from a gay/lesbian conception in urban America today. In simple terms, adolescents who come out in Chicago are semisecretly initiated into a youth group; they graduate from being "homosexual" to being gay in their adult lives.

A generation ago, coming out was a secret incorporation into the surreptitious "homosexual" community. The category change from heterosexual to homosexual stigmatized and discredited personhood. Without institutional support, the pejorative cultural meanings of sexual identity category change reduced the problem to one of "simple" category change in individual self-representation. "Most persons who eventually identify themselves as homosexual," Dank once argued, "require a change in the meaning of the cognitive category homosexual before they can place themselves in the category."[85] The stigmatized signs of homosexuality were not enviable. There was no gay and lesbian movement and no social institutions available to promote positive identifications with the category gay. To come out in the late 1960s was for Dank's respondents a process of finding sex contacts in the bars, public toilets, the armed services, etc. By the 1970s, however, the concept of a "gay self" distinct from sexual contact had crept into the discourse of coming out. Mere cognitive change was no longer the issue. For this generation, "The emergence of the gay self thus renders the presentation of the self problematic. The lesbian must take into account the factors of stigma and the risks attendant to the revelation of her gay identity in most social settings apart from the community of her own. . . . The relationship of the gay self to the straight world is mediated through secrecy."[86] Coming out meant something very different to these people than it does at Horizons because the concept of a "gay self" was incomplete, owing to the suppressions of the old homosexual cultural system.

Adolescent coming out at Horizons not only alters selfhood; it refigures their social interactions, their statuses as actors, and their positive regard for gay relationships across time and space. Two cultural systems—the homosexual and the gay—have come into place, and their signs and symbols now compete to create divergent pathways to development. The consequences of socialization into gay versus homosexual meaning systems differ dramatically. The existence of each system predicates the meanings of coming out for the persons and groups involved. The anthropologist Max Gluckman once predicted that ritualization would occur in those arenas of complex societies in which significant "overlap" and "contradiction" made multiplex relationships conflictual, breaking down a "segregation of roles, and a segregation of moral judgments."[87] The rituals of coming out have emerged to energize and gracefully mediate the conflict and breakdown of the older homosexual system. This account does not address the underlying structural causes of homophobia, which is crucial; however, it does have the merit of explaining why sexuality remains a focus of the coming out ritual not only in the homosexual but in the gay cultural system. The breakdown of the segregation of moral judgments challenges stigma and discrimination. But coming out as gay or lesbian now violates the social conditions of homophobia far more than the old secrecy of homosexuality.

The coming-out processes of previous cohorts was incomplete because its structural supports were minimal and the oppression associated with it was so great. The gay and lesbian movement had to emerge and press for full social rights to facilitate the new cultural system. In doing so, however, it did not abolish the stigmata of the cultural category "homosexuality." Rather, it substituted for it a new social personae: gay/lesbian. To change social personhood from homosexual to gay among youths, the ritualization of status and meaning changes is absolutely necessary through social groups like that of Horizons. The Gay Pride Day Parade in particular is the key social event of adolescent gay development that graduates the person from "homosexuality" to "gay." However, no single event is constitutive of being socially/psychologically "pubertally" gay or lesbian. Each successive event leads to new social claims and relationships, the sum of which confirms being "gay," with its ultimate claims to social acceptance in contemporary society.

Notes

Support for this study comes from a grant awarded by the Spencer Foundation (G. Herdt, principal investigator), whose generous assistance is gratefully acknowledged. My collaborator in this study, Andrew Boxer (director, Center for the Study of Adolescence, Michael Reese Hospital and Clinics), is a full partner in the project. We have been assisted by our colleagues Dr. Floyd Irvin, a clinical psychologist (Michael Reese Hospital), and anthropologist Richard Herrell (University of Chicago). Our interdisciplinary study utilizes ethnographic techniques to examine sociocultural processes in the broader community and within the youth group and also individual interviews conducted with teenagers in private. Our interview protocol takes about three hours to administer. A separate interview study of fifty parents is also being conducted. This chapter concerns itself largely with the ethnographic component of the study. We are immensely grateful to Horizons Social Services for its support. We are particularly grateful for the continuing support of Bruce Koff. I wish to thank my colleagues Andrew Boxer, Ellen Lewin, Stephen Murray, Shelly Balmer, Robert Stoller, Barry Adam, and Richard Herrell for comments on this chapter. I alone am responsible for its shortcomings.

1. On public declaration, see John Lee, "Going Public: A Study in the Sociology of Homosexual Liberations," *Journal of Homosexuality* 3 (1978): 49–78. On private or secret contexts, see G. Herdt, *Sambia: Ritual and Gender in New Guinea* (New York: Holt, Rinehart & Winston, 1987). On "being homosexual," see J. Weeks, *Sex, Politics, and Society: The Regulation of Sexuality since 1800* (London: Longman, 1981).
2. T. S. Weinberg, *Gay Men, Gay Selves* (New York: Irvington, 1983).
3. Gilbert Herdt, "Introduction: Gay and Lesbian Youth, Emergent Identities and Cultural Scenes at Home and Abroad," in *Adolescence and Homosexuality*, ed. Gilbert Herdt (New York: Harrington, 1989).
4. B. Dank, "Coming Out in the Gay World," *Psychiatry* 34 (1971): 180–97.
5. V. Cass, "Homosexual Identity: A Concept in Need of a Definition," *Journal of Homosexuality* 9 (1982): 105–26; H. Minton and G. J. McDonald, "Homosexual Identity Formation as a Developmental Process," *Journal of Homosexuality* 9 (1983): 91–104; R. R. Troiden, "The Formation of Homosexual Identities and Roles," in Herdt, ed., *Adolescence and Homosexuality*.
6. S. O. Murray, *Social Theory, Homosexual Realities* (New York: Gai Saber, 1984).
7. J. Carrier, "Homosexual Behavior in Cross-cultural Perspective," in *Homosexual*

Behavior: A Modern Reappraisal, ed. J. Marmor (New York: Basic, 1980), pp. 100–122.

8. Joseph Harry, *Gay Children Grown Up* (New York: Praeger, 1982); J. Carrier, review of *Homosexualities,* by A. Bell and M. Weinberg, *Journal of Sex Research* 17 (1982): 38–41.

9. Herdt, "Introduction: Gay and Lesbian Youth."

10. M. R. Allen, *Male Cults and Secret Initiations in Melanesia* (Melbourne: Melbourne University Press, 1967); J. La Fontaine, *Initiation Rites* (New York: Penguin, 1985).

11. G. Herdt, *Guardians of the Flutes: Idioms of Masculinity* (New York: McGraw-Hill, 1981), and *Sambia.*

12. A. Van Gennep, *Rites of Passage* (Chicago: University of Chicago Press, 1960), p. 81.

13. K. Jay and A. Young, *The Gay Report* (New York: Summit, 1977).

14. B. Ponse, "Secrecy in the Lesbian World," *Urban Life* 5 (1976): 313–38; K. Read, *Other Voices* (Toronto: Chandler & Sharpe, 1980).

15. A. P. Bell, M. S. Weinberg, and S. Hammersmith, *Sexual Preference* (Bloomington: Indiana University Press, 1981).

16. Jay and Young, *The Gay Report;* A. Fricke, *Reflections of a Rock Lobster* (Boston: Alyson, 1981).

17. C. Geertz, "From the Native's Point of View: On the Nature of Anthropological Understanding," in *Meaning in Anthropology,* ed. K. Basso and H. Selby (Albuquerque: School for American Research and University of New Mexico Press, 1976), pp. 221–37.

18. C. Gilligan, *In a Different Voice* (Cambridge, Mass.: Harvard University Press, 1982).

19. On transformations in gendered worlds, see Herdt, *Sambia;* on changes in cognitive category or self-identity, see Cass, "Homosexual Identity."

20. Camille Gerstell, D. Feraios, and Gilbert Herdt, "Widening Circles: An Ethnographic Profile of a Youth Group," in Herdt, ed., *Adolescence and Homosexuality,* pp. 211–28.

21. E. Hooker, "An Empirical Study of Some Relations between Sexual Patterns and Gender Identity in Male Homosexuals," in *Sex Research: New Developments,* ed. J. Money (New York: Holt, Rinehart & Winston, 1965), pp. 24–52; Read, *Other Voices.*

22. Herdt, "Introduction: Gay and Lesbian Youth."

23. Glen H. Elder, Jr., "Adolescence in Historical Perspective," in *Handbook of Adolescent Psychology,* ed. Joseph Adelson (New York: Wiley, 1980), pp. 3–46; I. Roscow, "What Is Cohort and Why?" *Human Development* 21 (1978): 65–75.

24. I have little data on this cohort from Chicago, but, for an important historical study from the East Coast, see George Chauncey, Jr., "Christian Brotherhood or Sexual Perversion? Homosexual Identities and the Construction of Sexual Boundaries in the World War One Era," *Journal of Social History* 19 (1985): 198–211.

25. J. D'Emilio, *Sexual Politics, Sexual Communities* (Chicago: University of Chicago Press, 1983), p. 31. See also Allan Berube, *Coming Out under Fire* (New York: Free Press, 1990).

26. Monika Kehoe, "Lesbians over 65: A Triply Invisible Minority," *Journal of Homosexuality* 14 (1986): 253–76.

27. K. Vacha, *Quiet Fire* (Trumansburg, N.Y.: Crossing, 1985).

28. K. Plummer, *Sexual Stigma* (Boston: Routledge & Kegan Paul, 1975).

29. B. Adam, *The Rise of a Gay and Lesbian Movement* (Boston: Twayne, 1987).

30. John Gagnon, "Disease and Desire," *Daedalus* 118, no. 3 (1989): 47–77.

31. On Greenwich Village, see M. Levine, ed., *Gay Men* (New York: Harper & Row, 1979). On the Castro, see Manuel Castells, *The City and the Grass Roots: A Cross-cultural Theory of Urban Social Movements* (Berkeley and Los Angeles: University of California Press, 1983), pp. 138–68.

32. Weeks, *Sex, Politics, and Society,* pp. 15–16.

33. R. Shilts, *And the Band Played On* (New York: St. Martin's, 1987), p. 209; D. A. Feldman and T. M. Johnson, introduction to *The Social Dimension of AIDS: Methods and Theory* (New York: Praeger, 1986), pp. 1–12.

34. Shilts, *And the Band Played On.*

35. This literature is reviewed in A. M. Boxer and B. Cohler, "Life Course of Gay and Lesbian Youth: An Immodest Proposal for the Study of Lives," in Herdt, ed., *Adolescence and Homosexuality.*

36. Bell et al., *Sexual Preference.* See also Carrier, "Homosexual Behavior in Cross-cultural Perspective"; and Herdt, "Introduction: Gay and Lesbian Youth."

37. Bell et al., *Sexual Preference,* p. 10.

38. Herdt, "Introduction: Gay and Lesbian Youth"; G. Herdt and A. Boxer, "Ethnographic Issues in the Study of AIDS," *Journal of Sex Research* 28 (1991): 171–87.

39. John Martin et al., "The Impact of AIDS on a Gay Community: Changes in Sexual Behavior, Substance Use, and Mental Health," *American Journal of Community Psychology* (in press); Charles F. Turner et al., *AIDS, Sexual Behavior and Intravenous Drug Use* (Washington, D.C.: National Academy Press, 1989). On the eugenics movement, see A. M. Brandt, *No Magic Bullet* (Oxford: Oxford University Press, 1985), p. 19.

40. On alcoholism, Kus remarks, "Unlike the heterosexual alcoholic, the gay man coming into A.A. is usually severely self-homophobic. Indeed, research has shown that this internalized homophobia may very well explain the etiology and the high incidence of alcoholism in gay American men" (Kus 1987:267). Historically, D'Emilio (*Sexual Politics,* pp. 32–33) identifies the gay bar as the key symbol of social organization for early cohorts.

41. The arguments suggested here cannot be extended into rural communities, where our knowledge is fragmentary and outdated (but see Charles Silverstein, *Man to Man* [New York: Morrow, 1981]; and, on suburban gays, chapter 6). Impressionistic accounts from nonanthropologists suggest a universalizing process of gay identity construction in major urban capitals of the world (see Dennis Altman, *The Homosexualization of America, the Americanization of the Homosexual* [New York: St. Martin's, 1982]; and Philipe Aries, "Thoughts on the History of Homosexuality," in *Western Sexuality,* ed. P. Aries and A. Bejin (London: Blackwell, 1986), pp. 62–75; Aries is reviewed in Herdt, "Introduction: Gay and Lesbian Youth"). These accounts, however, are probably inaccurate in their insensitivity to local meaning systems, even in urban settings (see Carrier, "Homosexual Behavior in Cross-cultural Perspective").

42. My colleague Richard Herrell is the primary ethnographer for this component of our study.

43. Castells, "Cultural Identity, Sexual Liberation and Urban Structure."

44. N. Algren, *Chicago: City on the Make* (Chicago: University of Chicago Press, 1987), p. 26.

45. We use the real name of the agency at its request. All other names in this report are pseudonyms, however.

46. Van Gennep, *Rites of Passage,* p. 67.

47. E. Goffman, *Asylums* (Garden City, N.Y.: Anchor, 1961).

48. A. M. Boxer, J. Cook, and G. Herdt, "Double Jeopardy: Identity Transitions and Parent-Child Relations among Gay and Lesbian Youth," in *Parent-Child Relations across the Lifespan,* ed. Karl Pillemer and K. McCartney (Hillsdale, N.J.: Erlbaum, in press).

49. Weinberg, *Gay Men, Gay Selves,* pp. 79ff.

50. J. Soares, "Black and Gay," in Levine, ed., *Gay Men,* pp. 10–15.

51. The *New York Times* reported this incident a few days later in a story on AIDS and violence.

52. Michelle Fine, "Sexuality, Schooling, and Adolescent Females: The Missing Discourse of Desire," *Harvard Educational Review* 58 (1988): 29–53.

53. Troiden, "The Formation of Homosexual Identities and Roles." On gender conventions, see E. Newton, *Mother Camp* (Toronto: Prentice-Hall, 1972).

54. How could I not quote Mel Brooks here? "Let's face it, sweetheart—without Jews, fags, and gypsies, there *is* no theatre" (*To Be or Not to Be,* 1983).

55. E. Goffman, *Stigma* (Englewood Cliffs, N.J.: Prentice-Hall, 1963).

56. Evelyn Hooker, "An Empirical Study of Some Relations between Sexual Patterns and Gender Identity in Male Homosexuals," in *Sex Research: New Developments,* ed. J. Money (New York: Holt, Rinehart & Winston, 1965), pp. 25–26.

57. Harry, *Gay Children Grown Up.*

58. Van Gennep, *Rites of Passage,* p. 8.

59. See the work of Barry Adam on the cooptation of gays and lesbians into mainstream middle-class values (*The Survival of Domination* [New York: Elsevier, 1978]).

60. Jay P. Paul, "The Bisexual Identity: An Idea without Social Recognition," *Journal of Homosexuality* 9 (1984): 45–65.

61. Gilbert Herdt, "Cross-cultural Forms of Homosexuality and the Concept 'Gay,'" in *Sexuality and Homosexuality,* a special issue of *Psychiatric Annals* 18 (1988): 37–39.

62. A. D. Martin and E. S. Hetrick, "The Stigmatization of Gay and Lesbian Adolescents," *Journal of Homosexuality* 15 (1988): 163–83.

63. Henry L. Minton, "Femininity in Men and Masculinity in Women: American Psychiatry and Psychology Portray Homosexuality in the 1930s," *Journal of Homosexuality* 13 (1986): 1–21; B. Ponse, *Identities in the Lesbian World: The Social Construction of Self* (Westport, Conn.: Greenwood, 1978), p. 31, n. 14; R. Scruton, *Sexual Desire* (New York: Free Press, 1986).

64. Herdt and Boxer, "Ethnographic Issues in the Study of AIDS."

65. We know from other studies that "homosexual" adults report that they passed as straight in high school, feeling alienated from heterosexual dating in peer groups,

and so did not learn how to date (see, e.g., J. Harry and W. Devall, *The Social Organization of Gay Males* [New York: Praeger, 1978]).

66. She looks young and blends in, although she is a heterosexual graduate student.

67. Read, *Other Voices*.

68. Since our study was completed, a coming-out group for those twenty-one and older has been formed.

69. Van Gennep, *Rites of Passage,* p. 75.

70. G. Herdt, "Homosexuality," in *The Encyclopedia of Religion,* 15 vols. (New York: Macmillan, 1987), 6:445–52; R. M. Keesing, introduction to *Rituals of Manhood,* ed. G. Herdt (Berkeley and Los Angeles: University of California Press, 1982), pp. 1–43.

71. V. Turner, "Les Rites des Passage," in *Forest of Symbols* (Ithaca, N.Y.: Cornell University Press, 1967).

72. A. Muller, *Parents Matter* (New York: Naiad, 1987).

73. Boxer et al., "To Tell or Not to Tell."

74. R. A. Bernstein, "My Daughter Is a Lesbian," *New York Times,* 24 February 1987; E. Blackwood, "Breaking the Mirror: The Construction of Lesbianism and the Anthropological Discourse on Homosexuality," in *Anthropology and Homosexual Behavior,* ed. E. Blackwood (New York: Haworth, 1986).

75. See Herdt 1989, "Introduction: Gay and Lesbian Youth."

76. Martin and Hetrick, "The Stigmatization of Gay and Lesbian Adolescents."

77. Herdt, *Guardians of the Flutes;* La Fontaine, *Initiation Rites;* Turner, "Les Rites des Passage."

78. L. L. Langness, "Ritual Power and Male Domination in the New Guinea Highlands," *Ethos* 2 (1974): 189–212.

79. C. Warren and B. Laslett, "Privacy and Secrecy: A Conceptual Comparison," in *Secrecy: A Cross-cultural Perspective,* ed. Stanton K. Tefft (New York: Human Sciences Press, 1980), pp. 24–34.

80. Shilts, *And the Band Played On.*

81. M. Douglas, *Purity and Danger* (London: Routledge & Kegan Paul, 1966); Shilts, *And the Band Played On.*

82. Van Gennep, *Rites of Passage,* p. 79.

83. On "homosexual" and "gay" as communities or cultures, see Murray, *Social Theory, Homosexual Realities;* D. G. Wolf, *The Lesbian Community* (Berkeley and Los Angeles: University of California Press, 1979); as ghettos, see Levine, ed., *Gay Men;* and as life-styles, see Read, *Other Voices.*

84. M. Pollak, "Male Homosexuality—or Happiness in the Ghetto," in *Western Sexuality: Practice and Precept in Past and Present Times,* ed. P. Aries and A. Bejin (London: Blackwell, 1986).

85. Dank, "Coming Out in the Gay World," p. 189.

86. Ponse, "Secrecy in the Lesbian World," p. 336.

87. M. Gluckman, *Essays in the Ritual of Social Relations* (Manchester: Manchester University Press, 1962).

TWO

The Life and Death of Gay Clones

Martin P. Levine

The aims, then, of a sociological approach to homosexuality are to begin to define the factors—both individual and situational—that predispose a homosexual to follow one path as against others; to spell out the contingencies that will shape the career that has been embarked upon; and to trace out the patterns of living in both their pedestrian and their seemingly exotic aspects. Only then will we begin to understand the homosexual. This pursuit must inevitably bring us—though from a particular angle—to those complex matrices wherein most human behavior is fashioned.

—WILLIAM SIMON AND JOHN H. GAGNON
"Homosexuality: The Formulation of a Sociological Perspective"

More than two decades ago, William Simon and John Gagnon formulated the first constructionist explanation for the sociocultural organization of gay life. Taking a cue from symbolic interactionist theory, they contextualized the formation of gay life, arguing that "the patterns of adult homosexuality are consequent upon the social structure and values that surround the homosexual after he becomes or conceives of himself as homosexual."[1] In this way, they traced the origin of gay life to the elements of surrounding cultures and social structures.

In other works, Simon and Gagnon stress the role of socialization in the evolution of gay sociocultural patterns.[2] Like most sociologists and anthropologists, they argue that people acquire the cultural values, beliefs, norms, and roles that organize and direct their behavior through socialization into the prevailing sociocultural order. In addition, they feel that patterned regularities in social life occur as a result of individuals shaping their behavior around these sociocultural directives.

According to Simon and Gagnon, gay patterns emerge similarly in societies lacking a separate socialization process for adult homosexuality. They claim that in these cultures men who eventually become gay undergo essentially the same socialization process as other males. That is, they learn the same cultural values, beliefs, norms, and roles as other men. Moreover, they contend that regularities in gay life emerge as gay men shape their behavior within, between, and in reaction to these sociocultural prescriptions.

Subsequent constructionist explanations for gay life narrow the scope of Simon and Gagnon's rather broad formulation. Typically, these accounts appear in sociological studies of homosexuality framed from either a social labeling or a role perspective.[3] In social labeling studies, stigmatization accounts "for the forms homosexuality" takes, "whether in behavior, identity, or community":

> The single most important factor about homosexuality as it exists in this culture is the perceived hostility of the societal reactions that surround it. From this one critical factor flow many of the features that are distinctive about homosexuality. It renders the business of becoming a homosexual a process that is characterized by problems of access, problems of guilt, and problems of identity. It leads to the emergence of a subculture of homosexuality. It leads to a series of interaction problems involved with concealing the discreditable stigma. And it inhibits the development of stable relationships to a considerable degree.[4]

According to role theory, homosexual roles shape the patterns of gay life.[5] That is, regularities in gay life arise as gay men behaviorally enact the cultural expectations embedded in the homosexual role.

This chapter examines the validity of these three constructionist explanations of gay life for the forms of life associated with the gay clone, a social type that first appeared in the mid-1970s in the "gay ghettos" of America's largest cities.[6] Social scientists use the term "social type" to describe an informal role that is based on collective images of a particular kind of person.[7] The clone role reflected the gay world's image of this kind of gay man, a doped-up, sexed-out, Marlboro man.

Although the gay world derisively named this social type the clone, largely because of its uniform look and life-style, clones were the leading social type within gay ghettos until the advent of AIDS.[8] At this time, gay media, arts, and pornography promoted clones as the first post-Stonewall form of homosexual life. Clones came to symbolize the liberated gay man.[9]

The material presented here comes from a longitudinal field study conducted from 1977 to 1984 of a clone social world in New York's West Village. The fieldwork included observation and participant observation in such central meeting places within this world as bars, discos, and bathhouses. In addition, extensive participant observation was conducted among three distinct friendship cliques. Furthermore, unidentified interviews were conducted with both key informants and other participants. All three of these techniques have been used to collect follow-up data since the formal fieldwork ceased in 1984.

In what follows, I will show how Simon and Gagnon's constructionist explanation offers the best account for the patterns of clone life in the West Village. To support my argument, I will discuss the social context of the clone social world, the sociocultural organization of the gay social world, and the sociocultural organization of the clone social world. All undocumented words, phrases, and indented quotations in the third section come from my field notes. The words and phrases constitute gay argot and are defined in the notes; they are set off in the text by quotation marks.

The Social Context of the Clone Social World

America underwent profound social changes over the course of the last three decades.[10] During the 1960s and early 1970s, various student, gender, racial, and ethnic liberation movements struggled against the Vietnam War and social oppression. In particular, these movements removed many of the discriminatory sanctions applied against women and racial, ethnic, and sexual minorities and successfully altered the stigmatized cultural roles and identities assigned to these groups.[11] For example, the black movement effectively ended legalized discrimination in housing, employment, and public accommodations and taught African-Americans to be proud of their racial and cultural heritage, which profoundly reduced black people's internalized self-hatred and low self-esteem.[12]

There were also momentous shifts in culturally hegemonic values during the course of these decades.[13] At the end of the 1960s, the burgeoning counterculture spread a libertarian ethos among millions of young, urban, college-educated, and middle-class Americans, which seriously undermined the cultural dominance of the Protestant ethic.[14] In particular, the libertarian ethos deeply undercut the normative influence of the Protestant ethic's values sanctioning sacrifice and self-denial.

By the mid-1970s, the normative decline of the Protestant ethos permitted the rise of another set of values, known as the self-fulfillment ethic, which idealized gratification of all inner needs and desires.[15] The self-fulfillment ethic transformed the counterculture's libertarian ethos into a value set sanctioning unbridled hedonism, materialism, and expressiveness, which subsequently sparked massive consumerism and experimentation with sex and drugs among followers of this ethic.[16]

The altered social climate of the 1980s sharply curtailed the spread of the self-fulfillment ethic.[17] A contraction in disposable income among the middle class and an epidemic of incurable sexually transmitted diseases eroded the economic and physical basis for unrestrained self-gratification. That is, unchecked consumerism and erotic hedonism became impractical in an era of economic deterioration, genital herpes, hepatitis B, and AIDS. In addition, widespread aspirations for stable relationships further weakened belief in self-fulfillment. More precisely, emergent desires for more permanent relationships and social networks fostered widespread dissatisfaction with the "me-firstism" implicit in the pursuit of unbounded self-gratification.

The waning of the self-fulfillment ethic during the 1980s promoted the growth of alternative value sets that merged values from both the Protestant and the self-fulfillment ethics. Yankelovitch labeled these value sets the ethics of constraint and commitment.[18]

The constraint ethic held that biopsychosocial contingencies sharply restrict gratification of inner needs and desires. It contended that materialistic and hedonistic pursuits had to be weighed against economic, social, and physical limitations. As a result, it sanctioned a form of restrained hedonism in which sensual indulgence was tied to physical well-being and a form of expressive materialism in which materialistic pursuits were linked to autonomy and creativity. In this way, it idealized self-discipline in the quest for restrained hedonism and expressive materialism.

The commitment ethic perceived connectedness as a cultural ideal. Accordingly, it valued attachment to people, avocations, institutions, and communities and approved of self-sacrifice in the service of deeper and more meaningful relationships and sacred or expressive activities.

The ethics of constraint and commitment fostered ready acceptance of sobriety, health maintenance, and erotic limitations among those who endorsed these values.[19] Restrained hedonism prompted millions of urban, educated, middle-class Americans to forsake smoking, alcohol, drugs, and recreational sex for strict regimens of abstinence, exercise, nutritional diets, and relational sex. This in turn provoked widespread participation in twelve-step recovery programs for substance abuse, eating disorders, and "sexual addiction."[20] In addition, expressive materialism created enormous demands among this population for imaginative and self-reliant jobs. Finally, connectedness engendered tremendous commitment within this group to expressive hobbies, historic preservation, and community service.[21] In the sexual realm, it fostered adherence to relational scripts, which sanctioned obligation, fidelity, and romance between sexual partners.[22]

The Sociocultural Organization
of the Gay Social World

The social changes of the past three decades profoundly affected the forms of gay life. At the opening of the 1960s, American culture stigmatized homosexuality as a type of gender deviance that required strict social control.[23] That is, gay men were regarded as "failed men," as men who deviated from masculine norms because they were either mentally or morally disordered. In this way, gay men were relegated to cultural roles of "nelly queens," "hopeless neurotics," and "moral degenerates."[24]

The stigmatization of homosexuality fostered harsh social sanctions designed to isolate, treat, correct, or punish gay men. For example, most states criminalized homosexual contact, which exposed gay men to police harassment, imprisonment, and blackmail. Moreover, psychiatry regarded homosexuality as a treatable form of mental illness, which left gay men open to mandatory psychotherapy or psychiatric hospitalization. Finally, family and friends frequently taunted, ostracized, and even violently attacked gay men.

Stigmatization meant that the gay world of the sixties functioned as a deviant subculture.[25] This symbolic world constituted a relatively "impoverished cultural unit."[26] That is, the threat of sanction effectively limited structural and cultural elaboration within this world to covert sets of socially isolated, self-hating social networks and gathering places, which were primarily designed to facilitate social and sexual contacts and the management of stigma.[27]

Three techniques for neutralizing stigma largely shaped the patterns of life within this world: passing, minstrelization, and capitulation. Passing accounted for the secrecy that characterized this world and included a set of behaviors that was designed to hide a gay identity and world under a heterosexual facade. Minstrelization explained the patterns of cross-gendering associated with "camp," a behavioral style entailing the adoption of feminine dress, speech, and demeanor. Finally, capitulation accounted for the feelings of guilt, shame, and self-hatred associated with the damaged sense of self that resulted from believing that homosexuality was a form of gender deviance.[28]

Stigma management also engendered significant impediments to erotic expression during this period. The lack of anticipatory socialization for male homosexuality in our culture signified that men who eventually became gay experienced essentially the same erotic socialization as men who grew up to be straight.[29] Socialization agents taught both prehomosexual and preheterosexual youths the dictates of the male sexual script. Consequently, gay men acquired a recreational erotic code that held that sex was objectified, privatized, and phallocentric and an arena for demonstrating manly prowess.

Passing and capitulation prevented many gay men from engaging in the recreational sex associated with the male sexual script. The threat that recognition and police raids or entrapment posed to heterosexual passing forced some gay men to shun the opportunities for recreational contacts present in the sexual marketplace of bars, bathhouses, and public restrooms. In addition, the belief that same-sex desires constituted gender deviance blocked others from engaging in recreational sexual contacts.[30]

The gay liberation movement of the sixties fundamentally altered forms of gay life. Many early gay rights activists had participated in either countercultural, antiwar, or civil rights movements and were therefore prepared to advocate libertarian values and the destigmatization of homosexuality. For example, they championed an ethic sanctioning self-expression, especially in regard to experimentation with drugs and sex.[31] In addition, they promoted a construction of same-sex love that stripped homosexuality of its discrediting association with gender deviance. That is, they held that same-sex love was a moral, natural, and healthy form of erotic expression among men who typically conformed to cultural expectations for manly demeanor and appearance.[32] Finally, they actively campaigned to reduce the level of criminal, psychiatric, and social sanction and succeeded in forcing some localities either to repeal sodomy statutes or to cease police harassment of gay men, in compelling the mental health professions to remove same-sex love from the official list of psychological disorders, and in provoking a growing acceptance of gay men in the family, media, and workplace.[33]

The lessening of stigmatization reorganized the patterns of life within gay social worlds located in major urban centers.[34] For example, the reduction of legal and social sanctions removed most constraints against structural and cultural elaboration within these worlds. Accordingly, the range of gay services, traditions, gathering places, and cultural subgroupings widened and deepened: "The dozen largest urban areas of North America now have readily identifiable gay neighborhoods with heavy populations of same-sex couples. Each of these districts features not only openly gay bars and restaurants, but clothiers, bookstores, laundromats, a variety of shops, doctors, lawyers, dentists, and realtors that cater to a gay clientele."[35] In addition, these neighborhoods contained an array of gay sexual, recreational, cultural, religious, political, and professional scenes or subcultures.[36] In these areas, gay men could cruise for anonymous sex, join gay baseball teams, sing in gay choruses, attend gay studies groups, worship in gay churches or synagogues, work for gay Democratic or Republican clubs, see exhibitions of gay art, theater, and cinema, and participate in gay bankers, doctors, or lawyers organizations.

The weakening of sanction and the destigmatized definition of homosexuality also modified the forms of life associated with stigma neutralization. For example, the decline in sanction removed the grounds for heterosexual passing, which provoked many gay men to become openly gay. Moreover, the redefinition of homosexuality as a normal, healthy, masculine form of male sexuality erased the basis for the cross-

dressing connected with minstrelization, prompting a wholesale abandonment of camp attire, demeanor, and activities. In addition, this definition of same-sex love eliminated the reason for perceiving homosexuality as gender deviance and fostered a new pride and sense of validity
in being both gay and a man. Finally, along with the libertarian ethos,
the decrease in sanction and heightened self-esteem eradicated many
of the impediments to recreational sexual contacts, which provoked an
increase in anonymous erotic activity.[37]

The social changes of the 1970s and 1980s further strengthened
these emergent urban gay patterns. During the 1970s, the self-
fulfillment ethic sanctioned gratification of inner needs and desires,
and many urban gay men became openly gay, materialistic, and hedonistic. Consequently, the forms of urban gay life came to include consumerism, erotic exploration, recreational drug use, and disclosure of
sexual orientation.[38]

However, these patterns were forsaken during the early eighties. By
then, AIDS, a decline in discretionary income, and yearnings for stable
relationships caused unbridled self-gratification to be regarded as un-
sound behavior. That is, a fatal venereal disease, mounting medical and
caregiving expenses, and desires for permanent relationships made recreational sex, consumerism, and drug use appear untenable.[39]

By the mid-1980s, the ethics of constraint and commitment became
hegemonic within urban gay worlds. At this time, AIDS, economic
deterioration, and longings for secure relationships made urban gay
men embrace restrained hedonism, expressive materialism, and connectedness as cultural ideals. For example, the medical dangers associated with sex and poor health maintenance, coupled with a decrease
in disposable income, prompted these men to accept values linking
gratification of hedonistic and material desires with self-discipline for
the purpose of either physical and financial well-being or autonomy
and creativity. In addition, health concerns and longings for steady
relationships led them to endorse values sanctioning commitment, monogamy, coupling, and celibacy.[40]

The ethics of constraint and commitment provoked new forms of
life in urban gay worlds. The ideal of restrained hedonism fostered
ready acceptance of temperance, erotic restrictions, and health maintenance among urban gay men. These men increasingly gave up liquor,
cigarettes, drugs, and risky sex for rigid regimens of exercise, sleep,
diet, and safer sex. Many even entered twelve-step programs to "recover" from substance abuse and "sexual addiction." In addition, ex-

pressive materialism drove other gay men to work in fields demanding both creativity and autonomy. Finally, connectedness forced some men to become either caregivers for sick or dying friends and lovers or unpaid volunteers for community-based political or health organizations.[41]

The Sociocultural Organization of the Clone Social World

A unique set of sociocultural patterns distinguished the clone social world in the West Village from other gay cultural entities in New York City. The changes in the forms of life within this world between the 1970s and the 1980s paralleled the outbreak of the AIDS epidemic.

The Pre-AIDS Patterns of the 1970s

Prior to AIDS, the clone social world was structured around a group of socially isolated social networks and gathering places, networks and places segregated from the broader gay as well as the heterosexual world. That is, the participants in these networks and places were mainly clones.

The social networks included "cliques" and "crowds." Cliques functioned as friendship circles and met the men's basic social, emotional, and material needs. In this sense, they were surrogate families. A crowd consisted of a group of cliques that frequented the same meeting spot. For example, the Saint crowd involved the set of cliques that routinely gathered at The Saint disco. In addition, the members of a crowd usually either recognized or knew each other.

The crowds mixed in a round of meeting spots that was known as the "Circuit." The gathering places in the Circuit were mainly locales for social, recreational, or sexual activities. For example, the men dined in Circuit restaurants, worked out in Circuit gyms, cruised in Circuit bars, and had sex in Circuit bathhouses. In addition, the men attended Circuit meeting spots according to a fixed schedule called "Circuit hours." A retail clerk in his mid-twenties explained, "After work, we go to the gym, either the Y or the Bodycenter; then we stop by One Potato or Trilogy for dinner. On Friday nights, we cruise the Eagle and Spike. On Saturday nights, we go dancing at the Saint, and on Sunday nights, we go to the baths."

Three distinctive social patterns characterized the clone social world during this period. First, presentational strategies within this world were typically "butch."[42] For example, these men usually fashioned themselves after such archetypically masculine icons as body builders and blue-collar workers, and commonly wore work boots, flannel shirts, and button-up Levis and had gym bodies, short haircuts, and mustaches or beards.

Moreover, clones dressed in such a way as to highlight male erotic features and availability. For example, these men frequently wore form-fitting T-shirts and levis that outlined their musculature, genitals, and buttocks. To highlight the penis even further, they often wore no underwear. In addition, they usually wore keys and handkerchiefs that signaled preference for sexual acts and positions: "White vividly describes the effect of eroticized butchness: a strongly marked mouth and swimming soulful eyes (the effect of the mustache); a V shaped torso by metonymy from the open V of the half unbuttoned shirt above the sweaty chest; rounded buttocks squeezed in jeans, swelling out from the cinched-in waist, further emphasized by the charged erotic insignia of colored handkerchiefs and keys; a crotch instantly accessible through the buttons (bottom one already undone) and enlarged by being pressed, along with the scrotum, to one side."[43]

Furthermore, expressive strategies in Circuit gathering places evinced similar themes. For example, the decor and names of many Circuit meeting spots used western, leather, or high-tech motifs. One popular bar conveyed cowboy imagery through such furnishings as wagon wheels, corral posts, and western paintings, and staff uniforms consisted of cowboy hats, shirts, and boots. Other bars expressed this imagery through such names as Badlands or The Eagle.

The spatial design and names of some gathering places also articulated butchness. For example, many bars set aside specific areas for "cruising" and "tricking."[44] Some even showed pornographic films in backrooms. Other places manifested butchness in such names as The Cockring or The International Stud.

Second, erotic patterns within this world included cruising and tricking. Typically, clones cruised Circuit gathering places such as bars, bathhouses, and sex clubs for men who were their "type," that is, their erotic ideal, usually either good looking or "hung," "built," and butch.[45] Generally, clones cruised these men by situating themselves in a position to signal sexual interest and negotiate a time and place for tricking. In most cases, they tricked almost immediately after meeting.

A rough, uninhibited, phallocentric form of sexuality characterized tricking among clones. Tricking frequently involved "deep throating," "hard fucking," and "heavy tit work." For example, fellatio often included vigorously jamming the penis completely down the throat (deep throating), which frequently caused gagging or choking. Anal intercourse usually entailed strenuously ramming the penis entirely up the anus while painfully slapping the buttocks (hard fucking). Nipple stimulation commonly involved robustly sucking, pinching, or biting the nipples to the point of pain (heavy tit work).

Clones often used drugs to overcome pain during rough sex and heighten erotic responsiveness. "Pot," "poppers," and Quaaludes were particularly popular.[46] A thirty-something health professional reported, "I love to do poppers during sex because they cause the muscles in my ass and throat to relax, which allows me to suck dick and get fucked without gagging or feeling any pain."

Most tricks consisted of a single erotic encounter. That is, the men had sex once and never again. For example, a waiter in his twenties in a Circuit restaurant remarked, "I don't know why I give tricks my phone number. No one ever calls. Most of the time you trick with them and they don't even say hello to you the next time you see them."

Third, "partying" constituted the main recreational pattern among clones. These men regularly danced the night away in Circuit discos while "high" on such drugs as MDA, poppers, or cocaine.[47] Typically, the men took drugs at informal clique get-togethers prior to going to the club, usually for the purpose of sensual stimulation for partying. A financial analyst in his early thirties stated, "MDA gives me the energy to dance all night. When I am stoned on MDA I can really get into the music and lights. My legs feel rubbery, like they can move to every beat."

Partying largely occurred on weekend nights in Circuit clubs. On party nights, hundreds of drugged, bare-chested clones jammed the dance floor, where they danced feverishly to throbbing rhythms and dazzling lights while snorting poppers and throwing their arms and clenched fists into the air. The following account incisively depicts partying at the legendary Flamingo:

> As we entered the club at one in the morning (the doors had opened at midnight) I saw a room full of husky men, many of them shirtless, sipping beer or Coke. . . . Everyone in the audience could have been put on

professional display, since the crowd was extraordinarily muscular. . . . In the inner room people were dancing. . . . The light show was adequate but not obtrusive. . . . the blending of the records . . . the choice of music were superb. . . . Along one wall enthusiasts from the floor had leaped up onto a ledge and were grinding in dervish solitude. The mirror panels were frosted over with condensed sweat. One after another all the remaining shirts were peeled off. A stranger, face impassive, nosed up to us and soon was lending us his hanky soaked in ethyl chloride—a quick transit to the icy heart of a minor moon drifting around Saturn. Just as casually he stumbled off.[48]

The Post-AIDS Patterns of the 1980s

The distinctive sociocultural patterns of the clone social world largely dissolved during the 1980s. The men's previous erotic patterns meant that many clones were infected with HIV. That is, cruising and tricking had spread HIV infection widely among the men.

Many clones either became sick or died from AIDS. In fact, some of the earliest AIDS fatalities in New York City occurred among these men, and more than half the sample of three intensely studied cliques died. The rest were in varying stages of infection and illness. Only a handful tested negative for the HIV antibody.

AIDS-related diseases and fatalities caused clone structural entities either to collapse or to vanish. In most cases, the deaths of members broke cliques. For example, one clique lost six of its eight participants in three years. One survivor, a corporate executive in his late forties, commented, "Almost all the guys from my group have died. The lovers Tom and Jim went first in '82. Then Bob, Chad, and Ted in '83 and '84. Frank died a year later. Only Steve and I are left, but Steve has KS, and my lymph glands are swollen."[49]

In some cases, the burden of continuous sickness, caregiving, and dying split cliques. That is, emotional strains and pressures caused men to abandon the group. A free-lance writer in his thirties explained: "My clique fell apart after Seth, Bill, and Ed died. Al and Brian were afraid that one of us would get sick, so they moved to California. They just could not go through it again. After Seth died, Ben stopped returning our calls. I think he was pissed because he thought Bill, Ed, and I were not there enough for Seth." Moreover, the disintegration of cliques destroyed crowds. That is, the absence of familiar faces and acquaintances dissolved the social ties within crowds. A fashion designer in his late thirties remarked, "When I came here on Sunday evenings in the past, I would know at least half the bar. I could stand here and talk to different friends all night. Now I hardly know any one, and I don't recognize most of these faces. Most of the old crowd has either died or left town."

Furthermore, the demise of crowds plus official sanctions demolished the Circuit. For example, many clubs, gyms, and restaurants closed for lack of crowd patronage. In this regard, many men believed that lack of crowd cliental shut The Saint. A photographer in his thirties explained: "The Saint's shutdown came as no big surprise. The crowd that went there was dying off. AIDS killed it. I mean how could they keep it open with everyone dying. Each time I went, it was increasingly empty." In addition, local health officials closed bathhouses and sex clubs for being public health hazards.

The remains of the clone social structure blended into the broader gay world. That is, the surviving structural entities were integrated into other gay social worlds. For example, some clone cliques reconstituted themselves as friendship groups in the HIV social world. For example, two surviving members of one clone clique formed a new friendship circle with men from an HIV-positive support group. In addition, a few Circuit bars remained open because they successfully attracted younger gay crowds.

AIDS also altered the meaning of clone erotic, recreational, and presentational patterns. The relation between drug use, inadequate rest, and recreational sex with immunological damage and AIDS caused cruising, tricking, and partying to be perceived as unhealthy and self-destructive, and a widespread decline in these practices resulted. In addition, fear of AIDS erased the reason for eroticized butch imagery.

Several social patterns replaced the previous forms of clone life. First, butch presentational strategies were largely deeroticized. For example, clones still wore manly attire but in such a way as to camouflage musculature, genitals, and buttocks. That is, they wore underwear and looser T-shirts and levis. In addition, clones developed more natural physiques. In this regard, love handles became accepted as indicating health. Furthermore, most gathering places either ceased showing pornographic films or forbid sexual contact in backrooms.

Second, clone erotic patterns switched to safer and relational sex. Typically, clones defined safer sex as protected anal intercourse. In this vein, an actor in his twenties quipped, "The AIDIES [1980s] is the era of latex love." Indeed, the men routinely shared information about safe and comfortable use of condoms.

However, there was considerable ambiguity about the risk involved in other erotic acts. Almost all the men scoffed at official safer-sex guidelines for kissing and fellatio. Most felt that deep kissing was safe because of the low concentrations of HIV in saliva. They felt similarly about oral sex with no ejaculation or preseminal fluids because there was no exchange of body fluids. Hence, they regularly practiced these behaviors.

In addition, relational sex became normative among clones. That is, sex for most men occurred in the context of sociosexual relationships; they had sex mainly with dates, boyfriends, or lovers. In fact, some attended classes on how to date men at an AIDS service organization.

The relational ethos fostered new erotic attitudes. Most men now perceived coupling, monogamy, and celibacy as healthy and socially acceptable. An art dealer who was in his forties stated, "Ten years ago it was déclassé not to have sex. People thought you were weird if you did not trick. Now celibacy is in; people think you are healthy." Conversely, most men devalued routine recreational sex as dated and unhealthy. An educator in his mid-thirties commented while in a bar, "You see the guy over by the wall, the one groping the other guy. He is a real whore. I mean he still cruises the bar for tricks. I've seen him go home with three different people in the last week. You'd think he would know better, with AIDS and all that."

Third, health maintenance and community service became the chief recreational patterns among clones. Typically, the men hoped to boost their immune system through health maintenance. In this way, they felt that strict regimens of rest, diet, and exercise would keep them healthy. Hence, they regularly slept, took vitamins, ate health food, and exercised at health clubs. In addition, many practiced stress reduction and alternative forms of healing, including visualizations, homeopathy, and macrobiotic diets.

Community service chiefly involved caregiving and activism. The men cared for friends with AIDS, who were typically members of their clique. They made them dinner, paid their bills, cleaned their homes, and took them to doctors and hospitals. Moreover, they provided emotional support during the illness, offering love, acceptance, and companionship. At times, they even had power of attorney, with responsibility for making treatment decisions and implementing funeral arrangements. Clones also became unpaid volunteers in political action groups or AIDS service organizations. In particular, many became some of the earliest volunteers at Gay Men's Health Crisis. Others volunteered in more militant direct action groups such as Act-Up.

AIDS made volunteering socially acceptable among clones. Typically, the men devalued volunteering before the epidemic. Many even openly denigrated gay activists as boring. Others saw no need for activism since they did not believe that gay men were oppressed. AIDS forced them to question these assumptions. The government's inadequate response to the AIDS crisis painfully proved that gay men were indeed oppressed. Consequently, many became politicized, and they began to see the importance of volunteering for social and political change.

Conclusion

The material presented in this chapter shows that the best constructionist explanation for the sociocultural organization of clone life in the West Village is Simon and Gagnon's model. According to this model, elements of the surrounding culture and social structure largely shape the forms of life within the gay world. The model incorporates the explanatory factors associated with the other constructionist explanations for clone sociocultural patterns. That is, this model views homosexual stigma and roles as some of the sociocultural forces molding clone life.

Following Simon and Gagnon, the social context shaped the forms of clone life. That is, AIDS, gay liberation, male gender roles, and the ethics of self-fulfillment, constraint, and commitment molded and remolded sociocultural patterns within the clone social world. For example, gay liberation and the advent of AIDS significantly affected clone social structure. At first, gay liberation's success in lessening legal and social penalization of homosexuality in New York City engendered the formation of socially isolated cliques, crowds, and gathering places. Later, AIDS-related diseases and deaths either dissolved or socially integrated these structural forms into the broader gay world.

In addition, gay liberation, male gender roles, and self-fulfillment values shaped clone social patterns during the 1970s. Gay liberation's redefinition of same-sex love as a manly form of erotic expression provoked masculine identification among clones, which was conveyed through both butch presentational strategies and cruising, tricking, and partying. In particular, butch attire, muscles, and masculine environments vividly articulated the sense that clones were *men*. In a similar vein, the roughness, objectification, anonymity, and phallocentrism associated with cruising and tricking expressed such macho dictates as toughness and recreational sex. Finally, the endurance, impersonality, and risk taking connected with partying conveyed macho ruggedness and activity-centered forms of social interaction. The cultural ideal of self-gratification further encouraged these patterns, sanctioning the sexual and recreational hedonism inherent in cruising, tricking, and partying.

AIDS and the constraint and commitment ethics reformulated these forms in the 1980s. Health concerns encouraged acceptance of values associated with restrained hedonism, which provoked safer sex and health maintenance. These concerns also prompted endorsement of the ideal of connectedness, which fostered community service and relational sex.

Notes

This chapter is dedicated to the memory of Michael Robert Distler (1950–86). I would like to thank Dr. Kristine Anderson for her help in the preparation of this chapter.

1. William Simon and John H. Gagnon, "Homosexuality: The Formulation of a Sociological Perspective," *Journal of Health and Social Behavior* 8 (1967): 179.
2. See, e.g., John Gagnon and William Simon, *Sexual Conduct: The Social Sources of Human Sexuality* (Chicago: Aldine, 1973), chap. 5; William Simon and John H. Gagnon, "The Lesbians: A Preliminary Overview," in *Sexual Deviance,* ed. John H. Gagnon and William Simon (New York: Harper & Row, 1967), pp. 247–82.
3. For social labeling studies of male homosexuality, see Martin S. Weinberg and Colin J. Williams, *Male Homosexuals: Their Problems and Adaptions* (New York: Oxford University Press, 1974); Joseph Harry and William B. DeVall, *The Social Organization of Gay Males* (New York: Praeger, 1978); Laud Humphreys, *Out of the Closets: The Sociology of Homosexual Liberation* (Englewood Cliffs, N.J.: Prentice-Hall, 1972).
4. Carol A. B. Warren, "Homosexuality and Stigma," in *Homosexual Behavior: A Modern Reappraisal,* ed. Judd Marmor (New York: Basic, 1980), p. 139. Kenneth Plummer, *Sexual Stigma: An Interactionist Account* (Boston: Routledge & Kegan Paul, 1975), p. 102.
5. For a discussion of the social role theory of homosexuality, see Mary McIntosh, "The Homosexual Role," *Social Problems* 16 (1968): 182–92.

6. The term "gay ghetto" refers to an urban neighborhood housing a dense concentration of gay institutions and residents. For a discussion of the validity of labeling these areas as ghettos, see Martin P. Levine, "Gay Ghetto," *Journal of Homosexuality* 4 (1979): 363–77.

7. George A Theodorson and Achilles G. Theodorson, *A Modern Dictionary of Sociology* (New York: Crowell, 1969), p. 444.

8. See Michael Signorile, "Clone Wars," *Outweek*, 28 November 1990, pp. 39–45.

9. See Dennis Altman, *The Homosexualization of America, the Americanization of the Homosexual* (New York: St. Martin's, 1982), p. 103; and Randy Alfred, "Clones: A New Definition," *Advocate*, 18 March 1982, pp. 22–23.

10. For an overview of these movements and changes, see Charles A. Reich, *The Greening of America* (New York: Barton, 1970); Daniel Bell, *The Cultural Contradictions of Capitalism* (New York: Basic, 1976); Aldon D. Morris, *Origin of the Civil Rights Movement: Black Communities Organizing for Change* (New York: Free Press, 1984); Jo Freeman, *Politics of Women's Liberation* (New York: Longman, 1975); Edwin M. Schur, *The Awareness Trap: Self-Absorption Instead of Social Change* (New York: McGraw-Hill, 1976); and Daniel Yankelovitch, *New Rules: Searching for Self-Fulfillment in a World Turned Upside Down* (New York: Random House, 1981).

11. See Rhoda Lois Blumberg, *Civil Rights: The 1960 Freedom Struggle* (Boston: Twayne, 1984); and Myra Marx Ferree and Beth B. Hess, *Controversy and Coalition: The New Feminist Movement* (Boston: Twayne, 1985).

12. See Minion K. C. Morrison, *Black Political Mobilization: Leadership, Power, and Mass Behavior* (Albany: State University of New York Press, 1987).

13. See Yankelovitch, *New Rules*.

14. See Reich, *The Greening of America*.

15. See Yankelovitch, *New Rules*.

16. See Schur, *The Awareness Trap*.

17. See Yankelovitch, *New Rules*.

18. See Daniel Yankelovitch, "American Values: Changes and Stability," *Public Opinion* 6 (1984): 2–9.

19. Ibid.

20. Art Levine, "America's Addiction to Addictions," *U.S. News and World Report*, 5 February 1990, pp. 62–63. For a critical treatment of the concept of sexual addiction, see Martin P. Levine and Richard R. Troiden, "The Myth of Sexual Compulsivity," *Journal of Sex Research* 25 (1988): 47–48.

21. See Yankelovitch, "American Values."

22. See Levine and Troiden, "The Myth of Sexual Compulsivity."

23. I am grateful to Michael S. Kimmel for the concept of homosexuality as gender deviance.

24. For a discussion of the cultural roles for homosexuality, see the introduction to *Gay Men: The Sociology of Male Homosexuality*, ed. Martin P. Levine (New York: Harper & Row, 1979), pp. 1–16.

25. For a review of sanctions, see Humphreys, *Out of the Closets*. For an overview of legal sanctions against gay men during the 1960s, see Edwin M. Schur, *Crimes without Victims: Deviant Behavior and Public Policy: Abortion, Homosexuality, and Drug Addiction* (Englewood Cliffs, N.J.: Prentice-Hall, 1965). For a discussion of psychological conceptualizations and treatment of gay men in the 1960s, see

Marcel T. Saghir and Eli Robins, *Male and Female Homosexuality* (Baltimore: Wilkens, 1973); and Ronald Bayer, *Homosexuality and American Psychiatry* (New York: Basic, 1981). For a discussion of social sanctions against gay men, see Weinberg and Williams, *Male Homosexuals*. On deviance, see Howard S. Becker, *Outsiders: Studies in the Sociology of Deviance* (New York: Free Press, 1963).

26. Simon and Gagnon, "Homosexuality," p. 183.

27. See Laud Humphreys, "Exodus and Identity: The Emerging Gay Culture," in Levine, ed., *Gay Men*, pp. 134–47.

28. For a general discussion of stigma management, see Erving Goffman, *Stigma: Notes on the Management of Spoiled Identity* (Englewood Cliffs, N.J.: Prentice-Hall, 1963). For an overview of how techniques for neutralizing shaped forms of gay life, see Richard R. Troiden, *Gay and Lesbian Identity: A Sociological Analysis* (Dix Hills, N.Y.: General Hall, 1988), pp. 95–96. For a discussion of the patterns associated with passing, see Carol A. B. Warren, *Identity and Community in the Gay World* (New York: Wiley, 1974). For an overview of homosexual camp, see Esther Newton, *Mother Camp: Female Impersonators in America* (Englewood Cliffs, N.J.: Prentice-Hall, 1972). For a discussion of the effect of stigmatization on gay identity, see Humphreys, *Out of the Closets*, pp. 39–41.

29. See Gagnon and Simon, *Sexual Conduct*.

30. See Warren, *Identity and Community;* and Martin Duberman, "Gay in the Fifties," *Salmagundi* 58–59 (1982): 42–75.

31. See Dennis Altman, *Homosexual: Oppression and Liberation* (New York: Avon, 1971); Barry D. Adam, *The Rise of a Gay and Lesbian Movement* (Boston: Twayne, 1987); John D'Emilio, *Sexual Politics, Sexual Communities: The Making of a Homosexual Minority in the United States, 1940–1970* (Chicago: University of Chicago Press, 1983); Toby Marotta, *The Politics of Homosexuality* (Boston: Houghton Mifflin, 1981).

32. See Peter Fischer, *The Gay Mystique* (New York: Stein & Day, 1972).

33. See Don Teal, *The Gay Militants* (New York: Stein & Day, 1971).

34. See Laud Humphreys and Brian Miller, "Identities in the Emerging Gay Culture," in Marmor, ed., *Homosexual Behavior*, pp. 142–56.

35. Laud Humphreys, "Exodus and Identity," p. 139.

36. For an overview of sociocultural elaboration in urban gay ghettos, see John Alan Lee, "The Gay Connection," *Urban Life* 2 (1979): 175–98.

37. On changes in gay life-styles, see Altman, *The Homosexualization of America*, pp. 1–38. On the abandonment of camp, see Wayne Sage, "Inside the Colossal Closet," in Levine, ed., *Gay Men*, pp. 148–63. For a discussion of gay liberation's redefinition of homosexuality as masculine, see Marotta, *The Politics of Homosexuality*.

38. See Altman, *The Homosexualization of America*.

39. See Dennis Altman, *AIDS in the Mind of America* (Garden City, N.Y.: Anchor/Doubleday, 1986), pp. 82–109; and Andrew Holleran, "The Petrification of Clonestyle," *Christopher Street*, no. 69 (1982): 14–18.

40. John H. Gagnon, "Disease and Desire," *Daedalus* 118, no. 3 (1989): 47–78.

41. See Altman, *AIDS*, pp. 82–109; and Levine and Troiden, "The Myth of Sexual Compulsivity."

42. "Butch" refers to manliness.

43. Edmund White, *States of Desire* (New York: Dutton, 1980), pp. 45–46.

44. "Cruising" refers to the search for sexual partners, and "tricking" denotes anonymous sex.
45. "Hung" signifies having a large penis, and "built" indicates having a muscular body.
46. "Pot" refers to marijuana, "poppers" amyl nitrates. Quaaludes are barbiturates.
47. "Partying" denotes recreational drug use and disco dancing. "High" signifies drunk or stoned. MDA was a hallucinogenic drug with stimulant properties.
48. White, *States of Desire,* pp. 278–79.
49. "KS" refers to Kaposi's Sarcoma.

THREE

The Pursuit of the Wish: An Anthropological Perspective on Gay Male Subculture in Los Angeles

E. Michael Gorman

You came here to find the wish fulfilled in 3-D among the flowers, the evasive childhood projected insistently into adulthood. The make-believe among the awesome palmtrees, that the invitation of technicolored, gold-laced Movies, of perpetual sun and the invitation of the Last Frontier of Glorious Liberty (go barefoot and shirtless through the streets) have promised us long distance for oh so long.

—JOHN RECHY
City of Night

Culture moves rather like an octopus too—not all at once in a smoothly coordinated synergy of parts, a massive coaction of the whole, but by disjointed movements of this part, then that, and now the other, which somehow cumulate to directional change. Where, leaving cephalopods behind, in any given culture the first impulses toward progression will appear and how and to what degree they will spread through the system is at this stage of our understanding, if not wholly unpredictable, very largely so.

—CLIFFORD GEERTZ
The Interpretation of Cultures

This collection of essays provided me with an opportunity to reflect on and to begin to articulate important cultural themes at work among self-identified gay men. Others have of course done this as well.[1] The context in which I explore these issues currently is Los Angeles, whose gay community has been in many respects understudied. This essay was prompted in part by the exigencies of the AIDS epidemic and my own work over the last six and a half years as an applied anthropologist and epidemiologist. The dimensions of both applied anthropology and more traditional theoretical anthropological reflection provide critical perspectives from which to view questions of gay male identity.

I have argued that, for a forceful and positive cultural identity of homosexuality to emerge, core prohibitions of Western, especially Judaeo-Christian culture, as embodied in the Leviticus Holiness Code, must have been addressed.[2] The same prohibitions persist today. Indeed, the stigma and contamination attached to homosexuality, whether male or female, have been intensified by the HIV epidemic, which has in some ways confirmed the perception of homosexuality as deviant, dangerous, sinful, and in some ways *malem in se,* "evil in itself." Yet, despite the times, gay culture endures, and gay men and lesbians continue to come out of the closet and self-identify.

My earlier work focused in part on the rite of passage of coming out—that transition in personal status and fundamental transformation of self:

> Coming out entails participation in a gay collectivity and a gay social identity. "Gayness" is constituted by a set of symbols and meanings and a code for conduct . . . the concomitant significant feature of which is the coming out process during which one "becomes" gay, comes to an understanding of gay symbols and gay ideology, identifies with them and becomes oriented to the sensibilities of gay life. One comes to an acceptance which is a new perception of one's self. With regard to collective identity one defines oneself with respect to one's boundaries or differentiation from heterosexuals ("straights") and with respect to the commonalities and bonds one shares with other gays in terms of affiliation. Affiliation may also be signaled by political involvement in the gay civil rights movement and by developing a network of relationships which is primarily gay.[3]

This process has not stopped because of HIV. Individuals of all ages continue coming out, and the dynamics of affiliation and differentiation also continue, albeit on somewhat different terms. On a collective level, the community has had to deal with this "double stigma," as Kowalewski and others have called it, resulting in its ongoing transformation.[4] Stigma, of course, is a core issue for gay identity, one classically articulated by Plummer.[5] Yet, despite the deaths of tens of thousands of gay and bisexual men, it does not appear that the epidemic has resulted in any massive retreat to the closet. It has, however, forced us to examine what being gay means. This essay attempts to articulate that present experience, with the idea of providing some insight into this process and indications of where the community is going. Some of the important questions are, How is the gay male social world constructed at this time? What are its institutions, neighborhoods, friendship networks, and life-styles? How is it coping with such controversial issues as gender, aging, politics, health care, and the behavioral and psychological effects of the HIV epidemic? What can be said about differences among the various age cohorts, such as the pre-Stonewall cohort (i.e., those who came out before the Stonewall riots in New York in June 1969), the Stonewall generation (mostly baby boomers), and the post-Stonewall, post-AIDS cohorts? How might understanding gay life in a city like Los Angeles—a city of satellite populations, each with its own ethos and history—provide insight into salient cultural processes operating in the gay male subculture across the United States at this time?

Data for this essay were gathered in a variety of ways, including participant observation; unobtrusive observation at gay organizations, gatherings, meeting places and events from 1987 to 1989; and semi-structured and unstructured interviews with gay men, lesbians, and heterosexual men and women with ties to the gay community. I have interviewed a cross section of men and women representative of the diverse ethnic, socioeconomic, and age groups characteristic of Los Angeles.

Los Angeles as Ethnographic Context

Three of the most striking aspects of Los Angeles are its size, its diversity, and its status as a major urban center in transition. Los Angeles County extends over four thousand square miles, has some of the most varied scenery, climate, and terrain of any single county in the country, and is the home of some nine million people of diverse race, ethnicity, class, and religious tradition. Some eighty-five municipalities lie within its borders, cities like Los Angeles itself (the second largest city in the United States and itself extending over 470 square miles) and also Long Beach, Pasadena, Santa Monica, and West Hollywood. Each of these has its own distinctive characteristics, its own ethos.

If Los Angeles is a city of distances and diversity, it is also a city experiencing a shift in its status as it becomes a primary economic and cultural hub of the Pacific rim. It also remains influenced to a great degree by the movie, television, and recording industries, and there is a sense in which "Hollywood" is a very apt metaphor for the city. It is not only that so many people, including many gay people, are connected with the industry, but there is also a sense that this is a place where people come to experiment with their dreams. Gay Los Angeles reflects these characteristics; as John Rechy says in *City of Night,* it is a place where gays have come to find the wish fulfilled.

It is probable that the gay population of Los Angeles constitutes the second largest gay community in the country.[6] As identified by informants and gay guides (such as *Bob Damron's Address Book*), the community newspapers (*Frontiers, Reactions,* the *Advocate*), and the *Gay Community Yellow Pages,* there are four primary nodal points—West Hollywood, Silverlake, Long Beach, and Studio City and the San Fernando Valley—and several smaller ones, including Pomona (the San Gabriel Valley), Santa Monica (the Westside), and midtown.[7] Some would also include Palm Springs (in Riverside County) and Laguna Beach (in southern Orange County) as "belonging" to Los Angeles. In addition to having a well-developed gay community infrastructure, these cities are popular weekend destinations for gays from Los Angeles proper. In this essay, I am concerned with characterizing gay neighborhoods in Los Angeles proper, especially West Hollywood, Silverlake, and the San Fernando Valley. Most of the interviews and observations reported herein were undertaken in those sites. I will begin by describing something about Los Angeles's gay history, which is quite rich. Often there is the implication that gay culture began with Stonewall. It is therefore important to understand the past of the community under consideration.

Prologue: The Yellow Brick Road of the Past

GIRL:
This booklet has been procured for you through the kindness of your dear mother or perhaps your dear sister.

Obviously don't go leaving it around for your landlady, Sgt or CPO as the case may be, to look into. Keep it always in the envelope or otherwise suitably concealed.[8]

For decades prior to Stonewall, Los Angeles had numerous gay gathering places in various locales. The 1957 *Gay Girls' Guide* identified at least three downtown bars (Maxwell's, the Crown Jewel, and the Earl Hotel) and cruising areas along Fifth and Sixth ("the Run") and on the east side of Pershing Square.[9] The *Guide* indicated several bars in Hollywood (the Golden Carp, the Circle, the House of Ivy), Long Beach (the Rendezvous Club), and Santa Monica (Crystal Beach, the Tropical Village) as likely places to meet those "of the persuasion," and many of these institutions had existed for years. While West Hollywood would later be thought of by some as the heart of the gay community, historically neighborhoods closer to downtown such as Echo Park, Bunker Hill and Boyle Heights, Silverlake, and Mt. Washington/Highland Park all were inhabited by large numbers of homosexual men and women. Long Beach also had a gay area, including a gay beach, and by the 1930s gay European intellectuals, artists, and musicians had begun to settle in Santa Monica Canyon.

According to one informant who had lived in Los Angeles since 1943,

There was a sense of "usness" that existed even in the 1940s, and then as now there were different areas each of which had its distinctive styles. . . . But you had to be careful. That meant you stopped acting gay once you went through that door [of the bar], you straightened up your act or as we said "pinned up your bobby pins," and as soon as you got outside you did a kind of crawfish step which made it seem as if you were just passing. In some areas you could be stopped just for walking, particularly at night. I was stopped several times walking along Wilshire Boulevard during the war and asked by some cop "Hey, are you queer?" A wrong answer could end you up in jail.

Another man, who was in his seventies and who had spent his adult life as a homosexual, had been born and raised in Pasadena. He said, "There were always people around, and it was possible to meet others 'in the department'—I've met them everywhere from every walk of life—but it was much harder then than in recent years. . . . Life then was more fragmented and much more undercover; we've lived a fairly quiet life in the suburbs and have many straight friends who are sympathetic. One of the worst things in the past was entrapment by the police and the fear of exposure. I remember a terrible scandal in Pasadena in 1939."

Los Angeles was the site of a number of important developments in the history of the national gay civil rights movement, including the founding of the Mattachine Society in 1951 and of One, Inc., in 1953, both very important organizations. *One* magazine was published in Los Angeles from 1953 to 1968 (a comparable lesbian magazine, *Vice Versa,* had begun in 1947–48), and One Institute of Homophile Studies, under the direction of such men as Jim Kepner, Dorr Legg, and a Dr. Thomas M. Merit, offered some of the first courses on gay history, sociology, and culture in the United States. Another group, the Knights of the Clock, although short lived, was the first interracial group for gay men.

The early 1950s were times of great discrimination against and victimization of homosexuals, although one of the first organized attempts to fight such practices as homo baiting and entrapment was made in Los Angeles when the Committee to Outlaw Entrapment was established in 1952. The organization fought charges against one of its members and was successful in ultimately having the case dropped, an unprecedented occurrence. Other significant events in Los Angeles gay history include the Black Cat Bar riot against the police in Silverlake in 1967 and the founding of both the Metropolitan Community Church and Dignity, the gay Catholic organization, in 1968 and 1969, respectively.

The first Christopher Street West/Gay Pride Parade was held in Hollywood in June 1970, drawing thirty thousand people. By 1970, Los Angeles had begun to develop into one of the primary foci of gay migration in the country, along with San Francisco and New York. Like those cities, it developed a substantial network of gay-identified institutions, including bars, bathhouses, and social organizations, and more visible communities were established in Silverlake, West Hollywood, and Long Beach, as were enclaves in the suburbs, including the San Fernando and San Gabriel valleys.

The Organization of the Gay Social World
in West Hollywood

West Hollywood represents one of two major gay cultural and political centers in Los Angeles. A small (1.9 square miles) municipality edged between Beverly Hills on the west and old Hollywood on the east, West Hollywood contains a population of only thirty-eight thousand, but its influence far exceeds the size of either its population or its geographic boundaries. One man described it as a media event—a state of mind, as far removed from Kansas as you can get in southern California.[10] It is also the focal point of gay and lesbian political activity in Los Angeles, the highlight of which is the Christopher Street West/ Gay Pride Festival held each year in West Hollywood Park, drawing over 150,000 people.

The city has pioneered important social legislation in a variety of matters, including AIDS education and prevention and the prohibition of discrimination on the basis of sexual orientation or HIV status, and it was one of the first cities in the country to recognize domestic partnerships between two nonmarried adults. West Hollywood also prides itself on providing for its senior citizens, who account for over 20 percent of its population (many of them are Soviet Jewish immigrants). It goes without saying that the city has large numbers of gay men and lesbians and the largest number of openly gay elected officials in the United States. The style of West Hollywood is much influenced by the film, recording, and television industries, the design industry, public relations firms, and the numerous restaurants and hotels that employ many of its inhabitants. The tempo is energized and upbeat; among gay men, a clean-shaven, well-muscled look is "in," although one still finds a few men wearing moustaches. Beards are rare, and the clone look of the past has almost completely disappeared. One man observed, "Here there is emphasis on youth and differentiation from the look of the seventies—which some people associate with AIDS."

While there is ambivalence about West Hollywood's style, there is much agreement about its importance as a "gay space." One young Asian man described his impressions of West Hollywood this way: "I live in the Valley, and for me West Hollywood is plastic, very white, and youth oriented. But it is also uplifting, vibrant, positive. It's a place where gays from remote areas can go to and be proud of and not be hassled." Another man, one who had lived in West Hollywood for over ten years and who had been actively involved in the community, said, "For me, West Hollywood is an intense image that began before I arrived here—one of youthful, well-built men—a combination of surf, sand, and sun. It is our own city. It is a place where people can be open, obvious, and can be there in their gayness. It is a haven, a place to blow off the split in our lives."

In many respects, West Hollywood, the self-proclaimed "Creative City," has become a primary gay ritual and political center, perhaps the primary one in southern California. While geographically tiny, it exists as a symbol of gay culture and provides a safe haven for those who want to live an openly gay life-style. It is the most open of Los Angeles's satellite communities. In terms of gender, it is less "macho" in the traditional sense of that term than Silverlake, for example. In West Hollywood, there is a greater emphasis on youth and style. Its ethos is "lighter," and it has fewer institutions, such as leather bars, that cater to more "masculine"-oriented gay men. One traditional way of referring to West Hollywood is "boystown." The "boy" image and boyish and androgynous looks are more popular here than in Silverlake.

Silverlake

There's not the same urge in Los Angeles to go out every night for sex and dancing. During the week people stay home and watch TV or work on their houses. Their home improvement skills are often remarkable. Gay men do their own building, masonry, electrical wiring, plumbing. Nothing daunts them.[11]

West Hollywood's cross-town rival for cultural hegemony in Los Angeles's gay male world is Silverlake. Silverlake is quite different from West Hollywood in many respects. Silverlake is not a separate municipality but part of the city of Los Angeles proper, a few miles north of downtown. The gay community of Silverlake straddles the neighborhoods of Echo Park, Mt. Washington, and Highland Park, all of which have large numbers of gay men and might be considered part of the larger Silverlake community. Silverlake is an older residential area, originally developed in the 1920s around Lake Silver, a reservoir; to the north it nestles against the hills of Griffith Park. Topographically, while West Hollywood tends to be flat, Silverlake is quite hilly, with many narrow roads winding around the hills above the reservoir. It is also ethnically and racially diverse, having large Hispanic and Asian populations; this diversity is reflected in the variety of restaurants, clubs, and bars. Silverlake's major neighborhood ritual, the Sunset Junction Fair, is held each August at the intersection of Sunset and Santa Monica boulevards. Gay, Hispanic, and Asian neighborhood groups all participate.

Silverlake tends to be less affluent than West Hollywood; rents and property there are a little cheaper, although parts of the area are quite famous, with a number of homes designed and built by prominent California architects. Silverlake has thirty-three listings in the 1989 *Damron Guide,* including most of the more prominent leather/levi gathering places in southern California and a number of restaurants, clubs, and meeting spots. The "look" of Silverlake is quite different from that of West Hollywood; many more men there wear mustaches and beards, and there is less emphasis on fashion. One man, who happened to be a resident of West Hollywood, put it this way: "Silverlake men tend to be a little older, more mature. They have been out longer, and they know what they want. There are also more couples there, and they keep more to themselves."

One has the sense of Silverlake being a village, perhaps less overtly a gay enclave than West Hollywood and one that embodies a different kind of gay archetype than West Hollywood. Silverlake historically had the reputation of being "where the men are," and the quotation from Edmund White given above is an apt one for Silverlake and its environs. If West Hollywood were to represent gay Los Angeles's "anima," to use a Jungian metaphor, Silverlake would represent its "animus," with overtones of male sexual energy. It is in Silverlake that most of the motorcycle, leather, and military-uniform clubs meet. Silverlake and eastern Hollywood also have several of the few remaining bathhouses in Los Angeles, whereas more image-conscious West Hollywood has none. This may be due in part to a traditionally greater tolerance for gay sexual diversity in Silverlake, but this part of the city also has a reputation for a more "libertarian" style.

Another gay satellite area of Los Angeles is Studio City and the North Hollywood area of the San Fernando Valley, particularly along Ventura Boulevard. The *Damron Guide* lists nearly forty gay bars, restaurants, and establishments in the general area. The Valley is much more spread out and suburban than either Silverlake or West Hollywood, and there is less of a central focus and distinctive character per se to the community in this part of Los Angeles than in the other two neighborhoods. The proximity to both Hollywood and Silverlake puts the Valley within easy commuting distance of both these areas, yet the Valley people also have their own sense of identity. One man said, "Despite its being spread out, there is a strong sense of commitment to neighborhood and to supporting Valley institutions here." The most important gay cultural event in the Valley is the Gay Rodeo held each year in March, which attracts several thousand visitors. The Valley is quite suburban in feel, and its ethos might be described as a combination of West Hollywood and Silverlake.

In addition to these neighborhoods, there are areas such as Pomona, West Los Angeles, and midtown Los Angeles, each of which has gay institutions. Pomona has seven listings in the *Damron Guide,* West Los Angeles eight, and midtown five. These areas represent gathering places for gays who often live less openly gay life-styles and who prefer more mixed neighborhoods or the suburbs.

AIDS: The Tempering of a Community

The AIDS epidemic hit Los Angeles very early; the first five cases of pneumocystis were diagnosed in Los Angeles in 1981. By 1990, the county had recorded the second highest cumulative incidence of AIDS in the United States after New York. Over 95 percent of cases have been among gay and bisexual men; there have been few pediatric cases, and only about 2 percent of cases have been among women. In short, Los Angeles has a very different profile than that of East Coast cities.

While the social effect of AIDS generally has begun to be documented,[12] the particular social ecology of Los Angeles has not to date received a great deal of attention with regard to AIDS. The spectrum of the epidemic and its effect on gay life has been different there than in San Francisco, where the gay community was better organized politically and thus able to demand more resources.

By late 1982, several Los Angeles residents formed the first AIDS response agency, the AIDS Project Los Angeles. Since then, other organizations have formed to meet the growing and varied needs of the epidemic, including the Los Angeles Shanti Foundation; AID for AIDS; the Minority AIDS Project, which addresses the needs of a primarily black clientele; and Cara a Cara (Face to Face), a Hispanic AIDS service organization. However, whereas San Francisco and New York responded relatively quickly to the threat of AIDS, the Los Angeles County government was slow to recognize the extent of the local AIDS problem and took a cautious and reactionary approach to the epidemic. This was due in great part to control of the Department of Health Services by Los Angeles County's conservative Board of Supervisors, several of whom were unsympathetic to the needs of the most highly affected constituencies, that is, gays, minorities, and intravenous drug users. Already hard pressed financially owing to the cutbacks that resulted from the implementation of Proposition 13 in the late 1970s, the Department of Health Services faced a difficult and escalating AIDS-prevention and service-delivery problem by 1989.

How has the epidemic affected gay life? Certainly there have been significant institutional changes, and there have been behavioral changes as well, marked by a decline in rates of sexually transmitted diseases and hepatitis B among gay and bisexual men, although that decline appears not to have been as dramatic as in San Francisco or New York. Some have suggested that Los Angeles has allocated less money for prevention or for targeting the high-risk population. Still, there has been a marked change. One man said, "It used to be that sex was like brushing your teeth. This is no longer so." Another man said, "The degree of high-intensity sexuality has lessened. Just with my friends, it used to be we would talk about what we did last night; now everyone is doing less. Sex is careful, not carefree."

One of the more obvious changes has been the emergence of various safer-sex practices, especially "phone sex." For example, one Gay Pride Day issue of one of the most widely read local gay newspapers had seventeen pages of phone sex ads out of ninety-four pages of text and advertising. In fact, there has been a noticeable closing of many overtly sexual places such as bathhouses and sex clubs, although Los Angeles still has more bathhouses than any other city in North America. Three of these were closed in 1988 by the district attorney for condoning unsafe sexual practices. Most of the others had closed because people simply stopped frequenting them. The closing of the three baths did not cause tremendous controversy, unlike similar closings in San Francisco. One man who owned a business across the street from one of the three baths said, "It was fine with me they closed that place. They didn't give a damn about the neighborhood or the other businesses around here—including gay businesses—and any place that still allows unsafe sex should be closed." Another man provided a more cautionary view: "Many guys who go to those places are older and have gone there for years. Mostly they're not having unsafe sex, and the baths were one of the few places where they could be reached with education. Besides, after this, where will the district attorney stop?"

More than the institutions of gay life in Los Angeles has been transformed by the epidemic. Take the meaning that individuals attach to sex, for example. One man said, "For me, just sex for sex sake is *not*

OK. Spontaneity is out the window. What I loved in the past was going to bed with a man and not knowing what direction the sex would go in, what terrain it would lead to. There seems to be a lot of codification going on now. It seems split off from any sort of anchor in my soul." Yet gay men are not stopping sexual activity. One woman observed, "I don't see my gay male friends being less gay or homosexual. They still have sex. It's not something you just stop. It's like these hets who say, Why can't they stop? Well you just don't. I see more people at gay pride parades. They are still very much into parts, like they say, [Oh, look at that rear end!]. But I think they are doing things differently. I don't see them being less sexual—they're healthy sexual animals, and I don't mean animals in a bad way."

Another man said, "People are still concerned about the same thing with the sexual aspect tempered. They say, 'Still no boyfriend,' although some say, 'Why bother to go out?' What's behind that is that they do not want to. They feel it's not safe to meet someone—that the party is over. Others say, 'OK, this is what I have to do to continue the party.'" Of the change, one man said, "Sexuality has changed. I am inhibited, very much afraid; it affects how I am with men. It has not decreased my libido, but it has decreased my behavior."

In addition, the HIV epidemic has brought about a profound confrontation with grief, death, and dying. A 1989 random-digit-dial telephone survey of three hundred gay and bisexual men in gay neighborhoods of Los Angeles found that these men knew an average of eighteen persons diagnosed with AIDS or ARC and that about one in twelve knew fifty or more.[13]

Thus, the AIDS epidemic has had a profound effect on gay identity. One man put it this way: "In between the play and the grief we find ourselves. Before we only had sexuality to find ourselves conspicuously. As a community the most conspicuous thing we had was gay liberation. Now there are many more issues than just sex."

The seemingly unrelenting and inexorable toll of the AIDS epidemic is both difficult and painful to fathom. More than one informant likened it to a war: "You never know who is going to go next. Who can you depend on? Which dear friend will leave? Will I be one of the survivors? When will it be over?" One woman said, "Sometimes I can't believe this is happening. We have more friends who are dying than our parents. We can tell our parents where to get the best deals on funerals."

Like war, the AIDS epidemic is seen not just as being destructive but as inspiring heroism and a sense of community. It is generating a camaraderie and a great bonding and heroism. One man, a social worker, put it this way: "AIDS does have a good side. I keep hearing comments from hospitals, from agencies, saying the gay people handle this better. Their support systems, their friends, are there for them." A man in his twenties said, "AIDS is like a war we are desperately fighting to win, or sometimes I feel we are in a lifeboat trying to survive. . . . Sometimes you see the best qualities of a man in a lifeboat. The AIDS epidemic has done a lot to bind people together. AIDS is a cause, it has given us permission to show compassion for each other."

There has also been a sense of accommodation. Philosophically, one man observed, "AIDS forces us to look at ourselves and our world as we are. It confronts us with the most metaphysical of all our issues, and that ultimately may be the most positive effect. I can only see confrontation with those issues as a positive thing. In that sense we are lucky, just as every homosexual is lucky to be a homosexual, to have the opportunity to create a whole new set of rules for the game."

AIDS has also had an effect on gender issues. In the past, the role of sick individual and that of caretaker have both been filled largely by women, or at least by the unempowered in society. However, as gay men begin to deal with the realities and the scale of the HIV epidemic, with so much sickness and death, and therefore with the need to assume caretaking roles, more traditional gender roles have begun to be put aside.

How ironic this is, considering that only in the 1970s did gay men begin to celebrate the fact that they were men, not "sissies." To a certain extent, gay liberation meant confronting this basic gender identity conflict.

There were aspects of the gay liberation movement that emphasized such perceived "male" values as nonmonogamy and sexual experimentation. Part of the message of gay liberation was that gay men could be *men*—that is, as one man put it, "They weren't sissies." According to another, gay men "didn't necessarily like to trade recipes and were not all hairdressers." It was okay to like men—and the macho "clone" look was in. This was a radical step in the sense that it confronted stereotypes of the homosexual held by society. There had of course always been masculine or "butch" homosexual males, as they were referred to, but gay liberation allowed this aspect of gay culture to become much

more visible. With the advent of AIDS, however, the image of the gay
Marlboro man has of necessity softened.

Other Changes in Gay Life

One also has the sense that many Los Angeles gay men are spending
more time at home and with friends. This kind of description was
heard particularly often from gay men in their thirties or forties—the
cohort most affected by the AIDS epidemic. Many of these men have
had friends or lovers die, and many are seropositive themselves. "Slow-
ing down" is a way of conserving energy, perceived of as a resource in
short supply and therefore not to be squandered. Gay men are also
apparently recognizing that they must make themselves more available
to friends—whether to provide transportation to the doctors or to
play a quiet game of cards in the evening. "Stress reduction" is now a
common major goal.

Not all these changes can be attributed to AIDS, of course. Such
tendencies as settling down, deemphasizing sex, buying a house, coupling, and turning attention to more sedentary pursuits can be attributed to aging. Younger men have not been affected by the AIDS epidemic to the same degree as older men have. Younger men still
frequent bars and party, but there is much more awareness of AIDS.
One man in his twenties said, "I think guys my age seem to value
relationships more than when older guys were our age. Not so much
into empty sex or anonymous sex. I mean there's a hell of a lot of sex
going on, but practically everyone I talk to knows about AIDS." He
continued, "I mean the people my own age don't usually think about
dying—yet not one of us doesn't know someone who has died. You
just don't live so much on a day-to-day basis. When you take something for granted, you abuse it."

In the past few years, an even greater differentiation between
younger—those under thirty—and older gay men in Los Angeles has
developed. Some of those under thirty consider themselves part of the
"boy" movement, and at least one gay Los Angeles entrepreneur has
capitalized on the fact that younger gay men want their own identity
by organizing a group called the YMDC (Young Men's Dance Club),
which sponsors large parties and dances.

The "look" of these younger men is decidedly different from that of
the Stonewall cohort—clean shaven (even in some cases shaving chest

and body hair), more dressy in the sense of wearing designer-inspired clothes, and in some cases having a more stylized look. Here is the sense of a new gay image emerging—one distanced from the look of the Stonewall cohort and the specter of AIDS. Sex, however, continues. As one observer put it, "I spend a lot of time with the guys, and the male energy is still there, only maybe expressed differently."

For their part, "older" gay men—those over thirty-five—are not always comfortable with the new look. "I'll *always* have my moustache," asserted one man. "If I liked clean shaven, I'd have stayed straight." Another man said, "I am dating a guy in his early twenties, and he tells me he doesn't want to grow a moustache, but he likes it on me." Another said, "I was at a party last summer, and this cute young guy came up to me and said, 'I like older daddies.' It was a shock to me because I didn't consider thirty-nine old!"

One of the changes of the last decade that has been commented on most has to do with relationships between gay men and lesbians. One woman said, "It used to be I had a sense that gay men did not want to have anything to do with women. There was one feeling that women were not welcome in some gay male circles, and to be fair men were not welcome in women's bars. Also, women viewed gay male sexuality—I mean the anything goes, as many as possible mentality—as distasteful. Now things have changed. Men aren't as overtly obsessed with sexuality, and women are less militant." The same woman continued, "Things started to change when all of us started to grasp the severity of the situation, and by now most women I know have been involved in caregiving of male friends." Several men spoke similarly and said they felt the two communities had come closer together.

One of the primary indications of the changing times has been a growth in service organizations, especially AIDS-related service organizations. A very large number of gay men and lesbians have become involved as volunteers, and many more have contributed money to the care of those affected by the epidemic.

There has also been a tremendous increase in the number of nonsexual, social institutions, a trend that began in the 1970s. While there had for years been gay bowling and softball leagues, the 1980s saw a plethora of gay athletic clubs develop in Los Angeles as in other cities—from gay track clubs, to swimming teams, to soccer, to, most recently, football. In addition, there are gay hiking clubs, cooking clubs, and movie groups, and one special interest group was established in 1988 for gay men over forty that boasts a membership of over two hundred and a variety of activities—an interesting commentary on and recognition of aging as the first Stonewall cohort approaches middle age.

Religious and spiritually oriented groups have also had an effect on gay life since the late 1960s, when both the Metropolitan Community Church, a gay-oriented Protestant denomination, and Dignity, an organization for gay Catholics, were founded in Los Angeles. While both these and other religious organizations, such as the gay Jewish temple, grew and became firmly established in the 1970s, the 1980s saw an even greater increase in religious and metaphysical organizations. Some of these are in the tradition of healing cults and often focus on AIDS issues and concerns. As in any epidemic, disease and death, the seeming randomness of infection, and the experience of illness have catapulted many people into "spiritual consciousness" when they might not ordinarily have considered themselves religious. In addition, quite a number of "mainline" religious groups, including the Episcopal, Presbyterian, Methodist, Congregational, and Unitarian churches and a few Roman Catholic parishes, have made a point of welcoming lesbians and gay men.

One of the most notable developments has been the growth of chapters of the so-called twelve-step programs—after the twelve steps of Alcoholics Anonymous—directed at gay men and lesbians. These programs deal not only with alcoholism but also with drug addiction (Narcotics Anonymous, Cocaine Anonymous), codependency (Alanon), sexual addiction (Sexaholics Anonymous, Sexual Compulsives Anonymous, Sex and Love Addicts Anonymous), and overeating (Overeaters Anonymous) as well as with the problems faced by adult children of alcoholics. Most recently, a twelve-step program for those who are HIV positive (HIV Anonymous) was established. On any given night of the week, any number of these various groups will be meeting. There was such a great need for such programs in the Silverlake area that several years ago members of gay AA groups banded together and bought a centrally located residence, establishing a gay twelve-step meeting center. A similar center exists on the west side of Hollywood. There are also several gay and lesbian addiction treatment programs in Silverlake, which advertise in the gay press.

Perhaps the proliferation of such programs reflects the coming of age—or at least the arrival at middle age—of the baby-boom generation. Perhaps their establishment reflects a search for a more deeply rooted sense of community in a society that does not explicitly value communitarian sensibilities or kinship. Los Angeles is often described as a city where individualism and performance and status are particularly prized, yet it may be that in such a context other human needs are not easily met.

Epilogue

Into the 1990s, the gay community in Los Angeles finds itself increasingly established, coping with the AIDS epidemic, yet transformed by the experience. In many respects, the gay community is a community in transition.

For one thing, gay men in Los Angeles, as are the gay men in San Francisco that Scott Wirth writes about, are no longer preoccupied with the archetype of eternal youth, the *puer aeternus,* or Pan, the wild god of the woods and the field.[14] The community finds itself no longer in adolescence but rather increasingly taking on the roles and tasks of adulthood. This transformation is reflected politically, economically, demographically, sociologically, culturally, and with respect to gender issues.

Politically, the gay and lesbian community has begun to participate in quite visible ways in the larger political arena of Los Angeles, as are other ethnic and special interest groups. It is telling that, in the late 1980s, politicians—from City Council members, to the mayor of Los Angeles, from individuals running for the State Assembly to U.S. senators—began attending gay political functions in Los Angeles and listening to the demands of the community. This dialogue and the increasing political clout of the community have resulted in some significant civil rights legislation—in particular, attention to AIDS issues (including the protection of confidentiality).

Economically, the community has not only survived but become a viable economic entity, in some ways analogous to the economic force of other ethnic communities. Los Angeles is the only city in the United States to have two successful "gay" financial institutions (one a savings-and-loan association, the other a bank). The 1988 *Gay Community Yellow Pages* had 192 pages of advertising and listings, larger than many small cities in southern California. While the nature of gay businesses has changed over the decade (fewer sexual establishments, fewer bars), there has been an increase in the number of gay professional and business associations.

Demographically, the community continues to change, in four major respects. First, there appears to be an ongoing migration of younger gay men to Los Angeles, if on a smaller scale than in the 1970s. The emergence of Los Angeles as a major economic center on the Pacific rim as well as a major design and art center (in addition to its continuing preeminence in films, television, and music) attracts many young gay men and lesbians to the region. Second, there is at least the impression that this younger gay population is increasingly diverse racially and ethnically, and there are specific groups for gay Latinos, blacks, and Asians. While this trend began in the 1970s, there is the sense that these groups play increasingly important roles in the overall organization of the community. These ethnic, cultural, and racial differences do not always coexist easily, yet great effort has been made to ensure representative racial and ethnic participation in most gay organizations. Third, the original Stonewall-era gay cohort that came out in and/or migrated to Los Angeles in the 1970s is aging. Many of the changes described in this essay can be attributed to the advance of middle age in this important historical cohort; it will be important to follow these individuals as they age. Of particular concern will be their ability to adapt to the losses of so many of their numbers to AIDS, itself the fourth major demographic change. To date, most of the AIDS deaths in Los Angeles have been among gay men of this generation, and the effect of this trauma, with the attendant bereavement and guilt over surviving, will have very important implications for gay identity overall.

Sociologically, there continue to be institutional and life-style changes related to those other processes. The new decade sees a somewhat different configuration of gay-identified institutions, some in the locales where gays have always clustered, but others spread out in the expanding frontiers of the Los Angeles megalopolis. One interesting change seems to be the decline of the bar as the prototypical gay institution and the emergence of other kinds of gathering places (restaurants, community centers, bookstores).

Culturally, there is greater diversity and more indication of self-acceptance. Sex is less overt, and there is on some levels more public recognition of caring and concern and the need for community itself. There is a sense of both loss and sadness as well as a determination to carry on. There is a greater sense of accommodation between men and women and the straight world. One man said, "There seems to be a beginning, I say a beginning, of greater self-confidence and self-acceptance among ourselves. Some of us have buried so many, we have to ask, 'Was it worth it?' I think most of us believe it was and is."

Notes

The author would like to express his appreciation to all the people he interviewed, to members of the Los Angeles gay and lesbian community, and in particular to Jim Kepner, Lee Klosinski, Mark Kowalewski, Peter Nardi, and Amy Ross.

1. See, e.g., William Simon and John H. Gagnon, "Homosexuality: The Formulation of a Sociological Perspective," *Journal of Health and Social Behavior* 8 (1967): 177–85; Dennis Altman, *Homosexual: Oppression and Liberation* (New York: Avon, 1971); Kenneth Plummer, *Sexual Stigma: An Interactionist Account* (Boston: Routledge & Kegan Paul, 1975); Martin P. Levine, ed., *Gay Men: The Sociology of Gay Culture* (New York: Harper & Row, 1979); Laud Humphreys, "Exodus and Identity: The Emerging Gay Culture," in ibid.; R. Parker, "Acquired Immunodeficiency Syndrome in Urban Brazil," *Medical Anthropology Quarterly* 1, no. 2 (1987): 155–75; Richard R. Troiden, *Gay and Lesbian Identity: A Sociological Analysis* (Dix Hills, N.J.: General Hall, 1988).

2. See E. Michael Gorman, "A New Light on Zion" (Ph.D. diss., University of Chicago, 1980).

3. Ibid., p. 147.

4. See Mark Kowalewski, "Double Stigma and Boundary Maintenance," *Journal of Contemporary Ethnography* 17 (1988): 211–28; K. W. Payne, "The Double Stigma of AIDS" (paper presented at the annual meeting of the American Anthropological Association, Philadelphia, December 1986).

5. Plummer, *Sexual Stigma*.

6. It is commonly assumed that New York has the largest gay community; San Francisco has the most visible and highly organized gay community.

7. In some respects, these might be considered as enclaves or ghettos (or some variety thereof) in the classic sociological sense as articulated by Levine (see *Gay Men*) and Scott Wirth ("Reflections on Archetypal Aspects of AIDS and a Psychology of Gay Men," in *What to Do about AIDS,* ed. Leon McKusick [Berkeley and Los Angeles: University of California Press, 1986], pp. 133–41).

8. *Gay Girls' Guide to the USA and the Western World* (Los Angeles, 1957).

9. The same *Guide* noted, "The park or square forms the basic gay rendezvous in every city."

10. West Hollywood contains the largest clustering of gay-identified restaurants, bars, gyms, bookstores, motels, meeting places, and organizations in southern California, meriting some sixty entries in the 1989 *Bob Damron's Address Book,* a national gay guide.

11. Edmund White, *States of Desire* (New York: Dutton, 1980).

12. D. A. Feldman and T. M. Johnson, eds., *The Social Dimensions of AIDS: Method*

and Theory (New York: Praeger, 1986); R. Bolton, "AIDS and Ads: Behavior Change among Gay Men in Response to the AIDS Epidemic" (paper presented at the annual meeting of the Kroeber Anthropological Society, Berkeley, March 1986); E. M. Gorman, "AIDS Prevention and Risk Reduction Strategies: Anthropological Perspectives on Implementation and Evaluation" (paper presented at the annual meeting of the American Anthropological Association, Washington, D.C., December 1985); E. M. Gorman, "The AIDS Epidemic in San Francisco: Epidemiological and Anthropological Perspectives," in Anthropology and Epidemiology, ed. C. R. Jones, R. Stall, and S. M. Gifford (Dordrecht: Reidel, 1986), pp. 157–72; L. Kochems, "Meanings and Health Implications of Gay Men's Sexuality" (paper presented at the annual meeting of the American Anthropological Association, Chicago, November 1987); G. Herdt, "AIDS and Anthropology," Anthropology Today 3 (1987): 1–3; S. C. McCombie, "The Cultural Impact of the 'AIDS' Test: The American Experience," Social Science and Medicine 23 (1987): 455–59; N. G. Lang and J. A. Kotarba, "From Lifestyle to Minority: The Remedicalization of Homosexuality since AIDS" (paper presented at the annual meeting of the American Anthropological Association, Denver, November 1984).

13. E. M. Gorman, D. E. Kanouse, E. M. Yano, and S. Berry, "Telephone Survey of Self-identified Gay and Bisexual Men in Los Angeles County" (Santa Monica, Calif.: Rand Corp., 1990).

14. Wirth, "Reflections on Archetypal Aspects of AIDS."

FOUR

Components of Gay Community in San Francisco

Stephen O. Murray

No community that comprises ethnically diverse persons dispersed (albeit nonrandomly) through an urban, post-industrial metropolitan area is going to be monolithic.[1] Assertions about complex societies must necessarily be statistical distributions, not exceptionless pronouncements. However, given the history of derogation of gay men, it seems necessary to stress that there *are* evaluative norms as well as statistical ones in urban gay communities. Despite factors extenuating the extent of aid, gay men can (and do) reasonably expect other gay men to help them find jobs and places to live and to care for those who are stricken with AIDS. Similarly, despite a tolerance for not announcing that someone is gay in many circumstances and a lack of agreement about what "gay" means, there is a moral imperative *not* to deny gayness within the gay community.

In this chapter, I endeavor to show some patterning of diversity within the San Francisco gay community. I begin by reviewing "community" as a "technical term" in social science, showing that, insofar as the term can be applied in urban settings, it is appropriate to identify "gay community" as one. Turning from the usage of social scientists, I discuss what San Francisco gay men mean by "gay community." This ethnosemantic analysis of a folk category shows that gay self-identification has been and continues to be the most important criterion of membership in the native view. Using data from the same sample, I explore two aspects of the path to membership in the San Francisco gay community: "coming out" and migration. A "community" requires a sense of peoplehood in a place. "Coming out" is the folk term for recognition of the relevance of gay peoplehood for an individual. Although there is a sense in which one can identify oneself as part of a gay tradition with no particular location in space, those men who consider themselves part specifically of the San Francisco gay community live in the San Francisco Bay Area. Most of us originated elsewhere. Many of us also came out elsewhere. Systematic differences by ethnicity and by generation exist for all three phenomena considered in this chapter: conception of what "gay community" is, age of coming out, and the reasons for and experience of migration to San Francisco.

Numbers in what follows derive from responses of the first 159 respondents in a 1988 snowball sample of San Francisco Bay Area self-identified gay men.[2] This sample overrepresents Asian men if contrasted to the Multicenter AIDS Cohort Study (MACS) random sample of gay men from the nineteen San Francisco census tracts with the highest 1983 AIDS rates, centered on the Castro district, or with the random telephone sample of the San Francisco Bay Area conducted for the *San Francisco Examiner* in the spring of 1989.[3] Other ethnic representations, age, percentage in a relationship, age of initial homosexual experience, and educational attainment of the two samples are roughly equivalent (see table 1, which contrasts four San Francisco gay community samples with samples from four other U.S. cities).[4] Half my sample resides in the neighborhoods of the San Francisco (MACS) sample. The claims that I make without numbers are based on quasi-native status and on participant observation, living in the San Francisco gay community for the last decade and reading the local gay press, especially the abundant letter columns.[5]

Community as a Social Science Technical Term

Debate over the existence of "gay community" stems partly from the dissensus about what a "community" is[6] and partly from a separate standard for "gay community" in contrast to other kinds of urban communities.[7] North American gay communities fit all the criteria suggested by sociologists to define "community" as well or better than urban ethnic communities do.[8]

The first, commonsense component of "community" is territory. The imaginary "traditional" rural village is supposed to have been geographically distinct, internally homogeneous and harmonious, and untrammeled by external influences. Nowhere are rural villages entirely isolated from each other, and, in some places, the boundaries of rural villages are difficult to draw.[9] Demands for taxes, soldiers, and labor are levied from outside, and, even in extremely mountainous regions, there usually are some persons oriented beyond the immediate locale to larger worlds.[10] Intravillage variability and conflict are more common than anthropologists once supposed.[11]

To make communities out of geographic aggregates, people must experience spatial boundaries as important ways of conceiving and distinguishing kinds of people within those boundaries.[12] Geography must be supplemented by endogamy, restriction of trade, local cults, and other such social creations to make socially salient boundaries.[13] Isolation and propinquity alone do not produce solidarity. Contrarily, seemingly trivial similarities (such as living in a red housing project rather than a green one or on one side of a street rather than another) may come to symbolize distinctiveness important enough to lead to collective action, and even to violence.[14]

North American cities lack walled-in ghettoes. Nor do checkpoints prevent the flow of persons between perfectly segregated areas.[15] Thus, one may travel from a predominantly Italian territory to a predominantly Chinese or a predominantly gay one in San Francisco. None of these areas is inhabited exclusively by Italian, Chinese, or gay residents; yet residents of a city are able to report where such communities are. At least they can specify where the centers are. Boundaries are often not distinctly conceived. Categories of everyday cognition are generally fuzzy sets.[16]

Several neighborhoods with lesbian and/or gay residential concentrations exist in large cities.[17] Clustering of recreational facilities, particularly nocturnal ones such as bars, fosters in-group perceptions of a gay or lesbian territory. The existence of distinctive institutions is more salient to the identification of a community—for both insiders and outsiders—than residential segregation or concentration.[18] Over the course of the 1970s, gay men in European and North American cities developed a fairly complete set of basic social services beyond the bars.[19] These included bookstores, churches, travel agencies, periodicals, political clubs, historical societies, charities, a savings-and-loan as-

Table 1 Gay Community Characteristics

Characteristic	Sample									
	SF, This Study	Random SF MACS Sample[a]	Random Telephone SF Sample[b]	Non-random SF[c]	Los Angeles MACS[d]	Chicago MACS[e]	New York City[f]	Pittsburgh MACS[g]	SF White, ca. 1969[h]	SF Black, ca. 1969[h]
Mean education	15.7					16.3	16.5		15.6	15.1
Percentage with some college	82	90	88	70	89	88	94	81	75	77
Mean age in 1988	43	40.5	37	40	35	35	39	35	37	27
Percentage white	71	89	77[i]	91	95	93	87	96		
Percentage in a relationship	57[j]		58[j]	58		53	43		51	58
Mean age at which began homosexual activity	16.5				17	19		17	23[k]	21[k]
Mean age at coming out	24.2	21.3[l]								

a Michael Samuel and Warren Winkelstein, "Prevalence of HIV in Ethnic Minority Homosexual/Bisexual Men," *Journal of the American Medical Association* 257 (1987): 1901–2; Warren Winkelstein et al., "Sexual Practices and Risk of Infection by the Human Immunodeficiency Virus," *Journal of the American Medical Association* 257 (1987): 321–25, and "The San Francisco Men's Health Study," *American Journal of Public Health* 78 (1988): 472–74.

b Larry D. Hatfield, "Gays Say Life Is Getting Better," *San Francisco Examiner*, 6 June 1989, A15–A19.

c Leon McKusick, William Horstman, and Arthur Carfagni, "AIDS and Sexual Behavior Reported by Gay Men in San Francisco," *American Journal of Public Health* 75 (1985): 493–96, "Reported Changes in the Sexual Behavior of Men at Risk for AIDS, San Francisco, 1982–84," *Public Health Reports* 100 (1985): 622–29, and "Longitudinal Predictors of Reduction in Unprotected Anal Intercourse among Gay Men in San Francisco," *American Journal of Public Health* 80 (1990): 978–83.

d Richard A. Kaslow et al., "The Multi-Center AIDS Cohort Study," *American Journal of Epidemiology* 126 (1987): 310–18.

e Ronald C. Kessler et al., "Effects of HIV Infection, Perceived Health and Clinical Status on a Cohort at Risk for AIDS," *Social Science and Medicine* 27 (1988): 569–78.

f John L. Martin and Laura Dean, "Developing a Community Sample of Gay Men for an Epidemiologic Study of AIDS," *American Behavioral Scientist* 33 (1990): 546–61; John L. Martin, Laura Dean, Marc García, and William Hall, "The Impact of AIDS on a Gay Community," *American Journal of Community Psychology* 17 (1989): 269–93.

g Ronald O. Valdiserri et al., "Variables Influencing Condom Use in a Cohort of Gay and Bisexual Men," *American Journal of Public Health* 78 (1988): 801–5.

h Alan P. Bell and Martin S. Weinberg, *Homosexualities* (New York: Simon & Schuster, 1978).

i Figure includes lesbians as well as gay men.

j Figure inferred from "living with someone."

k Age of first affair, which is generally later than first sexual activity.

l Mean age at which first socialized as gay. In contrast, mean age at which first thought of self as gay was 18.7.

sociation, etc. Indeed, an entire *Gay Yellow Pages* in San Francisco features myriad other gay businesses and services, just as do the *Hispanic Yellow Pages* and *Chinese Yellow Pages* there.

Contemporary gay (and also lesbian) urban North American enclaves differ from those of ethnic immigrants (past and present) in some important ways. In contrast to relatively impoverished immigrants speaking an alien language whom sociologists expect to form distinct (ethnic) institutions, gay men were relatively integrated into the full range of occupations and mostly had native command of English before gay institutional elaboration began. Most gay persons could and did "pass" in everyday life.[20] We *chose* to interact with our "own kind" rather than being restricted to those who spoke the same (minority) language.[21] Given a previous homosexual exogamy (a preference for straight "trade" rather than for "sisters" as sexual partners), sexual endogamy (self-identified gay men coupling with other self-identified gay men) was crucial to the formation of gay pride, consciousness, and collective action.[22]

Some men who engage in recurrent homosexual behavior do not recognize "sexual orientation" as defining any important component of their self.[23] They do not see a "we" that has anything important in common and, therefore, see no reason to associate with openly gay men in nonsexual interaction. Yet there are also people who feel that they have a distinct sensibility that they share with other gay people. Some individuals fight the expectation to be part of any such "we," while others eagerly seek a sense of community. Consciousness of kind is neither innate nor automatic; rather, it emerges over time, depending on the conception of an experience with others of a kind. This is true of ethnic consciousness as much as of gay consciousness.[24]

Social stigmas inhibit identification. Sometimes, however, a critical mass develops to challenge a stigma—either by asserting, "We are not like that," or by proclaiming, "The ways we are different are fine or even valuable." Stigmas then become badges of honor. They may also become stimuli to collective action challenging discrimination and affirming the value of the group's formerly stigmatized characteristics.[25] In a pluralistic society, group identification is an achieved status, not automatically and irrevocably established at birth or in primary socialization.[26]

Advocates and adversaries both foster collective identification, which is a necessary (but not sufficient) prerequisite to collective action. Definitions of a "kind of person" are used by some opportunistic politicians to advance minorities' status and by others to organize against minorities' gains—and sometimes against the very existence in a society of such a people. Public discourse about the value or threat of a kind of person crystallizes the identification of some persons with a group while scaring off others from identification or even association with the stigmatized group. Partly through political conflict, some people defined categorically come to see themselves as having a common history and destiny distinct from others, public supporters, and public enemies. Gay leaders have pressed economic boycotts, political coordination, and mass demonstrations. Other moral entrepreneurs have promoted legal discrimination and harassment as well as the criminalization of homosexual behavior.[27] In response to police raids and the seeming acquiescence of the legal system with the assassination of gay San Francisco supervisor Harvey Milk, there were gay riots. Nonetheless, it bears stressing that even those who have the feeling of being part of a group may still not join in collective action, which is rarely— if ever—characteristic of any population. Homosexual behavior does not necessarily lead either to a gay identity or to general association with gay men. Even gay identity and gay association do not necessarily lead to gay collective action. One could substitute "ethnic derivation" and "ethnic" for "homosexual behavior" and "gay" in these antisyllogisms without loss of validity. Sporadic action by a self-selected vanguard is more common for class- or ethnic-based groups as well as for lesbians or gays.

A decade ago, I reviewed "technical" social science definitions of "community" and showed that "gay community" is as much of one as any other urban community.[28] Even more than the Toronto of the late 1970s that I took as an example, the San Francisco gay community (then or now) evinces the criterial features of "community." The most important of these in the community literatures are a concentration of interaction among those who identify themselves as gay into gay primary groups, concentration in space (of residence, but, more important, of community institutions) in specifiable territory, learned (though not monolithic) norms, institutional completeness, collective action, and a sense of shared history.

A Community, Not Just a Life-Style Enclave

Since that time, one influential interpretation of American culture, *Habits of the Heart,* by Robert Bellah and four colleagues, has sought to preserve the sacred term "community" from application to what they term "lifestyle enclaves." This superficial, second-rate kind of grouping is based on "the narcissism of similarity" in patterns of leisure and consumption. "When we hear such phrases as 'the gay community' or 'the Japanese American community,'" they write, "we need to know a great deal before we can decide the degree to which they are genuine communities and the degree to which they are lifestyle enclaves."[29] Given the wide distribution of *Habits of the Heart,* it seems necessary again to address the question of the applicability of "community" to "gay community."

One criterion of "community" for Bellah et al. is "to reproduce the entire institutional complex of a functioning society . . . even, as far as possible in urban settings."[30] If, as I think I demonstrated, gay Toronto met this test in the late 1970s, San Francisco, then or now, has more instances of every institution, including four gay political clubs (one Republican and three Democratic: Alice B. Toklas, Harvey Milk, Stonewall), its own health services (including Operation Concern, 18th Street Services, and, earlier, Pride Foundation), and two rival weekly newspapers (the *Sentinel* and the *Bay Area Reporter;* earlier in the decade there was also the *Voice,* and there is now also the monthly *Coming Up!* and the quarterly *Outlook*).[31] Almost all these predate the efflorescence of AIDS organizations—protest ones such as Mobilization Against AIDS, Stop AIDS Now, and two Act-Up groups and service ones such as Open-Hand, the AIDS Emergency Fund, the AIDS Foundation, the Shanti Project, and others.

The most important criterion to Bellah et al., deeply concerned as they are about the failure of civic involvement in ultraindividualist America, is the extent to which serious commitments among geographically concentrated people similar in life-style "carry them beyond private life into public endeavors."[32] It seems to me that, even before the trauma of AIDS launched major political and charitable initiatives, San Francisco was already notable for gay political involvement in neighborhood, environmental, educational, labor, arts, and civil rights issues. These concerns extended beyond protecting and advancing specifically gay self-interests. In a long-running political battle in which the interests of "downtown" are pitted against "neighborhoods," gay county supervisors Harvey Milk and Harry Britt have been leaders in battles across a wide range of "progressive" causes, including height limitations on buildings, rent control, preserving open space from encroachment, civilian oversight of police, municipalization of electricity, etc. Although there are clearly gay male San Franciscans who oppose one or more of these policies, the heavily gay precincts consistently turn out the highest percentages of votes not just for the gay "progressive" candidates but for the more "leftist/progressive" straight candidates and for environmentalist state and local initiatives. In addition to elected officials, there are openly lesbian and gay members of the boards of most local political, charitable, and arts organizations.[33]

Beyond an active involvement in the civic culture of the Bay Area, the extraordinary mobilization to lobby for and care for persons with AIDS surely transcends hedonism and shared leisure of a "lifestyle enclave." The contributions of resources and extraordinary self-sacrifices by many gay San Francisco men protecting and caring for mortally ill peers constitutes compelling evidence that gay men share more than jargon, costumes, and transient sexual encounters. Although the larger society disvalues and seeks to undermine our relationships, gay men for the most part have stood by their lovers and friends rather than abandoning them. Whether in fund-raising or in providing services to persons with AIDS (and not just gay ones), over the past decade gay men have demonstrated their willingness to take on onerous burdens of caring for others. To put it mildly, it is hard to conceive the gay male response to AIDS as that of a "lifestyle enclave" with superficially committed individuals concerned only with narcissistic self-gratifications or reveling in "the narcissism of similarity" in consumptions patterns.

Bellah et al. further specify that "a real community" is "a 'community of memory,' one that does not forget its past. . . . Stories of collective history and exemplary individuals are an important part. . . . A genuine community of memory will also tell painful stories of shared suffering that sometimes creates deeper identities than success. . . . Where history and hope are forgotten and community means only the gathering of the similar, community degenerates into lifestyle enclave."[34] This certainly describes the gay community. Already in the late 1970s, I could write that "in recent years efforts to learn about the history of subordinated groups has gained momentum. The quest for forerunner heroes ('Shakespeare, Michelangelo and Me' or *From Jonathan to Gide*) has been supplemented by serious historical research on the everyday life of oppression."[35] As a survey of a gay bookstore or of history journals would show, this trend indeed gained momentum.

If Bellah and his associates examined the activities of either the gay or the Japanese-American community, they would see intense activity in preserving accounts of suffering in oral history projects and autobiographical publications as well as celebration of exemplary and of "common" members of each community. The AIDS quilt would seem to me to be a model of community-generated public remembrance. In addition to an efflorescence of professional historical scholarship on homosexual pasts, there are community-based groups collecting oral history in most American metropolises, including the very active San Francisco Bay Area Gay and Lesbian Historical Society.

The Native's View

Having shown that the gay community fits the new criterion for "community" as well as the older ones in social science discourse, I would like to turn from the outsider (etic) criteria of "community" to analyzing the native (emic) sense of what "gay community" means for those who consider themselves a part of it. Just before the first cases of AIDS appeared, Bob Poolman and I surveyed sixty-one gay-identified San Francisco men about their understanding of "gay community."[36] Based on pretest interviews, we framed questions systematically varying the criterial features suggested in the interviews. These were (1) having a gay identity, (2) living in a gay neighborhood, and (3) having (socializing with) mostly gay friends. We confirmed that, for most members of the gay community, gay identity is the salient, defining characteristic, not homosexual activity. As Michael, a white self-identified clone put it,

> It doesn't matter what you do in bed—or in the backrooms. Anyone who considers himself gay *is* gay.
> [How does someone come to consider himself gay?]
> God knows—and she ain't telling! Um, there's supposed to be a "gay sensibility," but again, there are people who are obviously straight who have it, and some very tacky fags. I'd have to say [that] it's who[m] you identify with. Like some of these straight people who I'd say have a "gay sensibility"—whatever that is—they're sort of "honorary faggots." There *are* people who consider it to be an honor, you know. There are others who have a lot of homosexual, um, "release" shall we say? Like they make it every day in some sordid tearoom, for instance, but would never admit

to being gay, even while they're sucking your cock, right? Well, to me they aren't gay.
[What are they? What would you call them?]
They're homosexual, but they aren't gay.
[And some people who have never had sex with another man are?]
Yeah, sure. The gay community is a state of mind, not body. Anyway, gay men aren't real concerned about excluding people from this elite [that] we consider ourselves to be. I've never heard of anyone's credential being challenged, like "I'm not going to believe you're gay until I fuck you."[37] We give everyone the benefit of the doubt. You wanna party with us? That's fine. You don't have to make it with other men if you don't want to. Your loss, if you don't, you know?

Craig, an African-American gay man interviewed in 1980, also stressed the "taste leader" self-conception of a gay vanguard, saying, "Not all homosexuals identify with being gay, and not all people who are gay identify with the community. Sex may be its starting point, but it's more whom you party with and have a good time with. It used to be political, but now, it's not. Now, it's mostly hanging around in gay places and being chic." Tony, a Filipino disco queen of that era, told me,

People standing out on the corner of Eighteenth and Castro or in Rinegold Alley at two in the morning [when bars close in California] aren't my idea of a community.
[What is *your* idea?]
Well, the Castro *is* a gay community, not just the corner where they flock to exhibit their sexuality. Who you want to be with *out* of bed is probably more important than who you want to be *in* bed with. I mean, who your friends are, where you go to socialize, not just who you fuck with.

In an earlier and more closeted milieu, Carol Warren distinguished gay identity from acknowledged homosexuality on the basis of sociation: "A gay identity implies affiliation with the gay community in a cultural and sociable sense. A homosexual, for the community, is one who both practices homosexuality and admits it, whereas a gay person is someone who does all that and also identifies and interacts with the gay world."[38]

We also asked about effeminacy and cross-dressing, not because we thought that these were components of the native view, but because homosexuality and gender deviance are so often conflated in the social science literature (and not just old literature!). In our initial interviews, we went through formal ("white room ethnography") questions that we thought would lead to nonresponse on questionnaires:

1. Are all effeminate men part of "the gay community"?
2. Are members of "the gay community" generally effeminate?
3. Are all men who dress as women part of "the gay community"?
4. Do members of "the gay community" generally wear women's clothes?

The answers to all four questions were negative, generally very negative ("Don't you know better?" or "What a stupid question!"). Nick, the informant most attuned to why we would ask questions to which we knew the answer would be strongly negative, commented,

Femme drag queen is the stereotype, and, of course, there *are* some, but most transvestites, and probably most men who seem effeminate are straight and *very* hostile to being regarded as gay. The compliment is returned. Most gay men are uncomfortable with drag queens and with flaming queens who reinforce the stereotype, and the drag queens are contemptuous of those they consider "male impersonators" and call "muscle queens" or "leather queens." Drag queens and flaming queens who aren't cross-dressers are tolerated, but [are] often objects of fear and loathing.

I think gay men generally like men and masculinity. You could even say we worship masculinity, so the effeminate stereotype is ludicrously wrong. Male homosexuality is "about" masculinity, not a form of femininity. Men who need women—who are, if you'll pardon the expression, "pussy whipped"—seem lacking in masculinity to many of us, though I'm told that in the "bad old days" [before the gay liberation consciousness of the 1970s] the supposedly straight man was a premium object of lust for fags. I don't know of anyone who seeks men who claim to be straight as a sex object, and I don't even understand how a [lover] relationship with one partner claiming to be straight would work. I deal with enough schizophrenia without seeking it out at home!
[Don't you think that boys who are regarded as effeminate are channeled into gay life?]
You mean everyone already thinks they're queer, so they become queer?
[Yes.]
No. I think they flee from homosexuality more than the jocks, who can suck cock and get fucked because they are respected in the masculine world of the locker room. . . . I don't mean to say that this kind of high school homosexuality usually leads to gay identification and the gay life or that the high school or college jocks who get off with each other generally recognize themselves as gay, either at the time or later, but I think

the really effeminate ones tend to be scared away from men and even from wanting men. The boys who are loving each other are the high-status jocks. Those who seem effeminate or [have] girls' interests aren't receiving any love from boys. How can they not see males as threatening: they're being attacked, not loved by men? . . .

[Do you think there is *any* relationship between what is understood by most American teenagers as femininity and masculinity and becoming members of "the gay community"?]

No. I think we include the whole femme-to-butch range in high school, perhaps with more of those boys who were completely caught up in the all-male world of athletics and had no interest in "mere girls," even though they may sometimes have rammed their cocks into some. And maybe with less of the boys who weren't interested in "male pursuits."

[By which you mean?]

Football, wrestling, cocksucking—things men do better.

Feminine appearance and dress were not just unimportant but exotic and incomprehensible in the gay male world of the late-1970s and the 1980s. Whatever the gender norms of the past may have been, masculine appearance, demeanor, and stoicism (literally, "taking it" without flinching so that sexual receptivity, too, was defined as masculine, not effeminizing) were the clone's norms.[39]

The style of the postclone, post-AIDS generation of young gay men (i.e., those coming out in the late 1980s and early 1990s, who for the most part were born after 1965) deemphasizes some of the masculinist markers of the clone epoch, in particular facial hair and pumped-up muscles, without reviving effeminacy as "the way to be gay." The "younger generation"—an ironic category for the baby boomers, who still see themselves as "the youth culture" in eternal opposition to establishment elders—is underrepresented in the survey reported here (but see chapter 1). However, the increased impatience with closetry represented by the tactic of publicizing the homosexuality of closeted officials and other public figures suggests that public identification as gay remains central to the conception of "gay community" for a new generation. Moreover, as will be shown below, the "younger generation" seems to be "coming out" at earlier ages than their elders did. Future research may show increased importance for friendship groups in their conception of "gay community," but I doubt that gender will increase in salience, even among those who regard clone masculinity as exaggerated or excessive.

In addition to the resolutely secular view expressed by informants involved in what is viewed as "hypermasculinity" or "the alienating hypersexuality" of the urban gay scene by some of their juniors and some of their age-mates,[40] there are a variety of gay spiritualities in which a gay vision transcends gender polarities. "Radical fairy consciousness" draws on exemplars from many cultures (e.g., Dionysos from ancient Greek religion, North American berdache, and historically untenable interpretations of witches persecuted through the history of European Christendom) to justify rejecting the violent, destructive strivings of patriarchal self-assertion, objectification (of self and others) in the lethal rituals of masculinity proving.[41] Within this syncretic or ecumenical worldview (homo)sexuality is no longer the "determining gauge": "Gay implies a social identity and consciousness actively chosen, while homosexual refers to a specific form of sexuality. It follows that the path of 'gay spirit' is not automatically adopted by everyone who has homosexual feelings [or engages in homosexual activities], nor is it necessarily limited to such individuals. It is merely a mode of personal growth commonly found among those who are gay."[42] This distinction between homosexual doing and gay being is common to gay politicos, gay spiritualists, and the "average clone in the street" who is not involved in either of those activities with their special discourses[43] and who is quite unready to renounce masculinity (or to cease making a sexual object of himself or of other men).

Eighty-eight percent of our 1980 sample considered gay-identified men who had never had a same-sex sexual experience to be part of the gay community. In contrast, only 43 percent included men within it who had had same-sex experience but recognized no gay self-identity. "Credentials don't often get challenged," as Nick said in part of the interview quoted above. Tsunayoshi, a Japanese-American gay man, reflected, "Some people say 'gay' is a practicing homosexual, but I think you are practicing just by being, even if you're only thinking about, fantasizing about men. Your mind is practicing?"

In replicating these questions with a sample of 159 gay-identified men in the San Francisco Bay Area in 1988, considerably fewer gay-identified men included non-gay-identified men who recurrently engaged in homosexual sex to be within the bounds of "gay community." Twenty-five percent of Asian gay men and 21 percent of Anglo gay men included within the gay community non-gay-identified men who involved in homosexual activity.[44] Anglo gay men in 1988 approxi-

mated the 1980 sample in including gay-identified men with no homosexual experience. Seventy-six percent included "gay virgins." Asian
gay men, who tended to have their first homosexual experiences later
than men of other ethnicities (see below), were far more reluctant to
include anyone without sexual experience within their conception of
"gay community": only 38 percent of them did. Otherwise, gay men
in 1988 emphasized identity as the sine qua non of gay community
even more than in 1980, as can be seen by comparing the 1980 and
1988 columns in table 2. Gay identity is close to sufficient basis for
including a man within "gay community."[45] The other proposed criteria are necessary additional requirements for only a few (2 percent
each if set 6 with only gay identity is compared to gay identity with
one of the other two features in sets 2 and 3 and with all three in
set 1).

We found in the 1980 data that those gay men who had at some
time been involved with a gay political organization were more than

Table 2   Percentage Including Set of Attributes in Category "Gay
Community," 1980, 1988

Set	Gay Identity	Gay Friendship	Gay Neighborhood	Percentage Including 1980	Percentage Including 1988
1	+	+	+	98	100
2	+	+	−	90	98
3	+	−	+	80	98
4	−	+	+	48	24
5	−	+	−	50	15
6	+	−	−	. . .	96
7	−	−	+	. . .	7

Set	Gay Identity	Homosexual Activity		Percentage Including 1980	Percentage Including 1988
8	+	−		88	73
9	−	+		43	18

Exclusively heterosexual women who socialize mostly with gay men	68
Lesbians who work with gay men for lesbian and gay rights or in AIDS organizations	100

five times more likely to exclude men involved in homosexual activity without a gay identity from their conception of the gay community than gay men with no gay political background. A gay political background had little effect on explaining variance in including other bundles of features. In the 1980 data, we also found a statistically significant linear increase in inclusiveness for all the combinations based on the year the respondent came out.

The proportion of those with some experience of gay political involvement was lower in the 1988 sample (35 percent) than in the 1980 sample. Moreover, the effects of such experience were attenuated. Those with some gay political involvement were 1.65 times more likely than those without any to include gay-identified men without sexual experience and 2.5 times more likely to exclude straight-identified men engaging in homosexual sexual activity from the category gay community. Gay political involvement continued to explain significant variance in inclusion of "gay virgins" in the 1988 data. Using stepwise regression, it was the most important explanatory variable ($r = .36$, $p < .001$), followed by a dichotomous white/nonwhite variable (raising the multiple to .463, $p < .001$), and a slight effect from coming out more recently (which raised the multiple r to .48, $p < .05$).[46] That is, white men who came out in more recent years were most likely to include gay virgins than were others.[47] As table 3 shows, white gay men were more than twice as likely to include gay virgins as were Asian gay men.[48] The linear increase on inclusiveness by coming-out year that we found in 1980 continued, but leveled off.[49] As already noted, the direct effect of gay political involvement was reduced (from 5:1 to 1.65:1 in differential acceptance).

For including non-gay-identified homosexually involved men in "gay community," the age at which one came out is the best predictor

Table 3   Acceptance of Gay Virgins and Non-Gay-Identified Homosexuals by Ethnicity

Ethnicity	Percentage Including Gay-Identified Virgins	Percentage Including Non-Gay-Identified Homosexuals	Number
White/Anglo	76	20	112
African American	50	50	8
Hispanic/Latino	50	43	14
Asian American	38	25	24

(r = .21, p < .01). Coming to grips with a gay identity seems to increase patience and tolerance for others, given the benefit of doubt that they have not sorted things out yet rather than that they are "denying their brothers." Hispanic and African Americans also are less insistent on gay identity and/or more focused on homosexuality than Anglo or Asian Americans (see both columns of percentages in table 3; multiple r = .28, p < .02, for this increase). A history of some gay political involvement is negatively related to including non-gay-identified homosexuals within the gay community (increasing the multiple r to .34, p < .02, for this increase in explained variance).[50] There was basically no variance to explain inclusion of lesbians: only one of the twenty-seven men asked excluded them.[51]

Identity

Accepting being gay is not just the most important criterion for establishing membership in the category "gay community" but the central moral imperative within it.[52] Denying one's self and brothers (and sisters) is the gravest sin. As with St. Peter, denial of identity to a hostile assailant is forgivable, but denial to one's self is viewed in retrospect as corrosive. Therefore, accepting homosexual inclinations is prescribed with varying degrees of gentleness and pressure to others.[53]

Members of the community recognize and respect that gay men come to terms with identifying themselves as gay at different ages and to differing extents of publicness. The pace of "coming out" is generally not challenged, and until very recently there has been a general taboo against forcing a "brother" out of the closet.[54] Men who identify themselves as gay are frequently tolerant of others who do not tell their coworkers or their families that they are gay. Although letting the assumption that one is straight pass without challenge in some situations is accepted, denying one is gay to men who identify themselves as gay and know about one's sexual habits (or who impute habits from captured glances or from noticing presence in particular locales) provokes denigration as a "closet queen" and direct challenge within gay settings. The prototypical response is a self-righteous, "Don't pretend to me, sister, I know better!"[55]

Coming out to natal family, coworkers, or other straight people is optional, but to accept being gay (at least simulating pride and rejecting shame) in the company of other gay men is as much a sign of adulthood as paternity is in other cultures. As Herdt argues, coming out is the most important rite of passage in gay life.[56] Although coming out is obviously in some sense a process rather than an event—and a process with varying durations, differing ceremonies, and differing ages of entry—gay men almost invariably point to one particular time when they graduated from misguided rejection of homosexuality to affirming their own gayness,[57] that is, from the (internalized) ignorant societal stigma to the more sophisticated understanding of the properly initiated and subsequently "in the know."[58] What gay men mean by "coming out" is usually some public acknowledgment, such as the first time they went to a gay bar or a gay meeting or told a friend.[59] The initiation rites are not strictly age demarcated, but the expected end result is acceptance of one's self as one member in a worthwhile people: "I'm OK, we're more than OK!"[60]

Despite the stigma of AIDS, openly gay men have not gone back into the closet in appreciable numbers, and some public figures (e.g., Roy Cohn, Malcolm Forbes, Liberace, and Rock Hudson) have been forced out of the closet by AIDS diagnoses.[61] In general, I see no reason to think that the rate of coming out has changed. There is a longer-term trend of coming out at younger ages, sooner after initial sexual experience (the age of which is rising slightly), and of ethnic differences, as can be seen in table 4. While the mean age of coming out for men before 1940 was 32.3, and while for those born between 1940 and 1944 it was still 27.6, the mean age dropped to 21.9 for those born between 1940 and 1949, to 21.0 for those born 1950–54,

Table 4   Mean Ages of First Homosexual Sexual Experience and of Coming Out by Ethnicity of Bay Area Gay Men

Ethnicity	Mean Age of First Homosexual Experience	Mean Age of Coming Out	Interim	Number
Black	13.2	27.6	14.4	9
Hispanic	14.6	23.1	8.5	14
White	16.4	24.4	8.0	112
Asian/Pacific	19.4	22.5	3.1	24
Total	16.5	24.2	7.7	159
Examiner random telephone sample of Bay Area gay men, reported duration between "when you knew you were gay and when you came out"			7.0	299

to 19.8 for those born 1955–59, and to 19.5 for those born 1960–69. This means that, beginning with the baby boom, gay men tended to come out soon after high school (those not going to college one year earlier on the average than those with some college or more education). The Chicago Horizons data extend the general trend of coming out at earlier ages to those born in the 1970s and coming out in the 1980s.[62]

Complicating this historical trend are ethnic differences. African-American men who eventually identify themselves as gay typically begin to have sex much earlier (mean age 13.2) than Asian/Pacific Islander men (mean age 19.2), yet come out later (African-American mean age of coming out is 27.6 in contrast to Asian/Pacific 22.5).[63] In general, those whose first homosexual experience was at an age younger than ten would come out at older ages than those whose first homosexual experience was at an older age.[64]

Migration

Coming out is the most important avenue to being a part of a gay community. Getting to where there are other gay-identified men is a secondary but still important prerequisite of being part of the San Francisco gay community, especially since only 4 percent of the sample were born in the Bay Area. At least since the end of the Second World War, some men have moved to San Francisco to "be gay." Some gay men continue to find it necessary to migrate to a metropolis in order to come to terms with internally recognized homosexuality. For instance, Peter, a white gay man in his late twenties, said, "I was always a homo and knew it, but I didn't deal with it until I got to New York." Similarly, Barry, an Asian-American in his early forties, told me that he knew he was attracted to men as early as primary school but waited until his education was complete (at age thirty), moved to San Francisco, and only then ventured for the first time into a gay bar to meet other gay men.

San Francisco has long been perceived as a place in which being gay is accepted, or tolerated, or "no big deal." For some, it is a place in which it is possible to live in a more or less all-gay world with few contacts other than those with gay people. For others, it is a place to be gay without being anomalous, that is, without being stigmatized by sexual orientation.

However, a perceived favorable social climate for gay sociation is only one factor among others determining individual and collective gay migration to San Francisco. Like all human behavior, migration is overdetermined: there is no single factor explaining the outcome. Moreover, just as gay identity is achieved and must then be maintained, someone around to be sampled for a retrospective study of migration has to have moved and stayed. The experiences of those who moved and then either moved on or retreated to the place of origin are necessarily missed by such sampling.[65] My sample can be considered the residues not only of migration but also of the process of gay identification.[66]

Before trying to model some of the variance in migration experiences of San Francisco gay men, I'd like to present some individual histories to show some of the variety of migration histories.

First is Larry. After release from the army, he went to college in his Midwestern home state, funded by the GI bill. On completion of his studies in the early 1950s, he wanted to move to California, which seemed to him the land of the future. He did not know anyone in southern California but had stayed in contact with a straight army buddy in San Francisco. Larry stayed with this friend until he found a job (the first full-time job of his life) and could afford to rent a place of his own.

Michael moved from the South in the mid-1960s because his lover was fed up with his job and wanted to move to a less oppressive climate. Michael was not especially enamored with his job or with the South and was willing to relocate. Both did piecework while getting established, and they separated within a year of arriving in San Francisco.

Jay went back to school in the early 1970s. On completing his studies in the late 1970s, he applied for academic jobs all over the country, without success. When a long-term relationship ended, he decided to move to New York City. However, a woman friend who was getting divorced asked if he would drive with her to San Francisco, where she was going to return to school. He agreed. They stayed with a friend of hers while apartment hunting. He worked for a temporary office work agency for a year before starting his own business.

Also in the late 1970s, Lance's friend Joe called his friend Michael and asked him to help Lance if he could when Lance arrived. Michael picked up Lance at the airport. He arranged for Michael to stay with his friend Jay (for Lance this was a friend of a friend of a friend) who had a vacant bedroom (the woman he moved with having decided that she was a lesbian and could not therefore continue to live with a man, even platonically). Jay not only provided free rent for six months but also arranged for Lance to work covertly (i.e., without a green card). Michael introduced Lance to his own extensive network, found work for him, and even negotiated free consultation with a (gay) immigration lawyer.

In the early 1980s, Bill visited a friend who had moved to San Francisco. At a party he met Michael. Bill spent the rest of his vacation with Michael. Michael visited Bill and invited him to move into his house. Michael mobilized his friends and either found or made a job for Bill when he moved.

In the mid-1980s, Peter was transferred by the multinational corporation for which he worked to the South Bay. He knew he wanted to live in the city and used the company's generous moving allowance to stay in a downtown hotel while he shopped for a house in a sunny part of San Francisco. He did not know any gay people in the Bay Area.

Larry and Peter say they moved to get better jobs. Bill and Michael say the primary reason for their moves was love. Jay first said that he never decided to move to San Francisco and that if I had to assign a reason it was to get away from his ex. Lance also wanted a change of scenery. All knew that San Francisco was reputed to be a good place for gay people to live and had some notion of greater sexual freedom there. All felt more comfortable being openly gay in San Francisco. Only Jay (and his woman friend)—and possibly Lance—was seeking more and/or different sex. All of them found jobs that they judged better and more satisfying than any they had had prior to migrating to the Bay Area, although it should be noted that Jay, Lance, and Larry were only entering the job market at the time they moved.

The diversity of experiences of even these few individuals shows that migration is not a single normative rite of passage for San Francisco gay men.[67] Moving was a stage of coming out for some. For others, it was more or less an accident. Some moved seeking love, others money. Some moved seeking a climate more tolerant of homosexuality, others a more temperate climate. Still others—those who went along with moves initiated by family, lovers, or employers—were not seeking anything in particular, not even change. It would be a mistake to imagine that gay men not native to the Bay Area thought about all the places in the country or the world they could live and picked San Francisco. Just as not everyone who changes jobs is looking for a new job,[68] not everyone who migrates is involved in a cost-benefit analysis of possible places to live. As Alden Speare noted, "The biggest problem with the application of a cost-benefit model to human migration may not be the crudeness of the actual calculation, but the fact that many people never make any calculation at all."[69] There are patterns of mobility, but these patterns are somewhere between the strict order of initiation rites in some small-scale Melanesian societies[70] and the atomistic rationalist calculus of neoclassical *homo economicus*.

Over the course of the 1980s, migration to what was once the gay Mecca seems to have slowed, and outmigration to the suburbs (and beyond, to the supposedly AIDS-free countryside) has been publicized in gay and straight print media (see chapter 6). The image of San Francisco as a haven of tolerance has also been tarnished by assassin Dan White and other murderers of gay men and by nationally publicized attacks on lesbians and gay men.

The extent to which men abandoned careers to come to the sexual playground of San Francisco in the 1970s was overestimated—most influentially, in 1980 by Edmund White in *States of Desire*.[71] Of my informants, 34 percent of the black and white men had jobs in San Francisco before moving, and 89 percent of these jobs were judged better than those that had been left behind. Moreover, it was the gay men who moved to San Francisco alone who considered the jobs they found in San Francisco better than the ones they had left. Twice as many of those moving by themselves as those moving with someone else reported their first job after migrating was better than the job they had before moving. Some of these men subordinated their own careers to those of a lover advancing his career by moving, but this does not fit with giving up everything to move to San Francisco's sexual scenes during the 1970s.[72]

Further challenging the view of giving up careers and jobs for marginal existence close to the sexual playground is the finding that those who moved to San Francisco in the liberation era (1969–80) were twice as likely to be better satisfied with their first Bay Area job than with the job they left behind in migrating than were men moving in the AIDS era of sexual suppression and repression (i.e., from 1981 onward).[73] Those with higher education, those who moved during the

1970s, and those with jobs arranged before moving were more likely to report that their initial San Francisco jobs were better than the jobs they had before moving. The first-order correlations of measures are listed in the first row of table 5.

More than half the men who moved to San Francisco did not have full-time jobs in the place from which they moved (88 percent of those who moved to San Francisco prior to 1969). Half those who did have a full-time job in the place from which they emigrated had a full-time job arranged in San Francisco before moving there. Of men who had a full-time job somewhere else and who moved to San Francisco before securing another, 30 percent found what they say were better jobs, and 38 percent initially took worse jobs.[74] This slight net downward mobility in job quality as assessed by migrants disappears when the seemingly more objective measure of difference in salary is substituted:[75] the median change was zero. There was a mean increase of $575, but, because this figure is composed of shifting values of the dollar over time, this number cannot be readily interpreted. Twelve percent reported earning less in their first San Francisco job than in

Table 5   Correlations and Means of Migration Variables

	Housing Satisfaction	Had Job before Migrated	Migrated Before 1970	Gay Political Involvement	Years of Education	Mean (%)	Standard Deviation
First job satisfaction	.29**	28**	−.21*	.02	.22*	20	40
Housing satisfaction		.24**	−.30**	.19*	.19*	58	49
Had job before migrating			−.22*	.22*	.43**	24	43
Migrated before 1970				−.14	−.20*		
Gay political involvement					.24**	41	49
Years of education						15.97	3.27

* $p < .05$.
** $p < .01$.

the one they had preceding migration. In contrast, 18 percent reported earning more. These data do not seem to be consistent with the view that migration to a gay center necessarily, or even usually, involves a sacrifice of job/career.

I do not mean to imply that no individuals had a hard time getting established in San Francisco; I did myself.[76] For those of us who left little or nothing behind (e.g., moving after finishing some level of school, after being laid off of a job, or during or after a divorce), the "in San Francisco" was not the most important part of "I had a hard time getting established in San Francisco," however. We did not necessarily have much to throw away by migrating—half of us not having a full-time job in the place from which we emigrated, for instance.

One recurrent problem for migrants to a place where many people wish to live is finding a job. Whether or not we had local networks to mobilize in order to find out about job possibilities, less than half received information that led to their first Bay Area job from personal contacts. Sixty-two percent of the San Francisco gay immigrants in my sample found out about the possibility of what became their first full-time San Francisco job through formal channels (want ads or employment agencies). Of those who were told about a job possibility by a person, 72 percent of the persons supplying what turned out to be salient information were gay or lesbian, 85 percent strong ties (friends or relatives), and 15 percent weak ties (friends of friends or acquaintances).[77]

Three-quarters of the gay Asian-Americans moved to San Francisco alone, but, contrary to claims that there is not gay chain migration,[78] 30 percent of the gay men queried moved to San Francisco with or to live with someone they knew before moving. This someone was a gay man in 83 percent of these cases. Varying by ethnicity, when they first moved to San Francisco, between a quarter (of Asian-Americans) and a half (of Anglos) stayed with someone they previously knew. Eighty-four percent of these were strong ties. Thus, combining these two measures, roughly half the gay male émigrés to San Francisco mobilized a preexisting network to the extent of receiving shelter on arrival. Presumably, not everyone who knew people in San Francisco well enough to stay with them actually did so. Some had arranged housing in advance of arrival. Some had lodging provided by employers as part of moving expenses. Still others chose not to impose on friends. Thirty percent of those who did not stay with anyone when they first moved knew one or more San Franciscans before moving. Half, thus, would be an underestimate of preexisting ties.

Of the twenty-three men who migrated to San Francisco before 1960,[79] only one reported his first San Francisco job being better than the one left behind when he moved. Thirty percent of later gay male immigrants reported that their first Bay Area job was better than the job they left when they migrated. Only half as many of the pre-1960 immigrants as those who migrated later (41 compared to 78 percent) report their overall satisfaction with their lives in San Francisco as being greater than in the places from which they moved.[80] The dissatisfactions that propelled them to migrate alone to San Francisco do not appear to have been resolved by residence in a promised land that does not flow with milk and honey.[81]

Gay Asian men moved to San Francisco alone more than gay men of other ethnicities (88 percent in contrast to 69). They were only half as likely to have jobs before moving as white gay men (25 percent compared to 54, $r = -.21, p < .02$). Somewhat fewer of the Asian gay men had full-time jobs prior to their move to the Bay area (19 percent in contrast to 30 percent of white gay men, $r = -.09$, $p > .19$).

Those who stayed with someone when first moving were somewhat more likely to find housing better than that occupied where they migrated from (77 vs. 60 percent). Those who already had jobs before moving found housing they judged to be better than what they left more often (95 vs. 40 percent), and more (75 percent) of those moving during the 1970s reported improved housing than did either their predecessors (53 percent) or followers (70 percent).

Enclave Economics

For those not struck down by AIDS, gay economic success continued during the 1980s, with careerism substituting for sex (as with our straight age-mates). As with the trend to coupling and settling down to domesticity, effects of aging supplement the effects of AIDS in promoting baby boomers now aged forty or older to invest their energy elsewhere than in sexual marketplaces. Business and property are (along with love and AIDS) major topics of conversation among gay men in the late 1980s and early 1990s.[82]

I hope to gather more data in order to look systematically at the gay enclave economy.[83] Only 7 percent of my informants worked in the

Castro (another 11 percent worked in the South of Market or Polk Gulch areas, where gay institutions are also somewhat concentrated). The mean annual income of those who worked in the Castro for gay employers was $17,583, in contrast to $20,500 for those working in the Castro for straight employers and $35,092 for those working elsewhere. The mean annual income for those working for gay-owned businesses (including self-employment) outside the Castro was $45,213, in contrast to $33,364 for those working for straight-owned businesses outside the Castro (medians were $35,000 and $25,000, respectively).[84]

The Castro data warrant further investigation of an enclave economy with lower wages for the "privilege" of working for/with one's "own kind," but it should be remembered that these means are based on data from only six men. It should also be noted that these six men were younger and less educated than the majority of the rest of the sample (with two years less mean education and no postgraduate education). Outside the Castro, gay men do better working for gay employers than they do working for straight employers. This is especially so for those who are self-employed. If there is gay exploitation of gay labor, it is concentrated in one gay ghetto within San Francisco.

Eighty-four percent of the men with jobs in the sample worked for straight employers, so what gay employers pay gay employees affects relatively few respondents. In the perception of the sample, 96 percent thought that gay employers paid gay employees the same amount of money as they paid straight employees for doing the same job, and 4 percent thought that gay employers paid gay employees more than they paid straight employees for doing the same job.[85] Of the seventeen who had gay supervisors at work, 24 percent thought that gay supervisors made greater demands on gay employees than on straight employees, while the remaining 76 percent thought that there was no difference. Dan, one of the former, complained,

> Perhaps it's because the company is so small rather than because it's gay. I know that it's generally the case that there is no ladder of advancement to higher-level positions in small companies, but working for a small gay company there is also this draining demand to work harder and make fewer demands because I'm supposed to have this great desire for a gay company to succeed. This is supposed to substitute for the gratification of higher earnings.
> [And you're more concerned about succeeding yourself?]

I like to see gay companies succeed, sure, but *I* would like to succeed, too. I'd like to share in the success more than I do. Instead, I'm supposed to be grateful to be able to work for the greater glory of gay enterprise and the greater profit of one gay enterpriser. And maybe, someday, more money will trickle down. Sounds Reagan Republican, doesn't it? But he [the gay owner] considers himself very progressive, still the radical he claims he was in college.

[And you're not grateful?]

Not grateful enough for him. I think [that] I'm grateful, but [I am] also resentful about, shall we say, *excessive* exploitation. I think I should share more in the profits, not that I deserve all of them.

Tsunayoshi similarly noted,

Everything is so fucking personal! I'm ungrateful or disloyal if I ask for anything, especially [for] more money. I think working for "your own kind" sets you up for extra guilt trips.

[Don't you think small companies where everyone knows everyone else expect more gratitude than larger companies, straight or gay?]

Sure, there has to be more personal expectations of employees from the top of a small company because you all know each other and see each other all the time, but I still think there's an *extra* load of guilt trips and management saying they are *personally* disappointed, as if you [the employee] aren't being a good "gay brother" if you want money they want to put back into the business. On the other hand, *they* don't consider that we might be disappointed in them as good "gay brothers" for what they put in their pockets instead of sharing with their "brothers." If we're brothers, we're "younger brothers" who don't deserve much; every-thing—in their view—is supposed to go to the eldest [i.e., primogeni-ture]. In this country, we expect that, without breaking up the family farm or family business, we should get a fairly equal inheritance. But we find we are not a real family, that we're being manipulated to be good little boys by an image of family, of being brothers working for the good of the gay family. The exact same thing happens for Japanese and Chi-nese: subordinate yourself to the good of the company, especially the family business. "We're all in this together, and I [the owner] happen to get more money, but be happy that 'our kind' is doing well, and take what I give you." We Asians have this Confucian "please step on me, that's what I'm on earth for" background, but lots of white gay men seem to share it without Asian family pressure and indoctrination [primary socialization] when it comes to working for gay-owned businesses. It must be pretty easy to manipulate people this way. I used to think it was only Asians, but I was wrong. Maybe it doesn't even take being [part of a] minority.

Even these two skeptical, class-conscious employees preferred working for and with gay men, and there are others who are so relieved at the comfort of being out of the closet on the job that they do not notice or report the kinds of underlying tensions about exploitation suggested by them. For instance, Alan reported, "I work harder than I would at a corporate, straight, higher-paying job, but it's worth it to me not to have to play the closet games, to have my sexual orientation taken for granted." Dave told me, "I want San Francisco to succeed. I want the company to succeed. In a way it's just a job, and not that exciting a job, but I think the world will be a better place if there are successful gay companies and if the City by the Bay can continue to be a beacon of gay acceptance and gay success." Intracultural variance, all over again!

Conclusion

Survey results challenge the widespread view that gay men abandoned careers to move to San Francisco, taking any job available just to live there. Edmund White's stereotype of a professional throwing away his career elsewhere to subsist as a waiter or security guard in San Francisco in order either to be gay in relative peace or to increase sexual opportunities does not seem to be the norm, if this sample's experiences are at all typical. Although there is some indication of lower wages for workers within the gay ghetto, these were not men trained as professionals. Those who were downwardly mobile in terms of job satisfaction and/or income were mostly those who moved with a partner and subordinated their career to the partner's, not those who moved alone to "the sexual frontier."

In terms of buffering the stress of migration, respondents who migrated prior to 1960 mostly lacked any social supports in the destination city. In subsequent decades, more than half the gay immigrants received information about jobs and places to live through strong ties. Many of the Asian gay men moved to the San Francisco Bay Area to complete school or immediately after completing it. They generally were not part of gay networks prior to migrating, often coming out only after moving to the Bay Area.

Temporal and ethnic differences exist in the conception of who is a part of "gay community," in the process of moving to a "gay capital city," in finding a place to live, and in finding a way to make a living. Nonetheless, in the experiences of an admittedly nonrandom sample of gay male San Franciscans, these events were more cushioned by gay networks than has been supposed. A diversity of personal paths leads to the San Francisco gay community. This chapter has mapped some of the patterning but should close by acknowledging considerable individual differences in experiences and in the meanings derived from experiences by those categorized as "gay" of this or that "ethnicity" and of one or another "age cohort."[86]

Notes

Earlier versions of portions of this chapter were presented at the 1988 annual meeting of the American Anthropological Association in Phoenix and the 1989 annual meeting of the American Sociological Association in San Francisco. Encouragement and helpful comments by Barry Adam, Phil Blumstein, Andy Boxer, Linda Coleman, Wayne Dynes, John Hart, Gil Herdt, the late Laud Humphreys, Sue-Ellen Jacobs, Paul Kay, John Lee, Marty Levine, Mary McIntosh, Brian Miller, Harvey Molotch, the late Kenneth Payne, Ken Plummer, Bob Poolman, Bill Simon, and Brett Turner and assistance in data collection from Bruce Brown, Gary Bukovnik, Norman Dale, Keelung Hong, and Brett Turner are gratefully acknowledged.

1. The 1980s saw an increasing number of gay ethnic organizations within the gay community in San Francisco. There have been fewer public complaints about overt discrimination in bars etc., although perceived lack of welcome and humiliating demands for multiple proof of identification are salient experiences for a number of gay men (and lesbians) of color. The impetus for these organizations has been not primarily negative reactions but positive pride in members' cultural background and wishes to provide mutual support as well as more socializing with "our own kind." Numerous "kinds" are available in San Francisco. Those that have been bases for gay organizations include Vietnamese, South Asians, Pacific Islanders, Latinos, Vietnamese, and an active chapter of the national federation of Black and White Men Together.

2. On snowball sampling, see Seymour Sudman and Graham Kalton, "New Developments in the Sampling of Special Populations," *Annual Review of Sociology* 12 (1986): 401–29; and John L. Martin and Laura Dean, "Developing a Community Sample of Gay Men for an Epidemiologic Study of AIDS," *American Behavioral Scientist* 33 (1990): 546–61.

3. Michael Samuel and Warren Winkelstein, "Prevalence of HIV in Ethnic Minority Homosexual/Bisexual Men," *Journal of the American Medical Association* 257 (1987): 1901–2; Larry D. Hatfield, "Gays Say Life Is Getting Better," *San Francisco Examiner,* 6 June 1989, pp. A15–A19; Warren Winkelstein et al., "Sexual Practices and Risk of Infection by the Human Immunodeficiency Virus," *Journal*

of the American Medical Association 257 (1987): 321–25, and "The San Francisco Men's Health Study," *American Journal of Public Health* 78 (1988): 472–74; Maria L. Ekstrand and Thomas J. Coates, "Maintenance of Safer Sexual Behaviors and Predictors of Risky Sex," *American Journal of Public Health* 80 (1990): 973–77. Whether this sample overrepresents gay Asian-Americans or whether they are less concentrated in the environs of the Castro district cannot definitively be settled, but I believe that the latter is the case and that gay Asians (and also Latinos and African-Americans) live in areas of ethnic residential concentration more than in areas of quasi-ethnic (gay) concentration. On quasi ethnicity and gay deassimilation, see Stephen O. Murray, "The Institutional Elaboration of a Quasi-Ethnic Community," *International Review of Modern Sociology* 9 (1979): 165–78. On conflicting loyalties, see Wayne S. Wooden, Harvey Kawasaki, and Raymond Mayeda, "Identity Maintenance of Japanese-American Gays," *Alternative Lifestyle* 6 (1983): 236–43; and Julius M. Johnson, "The Influence of Assimilation on the Psychosocial Adjustment of African-American Homosexual Men" (Ph.D. diss., California School of Professional Psychology, 1981).

4. Comparative San Francisco data are derived from Ekstrand and Coates, "Maintenance"; Hatfield, "Gays Say"; Winkelstein et al., "Sexual Practices," and "The San Francisco Men's Health Study"; Alan P. Bell and Martin S. Weinberg, *Homosexualities* (New York: Simon & Schuster, 1978); Leon McKusick, William Horstman, and Arthur Carfagni, "AIDS and Sexual Behavior Reported by Gay Men in San Francisco," *American Journal of Public Health* 75 (1985): 493–96; Leon McKusick et al., "Reported Changes in the Sexual Behavior of Men at Risk for AIDS, San Francisco, 1982–84," *Public Health Reports* 100 (1985): 622–29; and Leon McKusick et al., "Longitudinal Predictors of Reduction in Unprotected Anal Intercourse among Gay Men in San Francisco," *American Journal of Public Health* 80 (1990): 978–83. Data from other cities come from Richard A. Kaslow et al., "The Multi-center AIDS Cohort Study," *American Journal of Epidemiology* 126 (1987): 310–18; Ronald C. Kessler et al., "Effects of HIV Infection, Perceived Health and Clinical Status on a Cohort at Risk for AIDS," *Social Science and Medicine* 27 (1988): 569–78; John L. Martin, Laura Dean, Marc García, and William Hall, "The Impact of AIDS on a Gay Community," *American Journal of Community Psychology* 17 (1989): 269–93; Ronald O. Valdiserri et al., "Variables Influencing Condom Use in a Cohort of Gay and Bisexual Men," *American Journal of Public Health* 78 (1988): 801–5.

5. The devastation of gay men by AIDS in San Francisco is overwhelming. By the time this book is published, more than three times as many gay men in San Francisco will have died of AIDS than have all San Francisco men of whatever sexual orientation in all the wars in U.S. history. When one considers the national trauma and continuing recriminations about the senseless deaths of young men just during the war in Vietnam, and when one considers that no more than one in four men in San Francisco is gay identified (and probably far fewer), it is no surprise that the death and debilitation caused by AIDS have considerably affected the institutions and culture of the world's most visible gay community. As one Anglo gay man put it, "AIDS stalks us day and night, waking and even sleeping. It's not just getting sick [that] we have to worry about, but that someone is going to use AIDS as an excuse to attack us on the street or ship us off to a concentration camp." I am haunted by similar concerns and have written about them elsewhere (e.g., Stephen O. Murray, "A Loaded Gun: Some Thoughts on

American Concentration Camps and the AIDS Epidemic," *New York Native,* 27 July 1987, pp. 15–17; Stephen O. Murray and Kenneth W. Payne, "Medical Policy without Scientific Evidence: The Promiscuity Paradigm and AIDS," *California Sociologist* 11 [1988]: 13–54). Here, however, I am going to focus on some longer-term trends than just the 1980s and on factors other than AIDS in some changes in patterns of self-identification, group identification, and migration.

6. In addition to Toennies's contrast of *gemeinschaft* (community) to *gesellschaft* (society), it is necessary to deploy Schmalenbach's contrast of *gemeinschaft* to *bund* (communion). There may be *bunds* within the gay community, but the whole gay community is only a *bund* on Gay Freedom Day (see chapter 8), and not always even then.

7. This is typical of other concepts preceded by the adjective "gay." I have suggested that the invocation of such special standards for gay phenomena is a function of societal prejudice, including individual self-hatred (see Stephen O. Murray, "Fuzzy Sets and Abominations," *Man* 19 [1983]: 396–99, and *Social Theory, Homosexual Realities* [New York: Gay Academic Union, 1984]). Affixing "simple" labels on complex realities is the norm for social categories and certainly for aggregations of persons with multiplex ties inside and outside "boundaries" of "differences" that are labeled "communities" (Anthony P. Cohen, *The Symbolic Construction of Community* [New York: Tavistock, 1985], p. 101). In general, people share symbols without necessarily attaching identical meanings to them (see ibid., p. 15; Anthony F. C. Wallace, *Culture and Personality* [New York: Random House, 1961]; and Theodore Schwartz, "Where Is the Culture?" in *The Making of Psychological Anthropology,* ed. George Spindler [Berkeley: University of California Press, 1978], pp. 419–41).

8. Lesbian communities exhibit the same features, albeit to a lesser extent. On the cultural invention, essentialization (naturalization), and maintenance of "race," "ethnicity," and "lineage," see Julian Pitt-Rivers, "Race in Latin America," *Archives Européenees de Sociologie* 14 (1973): 3–31.

9. See Clifford Geertz, "Form and Variation in Balinese Village Structure," *American Anthropologist* 61 (1959): 991–1012; G. William Skinner, "Marketing and Social Structure in Rural China," *Journal of Asian Studies* 24 (1964): 3–23.

10. Robert K. Merton, "Patterns of Influence: Local and Cosmopolitan Influentials," in *Social Theory and Social Structure* (1949; New York: Free Press, 1968), pp. 441–74.

11. Although Robert Redfield is considered the chief perpetuator of this myth in his ideal type "folk society," his description of Chan Kom revealed quite virulent factionalism as well as considerable influence from outside the country, not just outside the village (see Robert Redfield, *The Village That Chose Progress* [Chicago: University of Chicago Press, 1950]).

12. These differences may be quite miniscule (see Michael Moerman, "Ethnic Identification in Complex Civilization: Who Are the Lue?" *American Anthropologist* 66 [1965]: 1215–30; Gerald D. Suttles, *The Social Construction of Communities* [Chicago: University of Chicago Press, 1972]. Cohen (*Symbolic Construction,* p. 74) generalized, "The community boundary is *not* drawn at the point where differentiation occurs. . . . The conceptualization and symbolization of the boundary from within is much more complex."

13. In *Explorations into Urban Studies* (Philadelphia: University of Pennsylvania Press, 1964), Melvin M. Webber argued for abandoning "place" in defining urban com-

munities: "In a very important sense, the functional process of urban communities are not placelike. . . . The idea of community has been tied to the idea of place. . . . But it is now becoming apparent that it is the accessibility rather than the propinquity aspect of 'place' that is the necessary condition. . . . Spatial distribution is not the crucial determinant of membership. . . . Interaction is" (pp. 108–10). David Ward, in his important historical study *Poverty, Ethnicity and the American City* (Cambridge: Cambridge University Press, 1989), also deemphasizes territorial bases (even residential segregation) for urban communities while emphasizing associational bases.

14. Suttles, *Social Construction,* pp. 156–232.

15. Even the Jewish ghetto within the Pale was not ethnically totally homogeneous (see Louis Wirth, *The Ghetto* [Chicago: University of Chicago Press, 1928], p. 3). Nor were the "defended neighborhoods" in the city on which the ecological approach to urban communities was based: "Very few of the defended neighborhoods in Chicago which Park, Burgess, and their followers described seem to have been exclusively or almost exclusively occupied by a single ethnic group" (*Social Construction,* p. 27).

16. Roger Brown, "Reference," *Cognition* 4 (1976): 125–33. See Lofti Zadeh, "Fuzzy Sets," *Information and Control* 8 (1965): 338–53; Paul Kay, "Tahitian Words for 'Class' and 'Race,'" *Publications de la Société des Océanistes* 39 (1978): 81–91; and Murray, *Social Theory,* pp. 19–21.

17. In San Francisco, these include the Castro and Potrero Hill (for lesbians and gay men), Valencia (for lesbians), Polk Gulch, and South of Market (for gay men). Similarly, in addition to Chinatown, there are at least two other concentrations of Chinese businesses and residences in San Francisco.

18. Residential concentration is indubitable, however (see Murray, "Institutional Elaboration," pp. 168–69).

19. Ibid., pp. 168–71; also see Murray, *Social Theory,* pp. 33–42.

20. On the invisibility of networks, see John Burnham, "Early References to Homosexual Communities in American Medical Writings," *Medical Aspects of Human Sexuality* 718 (1983): 34–49; John Grube "Natives and Settlers," *Journal of Homosexuality* 20 (1991): 119–35.

21. Of course, if "language" is taken metaphorically as "shared meaning," then no one else understands gay "language."

22. Lesbians may be relatively less affluent than gay men, but, like gay men, lesbians of all strata patronize distinctively lesbian/gay facilities, are likely to be in lesbian networks, and tend to endogamy in choosing sexual partners and to homosociality in choosing friends.

23. The classic exemplar is Laud Humphreys, *Tearoom Trade* (Chicago: Aldine, 1970).

24. See Tamotsu Shibutani and Kian Kwan, *Ethnic Stratification* (New York: Macmillan, 1965). Joseph R. Gusfielde (*Community* [Oxford: Blackwell, 1975], p. 35) defined community "as people who see themselves as having a common history and destiny different from others." Similarly, Cohen (*Symbolic Construction,* p. 16) wrote, "The quintessential referent of community is that its members make, or believe they make, a similar sense of things . . . and, further, that they think that that sense differs from one made elsewhere."

25. Erving Goffman, *Stigma* (Toronto: Prentice-Hall, 1963). On anticipatory socialization to gay roles, see Stephen O. Murray, "'The Homosexual Role,' Gay Roles,

and 'Homosexual Occupational Roles'" (paper presented at the annual meeting of the American Sociological Association, Chicago, 1987).

26. A classical example, "Chinese" being taught to regard themselves as "Chinese" in Hawaii, was provided by Clarence Glick ("The Relation between Position and Status in the Assimilation of the Chinese in Hawaii," *American Journal of Sociology* 47 [1942]: 667–79) decades before the recent "invention of tradition" discourse (such as Richard Handler, "On Sociocultural Discontinuity: Nationalism and Cultural Objectification in Québec," *Current Anthropology* 25 [1984]: 55–71; Jocelyn S. Linnekin, "Defining Tradition: Variations on the Hawaiian Identity," *American Ethnologist* 20 [1983]: 241–52). An interesting analysis of Haitian Americans being transformed into "black Americans" is provided by Tekle M. Woldemikael (*Becoming Black American: Haitians and American Institutions in Evanston, Illinois* [New York: AMS, 1989]).

27. On moral entrepreneurs, see Howard S. Becker, *Outsiders* (New York: Free Press, 1963), pp. 147–63; Joseph R. Gusfield, *Symbolic Crusade* (Urbana: University of Illinois Press, 1955); Louis A. Zurcher and R. George Kirkpatrick, *Citizens for Decency* (Austin: University of Texas Press, 1976); and Murray and Payne, "Medical Policy," pp. 27–44.

28. Murray, "Institutional Elaboration." For a defense of the applicability of "community" to cities, see Suttles, *Social Construction,* pp. 4–81. Some writers continue to dismiss "gay community" without providing examples of what they might consider "real communities." For example, Jan Z. Grover ("AIDS: Keywords," in *AIDS: Cultural Analysis, Cultural Activism,* ed. Douglas Crimp [Cambridge, Mass.: MIT Press, 1988], p. 24) asserts that gay people "are too diverse politically, economically, and demographically to be described meaningfully by such a term" but does not mention a people in American cities who are not also too diverse. In rejecting the locution "gay community," Richard Mohr (*Gays/Justice* [New York: Columbia University Press, 1988], pp. 12–13) at least suggests an alternative term—"a people"—with Jewish Americans as an analogue of "open-textured unity." Hate crimes are much more likely to be directed at gay men than at Jews in the United States in the late 1980s, so shared defense remains more salient for gay men than for Jews and other ethnic "communities." Despite their interest in stress-buffering social relationships, Martin and Dean ("Developing," p. 548) adopt a wholly intrapsychic operationalization ("private recognition that one was a homosexual or bisexual man") of "gay community."

29. Robert N. Bellah, Richard Madsen, William M. Sullivan, Ann Swidler, and Steven T. Tipton, *Habits of the Heart* (Berkeley and Los Angeles: University of California Press, 1985), pp. 72, 74–75.

30. Ibid., p. 73.

31. Murray "Institutional Elaboration." For other accounts of the growth and diversification of gay institutions during the late 1970s, see Manuel Castells, *The City and the Grassroots* (Berkeley and Los Angeles: University of California Press, 1983), pp. 138–68; John D'Emilio, "Gay Politics and Gay Community: The San Francisco Experience," *Socialist Review* 11 (1981): 77–104; Joseph Harry and William DeVall, *The Social Organization of Gay Males* (New York: Praeger, 1978); John Alan Lee, "The Gay Connection," *Urban Life* 8 (1979): 175–98, and "The Social Organization of Sexual risk," *Alternative Lifestyles* 2 (1979): 69–100; Martin P. Levine, ed., *Gay Men* (New York: Harper & Row, 1979), and "Gay Macho" (Ph.D. diss., New York University, 1986); and Murray, *Social Theory,* pp. 36–44.

32. Bellah et al., *Habits of the Heart*, p. 74.
33. In addition to two lesbians elected to the Board of Supervisors in 1990 and a gay man who was its president from 1988 to 1990 (this position goes to the highest vote getter in staggered elections for either six or five seats every two years), there are elected gay members of the Board of Education and the Community College Board, elected lesbian judges, and a number of mayoral appointees to various commissions.
34. Bellah et al., *Habits of the Heart*, pp. 153–54.
35. Murray, "Institutional Elaboration," p. 172.
36. Stephen O. Murray and Robert C. Poolman, Jr., "The Prototype Semantics of 'Gay Community,'" *Working Papers of the Language Behavior Research Laboratory*, vol. 50 (Berkeley, Calif., 1982). This paper was presented at the 1981 annual meeting of the Kroeber Anthropological Society in Berkeley and was then accepted for publication in *Forum Linguisticum*. The journal was delayed and delayed, and has apparently ceased publishing.
37. Something of an exception to this statement is the North American Gay Amateur Athletic Alliance, the governing body of the Gay Softball World Series, which requires that "individual city champions qualifying for the world series must verify all roster players are gay. According to NAGAAA's definition, gay describes a player whose majority of romantic encounters are with members of the same sex" (Steve Tracy, "Straights to Hell: Gay-Only Issue Clouds Gay Softball World Series," *Advocate*, no. 535 [1989]: 50). In that this requirement is one of self-identification, it does not provide an example of having to demonstrate sexual behavior to be included in a gay group or activity. This requirement is quite unusual, as the example of the Gay Games and other gay sports organizations also reported in the same article show.
38. Carol A. B. Warren, *Identity and Community in the Gay World* (New York: Wiley, 1974), p. 150.
39. Levine, *Gay Macho*; Murray, *Social Theory*, pp. 41–44; Joel Brodsky, "A Retrospective Ethnography of the Mineshaft," *Journal of Homosexuality* (in press).
40. Specifically, by Mark Thompson, *Gay Spirit* (New York: St. Martin's, 1988), p. 252.
41. The self-styled "Red Queen," Arthur Evans, labels rape, murder, fag bashing, etc. as "the patriarchal psychosis" (*The God of Ecstasy* [New York; St. Martin's, 1988], p. 178). On the construction of a continuity between native American berdache and urban gay Indians, especially in San Francisco, see Will Roscoe, *Living the Spirit* (New York: St. Martin's, 1988). See also Walter Williams, *The Spirit and the Flesh* (Boston: Beacon, 1986).
42. Will Roscoe, "What Child Is This?" *San Francisco Jung Institute Library Journal* 8 (1988): 48. In the first sentence, he is quoting from Thompson, *Gay Spirit*, p. xi.
43. Christian metaphors of communion and ecstasy shape the sense of themselves and rhetoric of self-conceptions of some gay men involved in AIDS service organizations and also in the rituals of the bathhouses and other sex-suffused locales in the pre-AIDS era (see Brodsky, "Mineshaft"). I would claim some continuities between the techniques of self-abnegation and transcendence through pain in S&M and the techniques of Christian mystics and also add that many Christian saints were familiar with "sins of the flesh" before renouncing them for "purity" as conceived in Christian cosmology.

44. On ethnic and historical differences in coming out, see below.
45. The original investigation was done at a time of pronounced lesbian separatism (see Deborah Goleman Wolf, *The Lesbian Community* [Berkeley and Los Angeles: University of California Press, 1979]). Only after preliminary results of this study were presented and Sue-Ellen Jacobs posed what should have been an obvious question about whether any women are considered by gay men in the late 1980s as part of "gay community" did I add the last two combinations of features, and I have not attempted to try to model a distinction between "gay community" and "gay and lesbian community." There are women who identify themselves as "gay" rather than as "lesbian." However, the lesbians who are involved in gay political and AIDS service organizations in the late 1980s are included within "gay community" by all the gay men who were asked.
46. The beta values for the model with the three variables that explained significant variation are .34 (gay political involvement), .33 (white), and .15 (coming-out year).
47. No doubt, this is related to the AIDS-phobic increase in celibacy, measured by Martin et al., "Impact," pp. 276–77.
48. Although the difference is not statistically significant, Asian men were also more likely to include non-gay-identified homosexually involved men than were Anglo men.
49. There was a slight, statistically insignificant negative relation between year of coming out and involvement with gay politics in the 1988 data in contrast to a steady rise through the 1980 data.
50. The beta values are .18 for coming-out age, .19 for black and Latino (vs. Anglo and Asian American), and -.19 for gay political involvement; i.e., each one separately explains an equivalent amount of variance.
51. I asked early respondents if AIDS had changed their conception of what "gay community" means. All said no, although several volunteered that the response to AIDS showed them that a larger gay community existed than they supposed and included a wider range of kinds of people than they had previously encountered or thought about.
52. There is normative pressure both from people who identify themselves as straight and from those who identify themselves as gay to take on a permanent classification consistent with the sex of one's usual sex partners (see Murray, "'The Homosexual Role'").
53. This may be a "cultural imperative" or the sum of individual conclusions about the therapeutic effects of ending denial. There are certainly plenty of folk maxims of the sort, "You'll never be happy (at peace, etc.) if you can't accept who you are." The term "denial," borrowed from the Freudian list of ego defenses, has been increasingly popular in American culture and is applied more appropriately to denying homosexuality than to many other phenomena to which it is applied. In my view, the earlier view of inauthenticity (more dominant in the 1960s and 1970s in American discourse, gay and other) has been medicalized, although the costs of denial (so far) are viewed as psychological rather than somatic. There are signs of attributing swifter mortality of some persons with AIDS to self-hatred, however, and I expect this medicalization to continue to expand its explanatory reach.
54. There is considerable suspicion that claims to be "bisexual" are a "cop-out" to

avoid the stigma of homosexuality (which is presumably at least a part of bisexual behavior), and there are essentializing pressures from both gay- and straight-identified persons to "choose what you really are." Although it would be difficult to measure, there may be more pressure on people who have sex with both men and women to abandon claims to a bisexual identity than to abandon heterosexual cover. The later "makes more sense." In the Levi-Straussian sense, it is "better to think" since it conforms to the binary operation of *la pensée humaine.* "Outing," i.e., publicizing the homosexuality of politicians and other public figures viewed as contributing to gay oppression and/or AIDS underfunding, is directed precisely at those who do not behave as "gay brothers" and whose homosexuality is perceived as nongay or antigay.

55. On this kind of social control in gay settings, see Sherri Cavan, "Interaction on Home Territories," *Berkeley Journal of Sociology* 7 (1963): 17–32, and "The Art of Gay Insults," *Anthropological Linguistics* 21 (1979): 211–23; and Grube, "Natives and Settlers." On other kinds of evaluative norms within locales for sexual encounters, see Martin S. Weinberg and Colin Williams, "Gay Baths and the Social Organization of Impersonal Sex," *Social Problems* 23 (1975): 124–36; John Alan Lee, *Getting Sex* (Don Mills, Ont.: General, 1978), and "Social Organization"; Levine, "Gay Macho"; and Brodsky, "Mineshaft."

56. See chapter 1. Even there the sacredness that many men feel in this transformation is understated. As with other social orders described in ethnographic literature, we cannot easily distinguish acquiescence with cultural views from acceptance of them. This is especially the case for bisexual behavior, which does not necessarily cease even with some public affirmation of a gay identity or following the symbolic extravaganza of a heterosexual wedding.

57. Only two of 158 men proffered a range rather than a specific age at which they came out. Although what step was crucial varies from individual to individual, nearly every gay man remembers a specific breakthrough. The genre "coming-out story" is relatively easy to tap, although details in it would probably be less reliable (on differential retention of memory and the use of inference to supplement memory, see Norman M. Bradburn, Lance J. Rips, and Steven K. Shevell, "Answering Autobiographical Questions," *Science* 236 [1987]: 157–61). Although the memory is generally very salient, several men said that in their view they were never in the closet, that everyone (including themselves) knew they were going to be fags from an early age.

58. In Spanish, a common nonperjorative term before the diffusion of the word "gay" was *entendido,* literally "in the know" (see Stephen O. Murray, "Lexical and Institutional Elaboration: The 'Species Homosexual' in Guatemala," *Anthropological Linguistics* 22 [1980]: 177–86). The transformation from considering persons involved in homosexuality "queer" (or *maricóns*) is a kind of conversion experience—but being converted to accepting gay people and accepting one's own gayness must be distinguished from sexual experience "turning" one homosexual.

59. As table 3 indicates, there is generally a lag between first homosexual experience and coming out (see Barry M. Dank, "Coming Out in the Gay World," *Psychiatry* 34 [1971]: 180–97; Richard R. Troiden and Erich Goode, "Variables Relating to the Acquisition of a Gay Identity," *Journal of Homosexuality* 5 [1980]: 383–92; and Hatfield, "Gays Say"; see also chapter 1). For those without child or adolescent homosexual experience, finding a man to have sex with is sometimes regarded as "coming out." In addition to the 6 percent who reported coming out

an age younger than the age at which they had their first homosexual experience, 17 percent reported coming out at the same age as the age of their first homosexual experience. Unfortunately, my data do not permit distinguishing those comings outs and first homosexual experiences that were regarded as simultaneous from those that occurred over the space of the same year. In commenting on this research, Mary McIntosh suggested that in the "preliberation" era "coming out" meant entering a public homosexual space such as a bar and thus was really a "coming into." More recently, "coming out" to family and friends has become more salient, but I think that venturing into the company of gay men with some presumption of commonality remains the dominant meaning of "coming out."

60. A feeling that one's own people are superior to other peoples is well-nigh universal, and overcoming societal stigma probably requires some sense of a counterelite. "Two, four, six, eight,/ gay's twice as good as straight" and the view of heightened gay sensibility are two examples of this affectation.

61. There has also been quite a boom of posthumous revelations by biographers of public figures such as Lord Keynes and Cary Grant.

62. By recruiting research subjects through an institution for those under the age of twenty-one, Andrew M. Boxer and Gilbert H. Herdt ("Safe Sex Concepts and Sexual Behavior among Gay and Lesbian Youth" [paper presented at the annual meeting of the American Anthropological Association, Phoenix, 1988]) necessarily underestimate age of coming out insofar as those who come out at older ages will not be sampled (see also chapter 1). Ethnic differences in their data have not yet been reported.

63. In the initial AIDS case-control study of urban gay men in 1981–82 ($N = 68$ and 211 cases and controls, respectively), more than half reported a sexual act (i.e., oral or anal sex) with a male by age sixteen years, approximately 20 percent by age 10, and 80 percent by age 20 (Harry W. Haverkos, William J. Bukoski, Jr., and Zili Amsel, "Initiation of Male Homosexual Behavior," *Journal of the American Medical Association* 262 [1989]: 501).

64. Having been slow to see this pattern, I did not gather any data on the early experiences and concealment practices. Three of the eight African-American gay men reported preteen homosexual experiences. These seemed to be sources of continued excitement for the two who provided some detail (I did not interview the third man myself).

65. Although moving on is also overdetermined, it does not seem unreasonable to suppose that those who moved to San Francisco and later left found it less than a promised land. The same day that I was revising this chapter, I chanced to read a letter in the *Bay Area Reporter* (15 November 1990, p. 8) by Scott Combs of Lawrence, Kansas, who wrote, "I'd rather live with upfront bigots than live in a place full of hypocritical, phony liberals," and asked, "What are the use of laws protecting people in San Francisco in employment regardless of sexual orientation when it is virtually impossible to get a decent job in the city? . . . It is full of employers who know that people want to live there and are willing to work for almost nothing. Average wages for all occupations combined may be slightly above the national average, but they in no way compensate for the cost of living." He is far from the only one to have given up the struggle to survive in the Bay Area, where homelessness is increasingly widespread. As he notes, "if you lose your job, you probably will not have a home for long."

66. It took comments by Wayne Dynes, Harvey Molotch, and Bill Simon on my

research for me fully to realize the "casualties" (or "dropouts") of both processes, who were unavailable for sampling, even though I knew that problems in differentiating those who migrated permanently from those who stayed home from those who moved back and forth and distinguishing migration from adjustment to a new locale are widespread conceptual problems in the literature on migration. The best review of attempts to conceptualize "migration" that I have encountered is Douglas S. Massey, "Social Structure, Household Strategies, and the Cumulative Causes of Migration," (paper presented at the annual meeting of the American Sociological Association, San Francisco, 1989). For an exemplary study of migration as a continuing individual and communal process (rather than a discrete event), involving returning for various lengths of time to the natal community, see Douglas S. Massey, Rafael Alarcón, Jorge Durand, and Humberto González, *Return to Aztlan: The Social Process of International Migration from Western Mexico* (Berkeley and Los Angeles: University of California Press, 1987).

67. An argument could certainly be made, however, for a liminal period immediately following migration for many.

68. See Mark S. Granovetter, *Getting a Job* (Cambridge, Mass.: Harvard University press, 1974); Stephen O. Murray, Joseph H. Rankin, and Dennis W. Magill, "Strong Ties and Academic Jobs," *Sociology of Work and Occupations* 8 (1981): 119–36.

69. Alden Speare, Jr., "A Cost-Benefit Model of Rural to Urban Migration in Taiwan," *Population Studies* 25 (1971): 130.

70. See Gilbert H. Herdt, *Ritualized Homosexuality in Melanesia* (Berkeley and Los Angeles: University of California Press, 1984).

71. Edmund White, *States of Desire* (New York: Dutton, 1980). A relative lack of achievement motivation is invoked by Martin and Dean ("Developing," p. 558), who describe San Francisco as "a magnate [presumably they mean magnet] for a more relaxed life-style in a physically attractive geographic area"—in contrast to New York City.

72. That primary socialization makes it especially difficult for either party in a male-male couple to subordinate his job/career to the other's is an important cultural stressor to which Gregory Baum was the first to alert me. With women's careers decreasingly subordinated to those of husbands, this stress on heterosexual relationships has increased in recent years.

73. For San Francisco, the liberation era could well be dated earlier (cf. Murray, *Social Theory*, pp. 30–32). There is not a marked discontinuity in 1965 (the time of the California Hall incident in San Francisco) or 1969 (the celebrated Stonewall riots in New York), so I have opted to distinguish a decade as the era of liberation. Demarcating the other end is at least as dubious since changes brought about by consciousness of AIDS did not begin with the identification of the first case cluster (in Los Angeles). This tripartite division of eras facilitates comparison with other studies, but I consider them very fuzzily bounded categories for different men in different places.

74. Only one African-American respondent had a job in the place from which he moved. He judged his first San Francisco job worse than the one he left, although the change in 1982 resulted in a $5,000 increase in annual earnings. Two of the Hispanic and one of the Asian men moving to San Francisco from places where they had jobs reported their first job there to be better, one Hispanic and two Asians worse.

75. The accuracy of recall of incomes is dubious. I am more confident in recall of the direction of change and put more weight on a contrast of those who reported increased earnings to those who reported decreased earnings than on the numbers reported, even if these were converted to constant dollars (an exercise in misplaced concreteness I have not undertaken). Harvey Molotch reminded me that the cost of living in the Bay Area is exceptionally high and that, depending on the place from which one migrated as well as when, a higher salary may not therefore indicate any real upward mobility and the same salary might indicate real/net downward mobility.

76. See Stephen O. Murray, "Urban Land Values, Public Safety, and Visible Gay Culture," *Sociologists' Lesbian and Gay Caucus Newsletter* 59 (1989): 7–8, challenging the view of privileged builders of gay ghettoes. It also bears stressing again that those who tried but failed to establish themselves in the Bay Area and moved back or moved on are not included in my sample.

77. Peter V. Marsden and Karen E. Campbell ("Measuring Tie Strength," *Social Forces* 63 [1985]: 482–501) compare various measures and make a case for this straightforward categorization of tie strength.

78. Murray, "Institutional Elaboration," p. 171.

79. All six men who served in World War II received honorable discharges.

80. None of the pre-1960 immigrants and 3.4% of the later immigrants judged living in the Bay Area less satisfying overall than living where they lived before moving. Two of these three men moved to stay with a lover.

81. It is certainly likely that the pioneers had a harder time than those who followed, lacking not only the access to a visible gay community but also the social support enjoyed by many of the latter immigrants. It is possible that the respondents are comparing their youth elsewhere with their middle or old age in San Francisco in the age of AIDS. Still another possible interpretation is that earlier immigrants were more negativist personalities. That the reason is not command of economic resources or a greater likelihood of living alone is demonstrated by comparing decade cohorts of gay male immigrants to San Francisco:

Mean Household and Per Capita Income in 1988 by Year of Arrival in San Francisco

Year of Immigration	Household Income ($)	Standard Deviation ($)	Per Capita Income ($)	Standard Deviation ($)	Percentage Living Alone	Number
Before 1960	111,000	165,177	57,542	80,176	33	12
1960–69	66,149	71,372	36,964	35,937	21	14
1970–79	55,829	49,161	37,228	25,428	54	41
1980–89	50,900	31,679	27,775	18,169	38	40

From Martin et al. ("Impact," p. 274), one might extrapolate that 85 percent of those living with someone else are living with a lover.

82. Some gay men still talk about dance clubs and anonymous sex, but the cultural focus has changed, and not just for the aging "clone generation."

83. Expecting to find patterns of "paying for the privilege" of working for quasi-ethnic fellows similar to what Jimy M. Sanders and Victor Nee ("Limits of Ethnic

Solidarity," *American Sociological Review* 52 [1987]: 745–73) found in San Francisco's Chinatown and Miami's Cuban businesses: preferential hiring, some cultural sheltering, observable examples of entrepreneurship, and lower wages than outside the ethnic enclave economy. For New York's Chinatown, Min Zhou and John R. Logan ("Returns on Human Capital in Ethnic Enclaves," *American Sociological Review* 54 [1989]: 820) also found that "enclave workers have worse jobs at lower pay" than minority workers outside the enclave.

84. The best predictor of earnings was education ($r = .35$, $p < .001$). Although a dummy variable, white/nonwhite, was not significantly correlated with earnings ($r = .15$, $p = .07$), an interaction of white and education was ($r = 26$, $p = .002$). Having a job before moving was also significantly correlated with earnings ($r = .22$, $p = .007$). Stepwise multiple regression eliminated the three variables statistically significantly but more weakly correlated than education. The mean annual earnings (standard deviation in parentheses) by ethnicity of respondents with any income were white, $37,681 ($36,889); African American, $45,500 ($31,086); Latino, $19,051 ($8,580); and Asian American, $27,546 ($12,088). The very large standard deviations suggest that medians are better indicators of central tendencies. These were $29,000, $25,000, $18,000, and $25,000, respectively. The seeming success of black gays is vitiated by the fact that half the black respondents had no income and are not included in these computations.

85. Unfortunately, I did not ask respondents if they thought working for gay employers was more or less lucrative than working for straight employers and cannot contrast the earning patterns to whatever those expectations are.

86. Many aspects of San Francisco gay life and changing culture have also not been discussed in this brief report. On changing patterns of sexual practice and drug use in the age of AIDS, see Martin et al., "Impact"; McKusick et al., "Longitudinal Predictors"; and Ekstrand and Coates, "Maintenance" (see also chapter 2). On the earlier political history of gay and lesbian communities in San Francisco, see Wolf, *Lesbian Community;* D'Emilio, "Gay Politics."

FIVE

Black Men and Their Same-Sex Desires and Behaviors

John L. Peterson

Virtually all the data on sexual behavior of black men in the United States are confined to studies of their sexual behavior with females.[1] Similar studies of the same-sex behavior of black males have been largely neglected. This neglect results in insufficient knowledge of the social and psychological factors that influence same-sex behavior among black males. This knowledge is needed even more now that some homosexual and bisexual behaviors of black males are associated with an increased risk of contracting AIDS.[2] Obviously, inferences about the same-sex behavior of black males cannot be derived from studies of their sexual behavior with females. Both the nature and the type of sexual behavior between men probably differ substantially from that between men and women. In the absence of data, researchers can offer only suggestions about the same-sex attractions and behaviors between black men. This chapter attempts to provide some of these suggestions.

The chapter begins with a discussion of the available data on the same-sex behavior of black males. Then it discusses various explanations for these men's self-identity as heterosexual despite their participation in homosexual behaviors. Also, for black men who self-identify as gay or homosexual, it examines the conflict that they may experience between their involvement in the black community and their involvement in the gay community. Antigay and antiblack sentiment is considered and the consequences on their life-styles as gay men. Finally, problems are discussed that interfere with their attempts to form and sustain male couple relationships.

Same-Sex Behaviors of Black Men

Because the same-sex behaviors of black men have rarely been studied, it is difficult to estimate how often black men engage in this type of sexual behavior. The classic Kinsey studies reported data only on white American men in their sample who had engaged in a homosexual act at least once.[3] However, other studies provide some impression of the homosexual experiences of black men. One study of college students found that 9 percent of heterosexual black males interviewed had received oral sex from another man and that 5 percent had performed oral sex on another man.[4] Further, in a study of prison inmates, 81 percent of black heterosexual males reported that they had engaged in sexual activity with another male while in prison. In this random sample ($N = 200$) of the prison population, black males were more likely than white males to engage in the insertor role during anal intercourse with other men.[5]

Data reported on self-identified gay men reveal that oral and anal intercourse were the two most frequently preferred homosexual activities of black men in San Francisco. In fact, 90 percent of black homosexual men ($N = 111$) in this study had experienced receptive anal intercourse.[6] More recently, studies of the risky sexual activities of black men during the AIDS epidemic have provided data on their same-sex behavior. One study of self-identified black gay and bisexual men ($N = 98$) in San Francisco, Oakland, and Berkeley found that bisexual men reported more sexual partners and more insertive and receptive anal intercourse with secondary partners than gay men. Gay and bisexual men differed little, however, in their sexual activities with their primary male partners.[7] Another San Francisco study reports data on the sexual behavior of a very small sample ($N = 29$) of black gay men whose sexual activity put them at high risk for AIDS. Results revealed that 65 percent of these men had participated in receptive anal intercourse with two or more male partners.[8] Admittedly, these data on same-sex behaviors of black men should be interpreted with caution. However, they provide some evidence that black men in the

United States participate in same-sex activity. Unfortunately, much more data is needed to describe the possible range and patterns of same-sex behaviors among black men accurately.

Self-Identity and Same-Sex Behavior

Black males may have extensive homosexual experience, but it may not affect their heterosexual identity. These heterosexual men may not label themselves homosexual because of the reasons they engage in homosexual behavior.[9] One motivation may be economic. For example, black male prostitutes who identify as heterosexual may become involved in homosexuality because they lack material resources or other financial opportunities. Their homosexual behavior does not preclude involvement in heterosexual relationships simply because they occasionally exchange sex for money or gifts from male partners. Also, a high level of unemployment among black men in the labor force has caused some black men to pursue illicit and criminal activities as a means of support.[10] One of these activities is the casual exchange of sex for drugs or money. Since the crack cocaine epidemic, such activity has increased in this drug culture, which is permissive regarding the range and frequency of sexual activity.[11]

Also, black males who self-identify as either heterosexual or bisexual may resort to homosexual behavior simply because a female partner is unavailable—as, for example, in prison or the military. In these situations, these men may protect themselves from the inference of homosexual identity, despite their homosexual activity, by engaging only in those homosexual activities that they consider to be masculine, such as the insertor role in oral and anal sex.[12] Sometimes their homosexual activities involve men whom they perceive as weaker and over whom they therefore exert sexual dominance and control.[13] At other times, their homosexual acts may be with male homosexuals or with male transvestites dressing as women.

Outside such situations, some black men who identify as heterosexual or bisexual may still participate in same-sex behaviors through anonymous sexual encounters in such public places as restrooms, steambath houses, and parks.[14] These men may use these outlets if their female partners are reluctant or unwilling to satisfy their physical desire for certain sexual acts, such as fellatio or anal intercourse. Those men who self-identify as bisexual may also derive physical pleasure from such sexual activities with both males and females. These men may engage in bisexual behavior sequentially or contemporaneously.[15]

These explanations provide some of the reasons why black men who self-identify as heterosexual engage in same-sex behavior. These men may perceive their homosexual behaviors as merely acts of erotic pleasure motivated by circumstance and performed without affection or emotional investment. They may participate in specific homosexual behaviors on occasion but not experience homosexual emotions toward their partner during the encounter. It seems plausible that black men who lack homosexual feelings in homosexual encounters are likely to define only their sexual behavior, and not their sexual identity, as homosexual.[16] This self-perception would allow them to justify their participation in homosexual activity and still sustain their heterosexual sexual orientation.

Dual Identities in Conflict: Black versus Gay

The number of black men who self-identify as gay or homosexual is unknown, although there are black men who consider themselves exclusively or mainly homosexual.[17] Regardless of their number, black gay men may not publicly disclose their sexual orientation because they anticipate disapproval by the black community. Some national data have revealed that blacks disapprove of homosexuality even slightly more than whites.[18] These strong antihomosexual attitudes can result in the stigmatization of black men who publicly disclose their homosexuality. Such stigma may be the reason that there is no distinct gay culture in the black community. Alternatively, some black men may resort to affiliation with the white gay community to pursue social opportunities with gay men. However, many black men may be dissuaded from affiliating with the white gay community because of experiences of racism and prejudice from some white gay men. Racial discrimination is not uncommon in gay bars, restaurants, and stores.[19] Faced with antigay attitudes in the black community and antiblack attitudes in the gay community, black gay men experience a severe conflict between their racial identity and their sexual orientation.

One basis for blacks' antihomosexual attitudes is the influence of religion and the black church.[20] Judeo-Christian views in the black church include certain literal interpretations of the Bible and acceptance of the doctrine of "natural law." Such fundamentalism views homosexuality as proscribed behavior because it is perverse and indecent and ultimately punishable by God. The doctrine of "natural law" is used to support this view of homosexual behavior as sinful sex—that is, sex that is biologically unnatural and not intended to result in procreation. Sexual behavior should occur only in marriage between males and females.

Beyond religion, another source of black antihomosexual attitudes is the influence of gender roles in black culture. Men and women are socialized to adopt conventional gender roles that emphasize physical and emotional intimacy between opposite-sex partners.[21] Male sex role expectations are intended to result in black men fulfilling their roles as husband and father. Homosexuality diminishes the number of men available for marriage and therefore constitutes a threat to the black family.

Similarly, homosexuality is felt to diminish the power status of black men relative to both black men and black women. Black males are more likely to be unemployed than black females because they experience greater economic discrimination.[22] As a consequence, many black males lack an important basis of male power in black relationships—the capability to contribute economically to the family. Since the economic capacity of black males is reduced, the need is heightened for them to demonstrate maleness in one of the other conventional ways. However, male homosexuality is viewed as further decreasing the status of black men because it emasculates them.[23] Black homosexual men are stereotyped as effeminate, weak, and unlike "real" men. To be a "man" in black culture is construed as having a primary sexual interest in women, and any man who lacks such interest is considered less than a man. This cultural belief equates masculinity in males with heterosexuality and femininity in males with homosexuality.[24] The belief is reinforced by the public's ability to recognize effeminate males as homosexual more often than they do masculine men.

Despite these reasons for antihomosexual attitudes, members of the black community may tacitly tolerate suspected homosexuality, but they are not likely to approve of it if publicly admitted. The assumption is that, while blacks will not condone homosexuality or support it publicly, they will allow it as long as it is secretive. Simply stated, "It is alright if everybody knows as long as nobody tells."[25] For this reason, black gay men may experience several costs in "coming out" and publicly disclosing their sexual identity.

One cost they may incur for admitting their homosexuality is the risk that the person they inform may disclose it to someone else. Disclosure relinquishes control of the privileged information. The confidant may not maintain one's privacy and may inadvertently or deliberately inform others. Consequently, another cost is the negative reaction of family members, heterosexual friends, and employers. If these persons disapprove of homosexuality, exposure could lead to loss of esteem and ridicule or rejection. Also, it could result in the loss of one's job. Even with legal protection, an employer could attempt to discriminate against homosexual employees, threatening termination on grounds other than homosexuality.

However, black gay men may also benefit by publicly disclosing their sexual orientation. These benefits vary, depending on whether one has come out to a few people or to many. For example, disclosure may reflect self-acceptance of one's own homosexuality, and such self-acceptance may enhance self-esteem. Disclosure could also produce better relationships with family and friends, relationships based on honesty rather than on deceit. The support received from such improved relationships may even strengthen self-acceptance. Finally, "coming out" may motivate black gay men to participate more fully in the gay community, where they are more likely to meet other gay men, because they are now less fearful of being identified as gay.

Unfortunately, involvement in the gay community may increase the likelihood that black gay men will experience racial discrimination. Since white gay men are socialized in the majority culture, their behavior can reflect the same racism as that which occurs in mainstream white society. This racism may be expressed in overt discrimination, such as systematic exclusion of blacks from jobs, housing, and social clubs. For example, the most notorious discrimination occurs through a process of "carding" nonwhites for admission to gay public facilities, such as bars. This process involves selective refusal of blacks by requiring several forms of picture identification not required for whites. Also, if blacks are admitted, they frequently encounter slower service than whites, and black staff are often not employed in these businesses.[26] Similarly, owners or managers may justify this inequitable treatment as economic self-interest, arguing that their white patrons prefer not to associate with blacks and that they will lose these patrons if blacks are admitted.

Another salient form of racism involves prejudice and discrimination toward blacks by whites on the basis of physical attraction. White gay men express racism toward black gay men through their standards of physical beauty and the influence of good looks on social relationships.[27] Modern gay culture promotes frequent sexual activity with multiple numbers of male partners, and many friendships are eventually formed from these sexual liaisons and affairs. The selection of sexual partners is often made on the basis of standards of physical beauty that typically exclude characteristics likely to be found among black men. These standards emphasize aesthetic preferences for Western European attributes in skin color, hair texture, and facial features. Since black gay men are unlikely to satisfy these standards, they are less likely to be chosen as sexual partners. Therefore, these biases in choosing friends and lovers result in frequent discrimination against blacks in white gay male culture.

Antigay and antiblack sentiment can cause black homosexual men to experience conflict between their racial and their sexual identities. This conflict involves a choice between active involvement in the black community or in the gay community. Involvement in the black community requires that black gay men remain closeted. Involvement in the gay community means that they must be prepared to respond to racial discrimination. This antagonism is increased by disagreements between blacks and gays over political and social issues, such as legalization of gay relationships. Agreement with one group may imply disagreement with the other. This conflict has suggested a distinction between black homosexuals who are black gays and those who are gay blacks.[28]

"Black gays" may be described as men whose allegiance is affected more by their blackness than by their gayness, who are more likely to be closeted or to identify themselves as bisexual, and who are often involved in the black community. Black gay men are more likely to base their self-identity on their race than on their sexual orientation. In comparison, "gay blacks" may be described as men whose allegiance is affected more by their sexual orientation than by their race, who are more likely to be open about their homosexual identity, and who are often involved in the white gay community.

The interests of black gay men are limited largely to matters that involve the black population. Their primary concern is with social and political issues that affect the black community. Therefore, their social and political participation usually occurs in the black community. They are reluctant to confront the black community over gay issues that may be interpreted as threatening their allegiance to the black population. However, they do not hesitate to confront the white population over issues of racism. While gay blacks may be concerned with issues in the black community, they are more likely to be involved in social and political activities in the gay community.

For these reasons, black gay men usually socialize in the black community. Within black culture, they are limited in developing a gay culture. To do so could be perceived as disloyal. Black homosexuality is tolerated only as long as it is closeted. The development of a black gay subculture would be doubly offensive because it would both legitimize and promote homosexuality. Consequently, black gays tend to lack the institutions available in mainstream gay culture, such as gay newspapers, gay organizations, and gay businesses. Gay bars may occasionally exist in black neighborhoods in urban cities, but they must rely on word of mouth to attract patrons. Without formal gay institutions, the opportunity for black gay men to socialize with each other is likely to depend on informal social networks. Friendships are frequently made at such social events as private parties and dances. However, the network that results is closed and therefore difficult to access if black gay men are new or closeted residents in the community.

In contrast, gay black men usually socialize in the urban gay ghetto. These men may be involved in largely white organizations in mainstream gay culture. These formal organizations include a variety of professional, political, civic, social, recreational, and sexual groups. They are likely to experience varying degrees of racial discrimination within these organizations. They may also become involved in interracial organizations to increase the likelihood of meeting men who are interested in blacks and to avoid those who are not. Such organizations also provide an institutional base from which gay blacks can advocate greater inclusion in and responsiveness from predominantly white organizations. A substantial proportion of gay black men may develop friendships with white men even though they may not restrict their friendships to whites. However, there are few opportunities to socialize with other blacks because of the greater number of white than black and other nonwhite men in mainstream gay culture. These differences between black gays and gay blacks also have consequences for the development of male couple relationships.

Black Male Couples

There are almost no data on black male couples despite the increased research on white male couples. In the absence of data, it is unclear how black homosexual men form and maintain their relationships as couples. Regardless of race, gay men experience the problems of locating and choosing their partners, forming relationships with their partners, and then sustaining their relationships. However, several issues relevant to black men may be discussed.

Locating Partners: Looking for Mr. Right

Black homosexual men may encounter difficulty in finding eligible partners for gay couple relationships. Black gay men have few sources for meeting other gay men in black communities. Those urban cities that have gay bars in black neighborhoods offer the most convenient opportunity to meet other gay (mostly black) men. Some black gays may go to heterosexual bars to meet other black gay men, especially in the suburbs and in rural areas, where there are few gay bars. The gay bar serves both social and sexual needs because gay men use it to find new sexual partners and to socialize with friends.[29] Many couples may have met while cruising in bars. Such chance meeting does not, however, guarantee that a long-lasting relationship will be established. Suitable sexual partners may not make for suitable partners in a more serious relationship. And initial sexual dissatisfaction may diminish interest in determining other, nonsexual attractions between potential partners.

The private house party offers another social occasion for black gay men to meet other men who are available for gay relationships. Parties held in friends' homes provide a social setting in which black gay men can enjoy camaraderie without disguising their sexual orientation. The men invited to these events are members of the social cliques of the host or friends of the host. Such social events allow gay men to meet casually and to become acquainted prior to a sexual encounter. After the initial meeting, those men who desire to meet again can contact each other and make arrangements to date. Of course, there is no guarantee that even relationships thus formed will not end up as one-time sexual encounters. However, unlike bars, private parties offer gay men the opportunity to determine if they have common interests and thus form first impressions of each other on the basis of more than looks. There is, after all, more to a gay couple's relationship than good looks and good sex.

Gay black men, on the other hand, have many sources for meeting eligible partners for possible gay couple relationships. Their involvement in the gay community provides a wide range of opportunities to meet other gay men. Of course, these opportunities include gay bars.[30] The number and diversity of bars in urban areas allow patrons to select bars on the basis of their preferences for different types of services and clientele. Patrons may prefer discotheques for dancing and social bars for drinking and conversation. They may prefer "preppie" bars, which cater to young up-scale customers, or leather bars, which cater to older, hypermasculine customers. Bars offer opportunities to acquire new friends and acquaintances. Since couples can meet through friends, these friendship networks are useful sources for meeting eligible men. Friends can also provide other opportunities to meet eligible partners outside bars, such as through invitations to attend private social functions or to join gay organizations. However, such opportunities for black men may be limited because there are few blacks in mainstream gay culture or because of racism. Because of cultural barriers to blacks' participation in the gay community, there are fewer black than white men available with whom one can develop friendships. And because racism affects whites' choice of friends, there may be fewer opportunities to form interracial friendships. Thus, blacks' opportunities for courtship and mate selection through gay bars are limited. However, other options are available.

The classified sections of gay newspapers and magazines offer gay black men another way to find partners. Some advertisements are placed by professional models or escorts, soliciting services for payment. Others, more relevant to mate selection, are those personal ads placed by individuals seeking sexual or dating partners.[31] One study found that, in an analysis of all advertisements in which the advertiser's race was indicated, only 3 percent were black compared to 92 percent white and 5 percent neither black nor white.[32] Blacks of course may also have been among those advertisers who did not specify race.

Another alternative available to gay black men involved in the gay community is dating and matching services. These services are developed specifically for gay men to meet suitable partners for dating and couple relationships. For a nominal fee, they provide confidential, computerized matches between advertisers on the basis of information that each has provided. Photographs are also taken and shown to potential matches. Matches are made for a specified period until a suitable partner is found or until the client's membership has lapsed. No studies are available on the effectiveness of this mate selection process or on the people who have used it. However, beyond the fee required, the extensive use of questionnaire data increases the likelihood that these services attract more educated men. If this is so, it seems likely that black men who use such a service would be middle class.

Beyond ads and bars, the urban gay culture includes numerous opportunities to meet potential dates and mates through social, professional, political, and recreational organizations. Affiliation with such organizations can increase the pool of eligible partners from which to choose—not only members but members' friends as well. Involvement in these groups probably depends on personal interests and prior social contacts. Without such contacts, however, gay blacks may be either unaware of or uncomfortable joining these such organizations.

Choosing Partners for Gay Relationships

There are many possible attributes that black men may desire in the partners they choose for gay couple relationships, including physical attractiveness, race, age, social class, intelligence, social interests, and personality. However, the only recent data available on the desired characteristics for partners of black homosexual men are reported by Johnson from a small sample ($N = 60$) of black homosexual men in the San Francisco Bay Area.[33] This mail survey revealed differences in the racial preferences of black gays and gay blacks. Black-identified gay men were more likely to prefer other black men as their ideal lovers. Gay-identified black men were more likely to prefer white males as their ideal lovers. Also, more black-identified (25 percent) than gay-identified (5 percent) black homosexual men reported that they would not date white men in the future.

These findings are reminiscent of Bell and Weinberg's earlier findings that most black homosexual men ($N = 111$) had more white than black sexual partners. In this study of San Francisco white and black gays and lesbians, most black men (67 percent) reported that more than half their sexual partners had been white. In contrast, none of the white men reported that more than half their sexual partners had been black, and over 20 percent reported that none of their partners had been black.[34] Other studies reveal that the majority of white gay men in those samples prefer partners of the same race when they advertise for sexual partners.[35]

Interestingly, Bell and Weinberg's data for lesbians are consistent with those for white men but inconsistent with those for black men. Like white gay men, white lesbians preferred whites more than blacks as their sexual partners. In fact, the majority of white lesbians (72 percent) reported that none of their sexual partners had been black. However, in striking contrast to black homosexual men, only a minority (30 percent) of black lesbians reported more than half their sexual partners as white. Similar sex differences have been found among interracial heterosexual marriages. Black heterosexual men tend to marry white women about twice as often as black women marry white men.[36]

These data raise the possibility that gay black men experience difficulty forming relationships when their choices of partners are white. One reason for the difficulty may be attributed to differences in racial preferences between white and black men involved in mainstream gay culture—more black men prefer interracial relationships than white men. Regardless of the reasons, however, there are unequal opportunities for courtship and mate selection for gay black men who prefer white men.

There may be greater opportunities for those gay blacks who prefer partners of their own race. However, such opportunities depend on the proportion of black men in the gay community who desire same-race partners. Given cultural and racial barriers, it may be argued that the highest incidence of black men who self-identify as gay is in the black, not the gay, community. If this argument is correct, the pool of black men with same-race preferences is likely to be lower in the gay subculture than in the black culture. Further, black gay men are more likely to achieve success in forming same-race relationships than gay black men. Despite this advantage, cultural barriers, such as antihomosexual attitudes, also limit the extent to which black gays may become publicly involved in male couple relationships.

Forming Male Couple Relationships

Much research has disproved the view that white gay men are unable to develop male couple relationships.[37] However, the only data demonstrating the extent to which black homosexual men form couples are provided by Bell and Weinberg.[38] Of the black homosexual men ($N = 111$) sampled, many (58 percent) were currently involved in a steady gay couple relationship. Of those involved, most were "in love" with and living with their partner, and nearly half had been together from one year to more than five years. For most of these men (77 percent), this was not their first relationship. These findings increase the suspicion that many black homosexual men do form gay relationships.

This suspicion raises the question of how black men structure their relationships when they are formed. It has been assumed that gay couples typically resemble heterosexual couples—one male partner assumes the traditional "feminine" role of the wife and the other male partner the conventional "masculine" role of the husband in decision making, the division of household tasks, and sexual behavior. Again, the only data available are from Bell and Weinberg, who found little evidence of traditional gender-role behavior among their sample of black homosexual men who were involved in couple relationships. Less than 10 percent reported that either they or their partner usually assumed responsibility for household tasks or traditional masculine roles.

If gender does not structure gay male relationships, other factors that may provide a pattern for them are the age and social status of partners. Age and social class differences between male partners may be important factors that affect the balance of power, such as in decision making. Interestingly, Bell and Weinberg found that black male respondents reported that they were younger and had lower incomes than their partner. However, they also reported that these differences did not affect their relationships. The couples may have developed egalitarian relationships that prevented the disparity in age or income to affect the relationship negatively. For example, two-thirds of these respondents either totally or partially combined their income with their partner's income. Since decision making was not assessed, it is unclear how this decision was reached or how other differences were resolved.

One other structural aspect of male couple relationships is the sexual monogamy or sexual openness of the relationship. In contrast to heterosexuals, many gay men may not consider sexual monogamy the norm for their relationships.[39] Often, sexual openness is not construed as "infidelity" and as the cause of dissatisfaction with relationships by white gay couples. There is only minimal and indirect support for this assumption for blacks. Bell and Weinberg reported that most black homosexual men (90 percent) in their study had more than two male sexual partners within the past year. They did not compare these results for respondents who were currently in couples with those who were not. Nonetheless, so many of the black men had multiple sexual partners within the last year that this number had to include most of the respondents in gay relationships. Equivalent results were found for white gay males in this study. The limitations posed by the small sample size and geographic location warrant caution in interpreting these results. Much more data are needed examining how black homosexual men form and structure their relationships and the ways, if any, in which black gay and gay black men differ.

Sustaining Relationships:
Breaking Up Is Hard to Do

The final aspect considered for black male couples is the maintenance and durability of their relationships. Like white gay couples, black male couples probably experience many problems that can diminish the quality of gay marriages. Also, they lack the social, legal, religious, or economic barriers to ending their relationships that exist for heterosexual marriages. A few explanations may be offered for the ways in which black male couples sustain their relationships.

One explanation is that some couples may develop the type of social support they need to maintain long-term relationships. Social support may buffer the stress experienced when couples develop problems. If black male couples have few support networks, they may lack sufficient resources to help maintain the relationship during periods of conflict. Family and friends are possible sources of such support. Many black homosexual men may be less likely to disclose their relationship to family than to friends and may therefore rely more on gay friends than on family members as their social support system. This social system can provide both emotional and material support to the partners to resolve their conflicts and to inhibit disruption of the relationship. Those gay men who lack such support are likely to have only limited opportunities to develop social networks of gay friends. They are also more likely to reside in communities where their relationships are not publicly acknowledged (e.g., suburban and rural areas).

Making various investments in their relationship may allow some black male couples to increase the stability of those relationships. Conflict is inevitable in all couples' relationships, both gay and heterosexual. Social and legal barriers inhibit partners from conveniently dissolving their relationships immediately when social conflict occurs. Those couples who are able to develop such barriers may reduce the likelihood that their relationship will dissolve before the conflicts are resolved. Tangible investments include shared property, shared material possessions, and joint financial resources. More intangible investments consist of trust, mutual values and understandings, and symbolic identity as a couple. Black male couples who frequently participate in the gay culture may derive further institutional support available in gay neighborhoods, such as gay churches, gay legal firms, gay realtors, and gay counselors.

Conclusion

This discussion has examined many issues related to the same-sex desires and behaviors of black men. When available, data were marshaled to support the suggestions offered. Clearly, more descriptive research is needed to discuss the homosexual behaviors and lifestyles of nonwhite men adequately. Major ethnographies and field surveys are needed on large samples of black homosexually active men. Also, these studies must be conducted in diverse geographic locations to increase the generalizability of the results. Studies are required to examine developmental and social differences among black homosexual males. It is unknown how age and social class influence awareness of and responsiveness to homosexual identity in black men. Research is needed to determine how black men who self-identify as gay differ in the choices they make regarding their life-styles. Research on black male couples would be useful to improve understanding of both heterosexual and homosexual relationships. Finally, and most important, this research would yield valuable knowledge that may reduce the stigma attributed to individuals who desire same-sex behaviors and life-styles. Given this neglected research, the prior discussion was intended to offer suggestions that may be useful to future studies of the same-sex behaviors and desires of black men.

Notes

1. For a review of this literature, see Jeanne Brooks-Gunn and Frank F. Furstenberg, Jr., "Adolescent Sexual Behavior," *American Psychologist* 44 (1989): 249–57; Diane M. Morrison, "Adolescent Contraceptive Behavior: A Review," *Psychological Bulletin* 98 (1985): 538–68; Philip A. Belcastro, "Sexual Behavior Differences between Black and White Students," *Journal of Sex Research* 21 (1985): 56–67; and Martin S. Weinberg and Colin J. Williams, "Black Sexuality: A Test of Two Theories," *Journal of Sex Research* 25 (1988): 197–218.

2. For the initial research identifying this problem, see Roger Bakeman, Judith Rae Lumb, Rudolph E. Jackson, and Donald Walter Smith, "AIDS Risk-Group Profiles in Whites and Members of Minority Groups," *New England Journal of Medicine* 315 (1986): 191–92; Richard Selik, Kenneth G. Castro, and Marquerite Pappaioanou, "Distribution of AIDS Cases by Racial/Ethnic Group and Exposure Category, United States, June 1981–July 4, 1988," *Morbidity and Mortality Weekly Report* 37, no. 3 (1988): 1–10.

3. Alfred C. Kinsey, Wardell B. Pomeroy, and Clyde E. Martin, *Sexual Behavior in the Human Male* (Philadelphia: Saunders, 1948).

4. Belcastro, "Sexual Behavior Differences."

5. Wayne S. Wooden and Jay J. Parker, *Men behind Bars* (New York: Plenum, 1982).

6. Alan P. Bell and Martin S. Weinberg, *Homosexualities: A Study of Diversity among Men and Women* (New York: Simon & Schuster, 1978).

7. John L. Peterson, Thomas J. Coates, Joseph A. Catania, Norman Hearst, Lee Middleton, and Bobby Hilliard, "Risky Sexual Behaviors and Condom Use among African-American and Bisexual Men in the San Francisco Bay Area" (San Francisco: University of California, Department of Medicine, 1991, typescript).

8. Michael Samuel and Warren Winkelstein, Jr., "Prevalence of Human Immunodeficiency Virus Infection in Ethnic Minority Homosexual/Bisexual Men," *Journal of the American Medical Association* 257 (1987): 1901.

9. For a thorough discussion of these issues, see John DeLamater, "The Social Control of Sexuality," *Annual Review of Sociology* 7 (1981): 263–90; Philip Blumstein

and Pepper Schwartz, "Bisexuality: Some Social Psychological Issues," *Journal of Social Issues* 33 (1977): 30–45; Laud Humphreys, *Tea Room Trade: Impersonal Sex in Public Places* (Chicago: Aldine, 1970); Albert J. Reiss, "The Social Organization of Queers and Peers," *Social Problems* 9 (1961): 102–20.

10. An excellent discussion of this dilemma is offered in Vernon M. Briggs, Jr., "The Growth and Composition of the U.S. Labor Force," *Science* 238 (1987): 176–80; and Timothy Joe, "The Other Side of Black Female-headed Families: The Status of Adult Black Men," *Family Planning Perspective* 19 (1987): 74–76.

11. Mindy Thompson Fullilove and Robert E. Fullilove III, "Intersecting Epidemics: Black Teen Crack Use and Sexually Transmitted Disease," *Journal of the American Medical Women's Association* 44 (1989): 146–53.

12. Joseph M. Carrier, "Mexican Male Bisexuality," in *Bisexualities: Theory and Research,* ed. Fritz Klein and Timothy J. Wolf (New York: Haworth, 1985), pp. 75–85; Richard Parker, "Masculinity, Femininity, and Homosexuality," *Journal of Homosexuality* 11 (1985): 155–64; Wooden and Parker, *Men behind Bars.*

13. John H. Gagnon and William Simon, *Sexual Conduct: The Social Sources of Human Sexuality* (Chicago: Aldine, 1973).

14. Humphreys, *Tea Room Trade.*

15. Jay P. Paul, "The Bisexual Identity: An Idea without Social Recognition," *Journal of Homosexuality* 9 (1984): 45–63.

16. Joseph Harry, "Sexual Orientation as Destiny," *Journal of Homosexuality* 10 (1984): 111–23; Kenneth Plummer, "Going Gay: Identities, Life Cycles and Lifestyles in the Male Gay World," in *The Theory and Practice of Homosexuality,* ed. John Hart and Diane Richardson (London: Routledge & Kegan Paul, 1981), pp. 93–110; Thomas S. Weinberg, "On 'Doing' and 'Being' Gay: Sexual Behavior and Homosexual Male Self-Identity," *Journal of Homosexuality* 4 (1978): 143–56; and Michael G. Shively and John P. De Cecco, "Components of Sexual Identity," *Journal of Homosexuality* 3 (1977): 41–49.

17. Bell and Weinberg, *Homosexualities.*

18. Albert D. Klassen, Colin J. Williams, and Eugene E. Levitt, *Sex and Morality in the U.S.* (Middletown, Conn.: Wesleyan University Press, 1989).

19. Stanley Crouch, "Gay Pride, Gay Prejudice," *Village Voice* 27 (April 1982): 11–12.

20. Larry Icard, "Black Gay Men and Conflicting Social Identities: Sexual Orientation versus Racial Identity," *Journal of Social Work and Human Sexuality* 4 (1985–86): 83–93.

21. Robert Staples, "Race, Liberalism-Conservatism and Premarital Sexual Permissiveness: A Bi-racial Comparison," *Journal of Marriage and the Family* 40 (1978): 733–42.

22. Briggs, "Growth of U.S. Labor"; Joe, "Other Side of Black."

23. Staples, "Race and Sexual Permissiveness."

24. Gagnon and Simon, *Sexual Conduct.*

25. Harlon Dalton, "AIDS in Blackface," *Daedalus* 118, no. 3 (1989): 205–27; Bell Hooks, "Homophobia in Black Communities," *Zeta* 1 (1988): 35–38.

26. Crouch, "Gay Pride."

27. Thomas Bean, "Racism from a Black Perspective," *Advocate* 339 (1 April 1982): 10–14.

28. Julius Johnson, "Influence of Assimilation on the Psychosocial Adjustment of Black Homosexual Men" (Ph.D. diss., California School of Professional Psychol-

ogy, 1982); Max C. Smith, "By the Year 2000," in *In the Life: A Black Gay Anthology,* ed. Joseph Beam (Boston: Alyson, 1986), pp. 224–29.

29. Philip Blumstein and Pepper Schwartz, *American Couples: Money, Work, Sex* (New York: Morrow, 1983).

30. Martin S. Weinberg and Colin J. Williams, *Male Homosexuals: Their Problems and Adaptations* (New York: Oxford University Press, 1974).

31. Mary Riege Laner, "Permanent Partner Priorities: Gay and Straight," in *Gay Relationships,* ed. John P. De Cecco (New York: Harrington Park, 1988), pp. 133–55; Mary Riege Laner and G. W. Levi Kamel, "Media Mating I: Newspaper 'Personals' Ads of Homosexual Men," in ibid., pp. 73–89; John Alan Lee, "Forbidden Colors of Love: Patterns of Gay Love and Gay Liberation," in ibid., pp. 11–32; Malcolm E. Lumby, "Men Who Advertise for Sex," in ibid., pp. 61–71.

32. Lee, "Forbidden Colors."

33. Johnson, "Assimilation of Black Men."

34. Bell and Weinberg, *Homosexualities.*

35. Laner, "Permanent Partner"; Laner and Kamel, "Media Mating"; Lumby, "Men Who Advertise for Sex."

36. Graham Spanier and P. Glick, "Mate Selection Differentials between Whites and Blacks in the United States," *Social Forces* 58 (1980): 707–25; E. Porterfield, "Black American Intermarriage in the United States," *Marriage and Family Review* 5 (1982): 17–34.

37. Letitia Anne Peplau, "Research on Homosexual Couples: An Overview," *Journal of Homosexuality* 8 (1982): 3–8; De Cecco, ed., *Gay Relationships;* Blumstein and Schwartz, "American Couples"; David P. McWhirter and Andrew M. Mattison, "The Male Couple: How Relationships Develop" (Englewood Cliffs, N.J.: Prentice-Hall, 1984).

38. Bell and Weinberg, *Homosexualities.*

39. Blumstein and Schwartz, "American Couples"; McWhirter and Mattison, "The Male Couple"; Peplau, "Homosexual Couples."

SIX

Nonghetto Gays: An Ethnography of Suburban Homosexuals

Frederick R. Lynch

In 1974, Joseph Harry found a strong relation between increasing city size and diversification of gay bars. Diversity of commercial scenes, suggested Harry, would attract increasing numbers of homosexuals looking for sexual contacts and lovers—just as cities were emerging as the centers of the "swinging singles" culture in the heterosexual world. Harry and William DeVall later added that larger cities give rise to additional social and cultural institutions that could form the basis of a gay community, including gay ghettos.[1]

Such observations were accurate in the 1970s. Since that time, several sociocultural trends have accelerated—or arisen anew—that may have affected the accessibility and desirability of urban areas for male homosexuals.

First, there has been the continuing shift of the U.S. population to the suburbs. Today, over half of all Americans reside in the suburbs, while only 30 percent remain in cities, which are perceived as increasingly beset with problems of high crime, poverty, racial tension, and social disorganization.

Second, the soaring costs of real estate and rents beginning in the late 1970s in the more popular urban enclaves in Los Angeles, New York, San Francisco, and other cities has undoubtedly affected the attitudes and plans of would-be urban migrants.

Third, it seems reasonable to assume that the deep recession of the early 1980s had an effect on social and geographic mobility—and, perhaps, on sexual mobility ("coming out") as well.

Fourth, especially among college students, there has been a sharp swing toward "careerism" and practicality in academic, career, and life-style choices. The recession of the early 1980s and the increasing competition for jobs as the baby-boom generation enters the marketplace have fueled this practical, utilitarian outlook. Insofar as homosexual activities have usually been a part of leisure time and space, preoccupation with jobs and home ownership and maintenance might be expected to mute concerns of gay life-styles.[2]

Finally, the advent of AIDS must have had some degree of adverse effect on the lure of the "swinging single" life-style for homosexuals and heterosexuals alike—at least insofar as the lure of multiple sexual partners is concerned. (Even before AIDS, these practices had become increasingly problematic owing to such sexually transmitted diseases as herpes and—especially for homosexual men—hepatitis B.)

How Does the Suburban Context Affect Homosexuals?

If most of the U.S. population now lives in the suburbs, and if the gay rights slogan "We are everywhere" has any validity, then it can be assumed that a significant number of homosexuals live and work in the suburbs. To extend Harry's thesis on urbanization, with increasing size of the suburbs, has there been a diversification of homosexual life-styles, even the growth of gay "satellite cultures."[3]

Suburban respondents have, apparently, been included in some previous studies of male homosexuals. Recent research on gay couples by Charles Silverstein and by David McWhirter and Andrew Mattison contains nationwide and countywide samples, respectively. One-third of Troiden's 150 respondents were from suburban Long Island. Suburban homosexuals were probably included in Harry and DeVall's "Detroit area" sample, which, in any case, was supplemented from a variety of sources. Barry Dank likewise engaged in a variety of methodological strategies for his classic study "Coming Out in the Gay World" and likely incorporated suburban homosexuals in his work. There were also suburban participants in impersonal sexual activities observed in an urban public park restroom by Laud Humphreys.[4]

While some suburbanites may have been nominally included in studies of male homosexuals, few researchers have singled out for *in-*

dependent focus the life-styles and problems of suburban homosexuals. A major exception is the study by T. S. Weinberg and Colin Williams. Though they expected to find a pronounced "urbanism effect" in subjects in cities of 250,000 or more compared to those in "outlying areas," the differences between the groups were small. Male homosexuals living in outlying areas (communities with populations ranging from 25,000 to 250,000) were slightly more circumspect in revealing their identities, worried more about exposure, "passed" (for heterosexual) more often, anticipated more intolerance and discrimination, had fewer homosexual relationships, less homosexual sex, less social involvement with homosexuals, and more social involvement with heterosexuals. On the basis of a sample of fifty males from New York City and fifty males from suburban Suffolk County and Minneapolis, Troiden and Goode stated, "We speculate that persons residing in large cities have greater access to gay opportunity structures and for this reason, perhaps, arrive at homosexual self-definitions at slightly younger mean ages than men who reside in less populous areas."[5]

Articles and accounts in gay-oriented publications suggest more detailed urban-suburban differences. However, such reports offer differing evaluations of the suburban settings. Here, for example, is C. Mack Gilliland writing in the 1982 Los Angeles *Gay Pride Parade Souvenir Program*:

> Homosexuality is a phenomenon of the city, or so much of the straight world believes, and the suburban gay and lesbian experience plays daily against all stereotypes that the other world holds. Few expect to find gay men and lesbians in the suburbs. When they do—at work, in the neighborhood, at the markets—suburban living to most gays and lesbians is akin to the role of the Old Lamplighter, going around hourly, gently one to one, turning lights on in people's heads—and learning, surprisingly, of being regarded not always with resentment or contempt, but mostly rewarded with a gentle respect, a curious fascination, and a new appreciation of oneself.[6]

Gilliland claimed to have "come out" to his high school students and found the reception cordial and curious.

Another communication from the suburbs about a year later was much more pessimistic. Writing in the gay-oriented *Los Angeles Blade* (13 July 1983), Dan Alonzo noted that, among his suburban teenage students, "gay means 'stupid and silly'" and "'faggot' remains the most humiliating insult a male teenager can give another." He also observed that several of his adult colleagues—and parents of students—were equally homophobic.

Is life for homosexuals in rapidly growing suburban areas refreshingly open and relaxed, as Gilliland would have us believe, or is it threatening and repressive, as Alonzo observed? Does suburban existence delay or complicate the formation and maintenance of homosexual identities (as suggested by Troiden and Goode) and/or inhibit involvement in homosexual social activities or the formation of love relationships (as found by Weinberg and Williams)? And what of the effects of the recession, soaring housing costs, and the onset of AIDS?

After discussing the methodological genesis of this ethnography, I shall turn to discussions of the formation of homosexual identities of suburban homosexual males and the development and maintenance of homosexual identities and life-styles (values, politics, and social involvement) in the initial, late-1980 phase of the four-year observation period, as contrasted with the final observations in mid-1985. Somewhat more briefly, I shall look at the nature and durability of homosexual friendships. Even more briefly, I then consider sex-role influences. Finally, conclusions are followed by an "AIDS Epilogue" update on the original field study.

A note on terminology: throughout the study I shall refer to the subjects of my study collectively as "homosexuals" rather than "gays." The reason for this is that the degree of self-acknowledgment and self-recognition of homosexual identity—a key element of being "gay"—varied enormously in the sample. Many were "out" insofar as they would go to a gay bar on a regular basis—but many were no further along than that. On the other hand (as in the previous sentence), I shall use the term "gay" to refer to gay bars, institutions, and subcultures as well as to individuals who were fully self-identified to themselves and significant others.

Methodological Genesis of the Current Study

This four-year ethnographic study of suburban homosexuals developed out of a project originally intended as a study of community conflict. In late 1980, I became aware of a rumor that a gay tavern might open on the outskirts of the conservative, upper-middle-class, suburban California community in which I resided. The purported location of this establishment was also quite close to a fundamentalist high school, several fast-food establishments, and sections of minority communities where youth gang activity was not unknown. This seemed to be a zesty recipe for future community conflict, so I began to track down the rumor at one of the largest suburban gay discos in southern California—the Crossroads—which was not far from the supposed location of the newer establishment.[7]

I discovered that the rumor was not so much false as premature. The new gay tavern—Kings—would not open until spring 1982. In addition, the opening and subsequent operation generated little harrassment or conflict by Kings' neighbors largely because Kings was slow to develop a steady, visible clientele—indeed, the tavern foundered for more than a year before it began to attract significant numbers of patrons, usually on weekends and especially on Sunday nights.

In the meantime, I had begun to notice and had become acquainted with two friendship groups: a group of about five single persons built around a gregarious twenty-three-year-old I shall call Skip Barrows and a second group made up of two couples and three single males that loosely formed around twenty-eight-year-old Sam Montana. I also became acquainted with a number of "peripheral members" or people who were known to members of one or both groups as well as to some "loners" in these settings.

Most persons regarded me in a curious, though somewhat friendly, manner as a sort of neuter "intellectual type" who "never went home with anyone." When I told them I was conducting a study of the opening of Kings, they were not surprised. And when I asked to interview them individually for a study that had now shifted to suburban homosexual life-styles, they cooperated to the fullest. I conducted twenty-six individual, in-depth interviews at my home, at theirs, or, sometimes (as in the case of tavern owners or managers), at either Kings or the Crossroads (the other large suburban tavern). About half these persons were members of one of two friendship groups: Sam Montana's or Skip Barrows's. Many of the rest were "part-time" or peripheral members of the group, but some were not attached to any particular network. Two of the interviews were with managers of suburban gay taverns.

The individual interviews with this "core sample" of twenty-six, white, mostly middle-class and service-sector male homosexuals were open ended in format. Aside from routine questions about social background, questions were focused on homosexual life histories, relationships with family, relatives, and straight and homosexual friends, attitudes toward and theories of homosexuality, attitudes toward politics, minority groups, and gay liberation, the desirability of long-term relationships, etc.

But the data obtained in the interview phase of the study became increasingly supplemented, supplanted, and sometimes contradicted by three additional years of direct and indirect observations and other data-gathering techniques in a variety of settings. I thus came to know some sociologically similar persons through "informal interviewing" and observation at least as well as some of those formally interviewed. Furthermore, the latter *continued to change* and evolve. Rather than obtaining a one-time "snapshot" of twenty-six people, I found myself recording a moving, changing "videotape" of these and other suburban homosexuals over a span of just over four years. The primary methodology thus shifted from interviews supplemented by short-term observation to ethnography supplemented (early in the study) by formal interviews. The style and methodology of this study, then, are more in the qualitative tradition of Carol Warren, Barbara Ponse, and Susan Krieger than the quantitative approach of Alan Bell and Martin Weinberg or Joseph Harry.[8]

This four-year field study of white, male, suburban homosexuals, then, is primarily a descriptive and suggestive account of the changing lives of a significant, yet largely unresearched, subpopulation of American society.

Key Characteristics of the Core Sample

First, it should be pointed out that most subjects lived and/or worked in suburban areas that were "of" but not "in" a major metropolitan area in California. Technically, they had access to large gay urban enclaves, and some subjects visited these areas from time to time. But trips to "boys town" were an hour's drive under the best of conditions. The rising costs of gasoline, the crackdown on drunk drivers, heavy traffic, and the added complications involved in making sexual contacts—especially on a long-standing basis—made frequent urban excursions "more hassle than it's worth." Most were unwilling to abandon jobs and/or living arrangements in the suburbs to migrate to gay-oriented areas in the city. One subject who did get involved in a major urban gay civic organization remarked, "The social life is definitely better in the city, but the standard of living is so much better out here."

In terms of social characteristics, the ages of the twenty-six persons formally interviewed ranged from twenty to fifty-nine, though three persons over fifty were not "central characters" in the study. The mean age of those interviewed was about thirty-two. Education ranged from twelve to seventeen years, while income ranged from $1,000 (one un-attached individual was unemployed at the time) to $60,000; the mean income was about $24,000. In terms of occupation, two were in the professional category, four were classified as managerial or administrative, three were teachers, one was self-employed, thirteen were in sales, service, or technical occupations, two were in the "skilled" category, and one was unemployed. (This occupational skew toward middle- to lower-level white-collar and/or service-sector jobs seems typical of studies of male homosexuals.)[9] All but two (who were half Hispanic) were Anglo.

Most of these persons were sufficiently aware of their homosexual leanings to have sought out and regularly patronized, on at least a weekend basis, one of the two larger suburban gay disco/taverns. As will be seen in the following discussion, most were entering —or had already entered—the "coming out" stage of homosexual identity formation.

Coming-Out Experiences of Suburban Homosexuals

This chapter is not meant as a formal, quantitative test of the theoretical models of gay identity formation offered by Dank, Plummer, Troiden, Coleman, and others.[10] These models were useful overall guides to the coming-out experiences of suburban homosexuals and were "confirmed" in several respects. Still, the combination of interview data and extended direct observation of the primary subjects suggests that the coming-out process is, indeed, a highly complex *negotiated* process in which the nature and/or boundaries of these "stages" can be difficult to define. For purposes of organizational focus, I shall primarily limit myself to Plummer's and Troiden's models, both of which posit that homosexuals pass through four stages: sensitization, signification, coming out, and then a fourth stage termed by Plummer "stabilization" and by Troiden "commitment."

In terms of the first stage—"sensitization"—in which "men gain experiences which *later* serve as sources for interpreting their feelings as homosexual,"[11] virtually all those interviewed recalled one or more same-sex physical contacts (usually mutual masturbation) in their childhood or adolescence—as do many heterosexuals as well. Though respondents were not specifically asked about early feelings of "feeling different" (sexually) from peers, seven did report such experiences—posited by Plummer and Troiden as highly typical of this stage. As proposed in the theoretical models, the sexual meaning of these feelings were not recognized at the time; only later were they reinterpreted in the light of an evolving homosexual orientation. Indeed, one such reinterpretation happened during an interview with Sid "Doc" Bonnelli, a forty-year-old doctor of osteopathy who was a core member of Skip's friendship group. Doc stated, "I remember when I was in junior high that there were one or two kids who were recognized as 'different,' and people called them queers or fairies. I was never tagged as one of them, though. I was kind of a loner; I was pushed into joining Boy Scouts by my parents. But I was in a car club, the Christian club, and had some close friends. But, now that I think of it, I can remember these feelings of erotic attraction toward guys in the showers in those days. Funny, I never thought of it 'till now."

About one-third of those formally interviewed specifically recalled being loners as children, and another five remembered being labeled a sissy or a queer. At the time, most rejected such taunts as true labels of their sexual natures. Another past and present trait often associated with homosexual life histories was that only two of those formally interviewed and none of those informally interviewed had ever or presently participated in organized sports activities—nor was there any interest in watching such events.

Perhaps more respondents would have reported more specific sensitization experiences if asked—or, in some cases, quizzed at length. A major surprise in the interviewing process was that just under half the subjects had devoted little deep thought to their biographies in terms of their homosexual evolution. When asked, "How do you explain or account for homosexuality in general and your own case in particular?" nearly 40 percent replied simply that they "hadn't thought about it much." Additional probing by the interviewer tended to yield only vague or superficial answers. This was especially true among younger subjects, who seemed to view their own sexual identities and the topic of homosexuality in a much more casual manner.

On the other hand, virtually all subjects formally interviewed detailed their personal "signification" stage—which typically entailed the questioning of heterosexual orientation and the recognition of potential homosexuality. For many, this occurred in their late teens or twenties, but a few encountered this stage somewhat earlier—usually by reading about homosexuality.

For example, one twenty-five-year-old subject reported such feelings at age twelve when he read and reread the portions on homosexuality in David Ruben's popular *Everything You've Always Wanted to Know about Sex:* "But I denied the idea that I was like them as there seemed to be so many whackos." (When this individual later entered his first gay bar at the age of twenty-three, he underwent "normalcy shock"[12] when he found that all homosexuals were not "whacko.")

Most respondents had some heterosexual dating experience during their signification stages, but such activities were found to be either immediately or progressively unrewarding. (Six of those formally interviewed had been heterosexually married.)

Plummer has written with regard to signification that "for some these changes are passed quickly; for others, they groan through the life span."[13] Indeed, what was especially striking in this study was that the difficulty of passage to anything like a "positive" gay identity was largely related to age, that is, the sociohistorical context in which the respondents moved through puberty and young adulthood. Those over 30 at the time of interview ($N = 16$) had sensitization experiences at a mean age of 12, encountered signification feelings at about age 22.6, and came out at around age 30. For those under 30 ($N = 10$), the corresponding figures are 13.8, 17.7, and 20.9. Such findings, then, confirm the effects of age or generational cohorts noted by Dank, Troiden and Goode, McDonald, and Warren.[14]

Coming Out and the Helping Hand

For those formally interviewed, the process of identifying oneself to oneself as homosexual, or "coming out," often involved a first visit to a gay bar. Such a decision often occurred through other social contacts with homosexuals; less frequently, the decision was made alone. Most of those in this study "tested"[15] themselves by going to a gay bar—often the major suburban bar, the Crossroads.

The decision to go to a gay bar, the act of crossing the threshold of such an establishment, was a major event vividly recalled by nearly half those formally interviewed. Tim Halston (thirty-seven at the time of the interview) was thirty-two when he took this major step:

> The first time I was taken to the Crossroads by my best friend's ex-wife and some of her friends. She was a beautician who had a lot of gay friends who went there. We stayed about three hours. Two weeks later, I went on my own. I thought I should start *doing* something. . . .
>
> So I drove down, watching the speed limit, and thought, "Oh, my God, I hope nobody sees my car because they'll know right where I'm going."
>
> I happened to get a good parking spot right across the street. I was almost like a schizophrenic. I sat there with the doors locked. I waited for cars to go by—anything for an excuse not to get out. . . . I just knew there would be somebody in the bar I knew. So I sat there for about thirty minutes until there was no one around. Then I got out and I ran across the street. I looked back and saw I'd left the headlights on, so I ran back across the street—and almost got run over by a car. Then I sat in my car again and waited and all the anxiety came back. I thought, "Here I am in this horrible hole all by myself!"
>
> Then I finally walked across the street and went in. You could hardly see it was so damn dark. So I walked over to the bar, got a drink, and walked around. I stood by the post near the front pool table. One of those old fools who probably sits at the bar all day and gets drunk came up and put his arm around me and said, "I'm lonely." So I said, "Buy yourself a dog," and walked away.

Tim eventually went back to the Crossroads and also visited other bars in the metropolitan center. He began acquiring gay friends through a homosexual best friend and through visits to the bars.

Tim Halston's case illustrates several points about beginning the coming out process in the suburbs. First, many subjects expressed "fear of the unknown" with regard to visiting gay commercial establishments in the gay ghetto city areas. They had heard through heterosexual friends and through media imagery that such places were "weird" and dangerous. Yet they also hesitated to visit the one or two major suburban bars for fear of "being seen"—a dilemma faced by persons who live in small towns.[16] A twenty-five-year-old respondent, who described his first visit to the Crossroads in terms highly similar to those of Tim Halston, did, indeed, immediately encounter an old college friend.

A second point with regard to Tim Halston's account of his first bar visit was the help offered by a friend—the *female* ex-wife of his best friend. Dank, Harry and DeVall, and Troiden all discuss the importance of the social contexts of coming out. As Troiden reports, "Meeting other gay men was the most common circumstance leading to homosexual self-definition." Troiden also found (as did Dank) that "self-definition and initial subcultural involvement took place quite closely together."[17] This was certainly true in this study.

Yet what has not been brought out fully in some other coming out studies is the role of guide, teacher, or "helping hand" in either the signification stage, the coming-out stage, or both. Silverstein has discussed the often benign and helpful role that older, more experienced homosexual men play with regard to younger homosexuals. Indeed, in this study five subjects were taken to bars or otherwise initiated into the gay subculture by men who were either the same age or older. Weinberg has also pointed out the importance to a man in the process of coming out of sustained contact with one or more homosexual males or "coaches" in "redefin[ing] his sexual activities and his own sexual identity as a homosexual." With regard to his sample of thirty males, however, Weinberg also observed that "this contact . . . usually came well after the onset of self-suspicion."[18]

But a rather interesting finding among respondents in this study was that five of the twelve persons who received such "coaching" or "helping hands" had received such aid from women. (If one counts help offered to two divorced subjects by female psychotherapists, the count rises to seven.) Furthermore, female helping hands tended to offer help earlier in the coming-out process than male counterparts. The findings of the formal interviews in this study indicated that women usually "raised the consciousness" of subjects somewhat earlier during the signification period than did males.

Thus, one subject was first taken to a gay bar by female coworkers at a department store where he worked part time. (He claimed to have no idea about his own homosexual tendencies at the time.) Another had his homosexual potential awakened through conversations with the lesbian mother of his fiancée. A third subject was first taken to a gay bar by his wife:

> Betty had met some gay friends while working for a department store, and she'd been to the Crossroads a couple of times with them. So they got me to go with them. At first, I was terrified of the place. But Betty seemed to enjoy the scene and would make comments on the men like, "Oh, he looks really hot." She'd invite some of them over to our table

and then back to our house, where we would have three-ways or where I would have sex with him in the spare bedroom. . . . Our own sex life had deteriorated from when we'd first been married, so I sort of just took this as sexual release . . . but later I found out that Betty had been seeing the store manager at our place when I was working swing shift. . . . When we got divorced, she moved in with another woman, and I now wonder if she wasn't going through some sort of lesbian thing when she started us going to the bar.

A fourth was first taken to a gay bar (when he was under the legal drinking age) by a female lesbian work supervisor:

I suspected I was gay, and I suspected my female supervisor was—she kept making remarks about the gorgeous girls that sometimes came up to the order window. So eventually she took me into the back room and said, "We need to talk." And she said, "I'm gay." And I responded, "So am I." She nearly fell on the floor. I wish I'd had a camera. . . .

So she said, "Why don't you come out to the bar with us?" I protested that I was under age, but she took me to the Crossroads before nine o'clock, when they started checking ID. I sat with her and her friends, and she started introducing me to these guys as they came along. I went there with her about every Saturday and Sunday for a while. I was never without her there for the first couple of months. By that time, I knew people—including the doorman. So I started going on my own.

The liberalization of sexual attitudes and rules of discussion during the 1970s may have made it easier for women to suggest such things to men—especially to young men. Indeed, the men who received helping hands from females were all under thirty when such aid was offered—in fact, two of them were under twenty.

A minority of those in this study had clearly begun homosexual "careers" in other settings. Three persons began to meet other homosexuals in a suburban park, while two subjects had homosexual encounters in occupational settings—"sensitization" types of experiences in that the events were defined by the subjects as "just sex" and not, at the time, as "homosexual." Three individuals quietly but rapidly developed homosexual identities by involvement in love affairs with other males—two of those in the military. For the rest, however, coming out usually awaited more sustained interaction with other self-admitted homosexuals—usually in a bar setting.

Only a minority of those formally or informally interviewed seemed to have ever desired psychological support services—such as rap groups or individual therapy or counseling. Those who had sought such services in the past had to find them as best they could. Most of the divorced subjects had been pressured to seek psychological help at the time of their divorce—with mixed results. (One of these men attempted to travel to collective counseling groups at the gay community center in the urban area but gave up after two trips as "it was just too far.") Two subjects in the study who sought counseling on a regular basis traveled to a therapist in the gay ghetto area.

Troiden has contended that entry into the fourth stage of commitment to homosexual identity involves the taking of a lover. By this qualification, then, most subjects in the early stage of this study were not officially or fully committed to a homosexual identity. Still, most were moderately to strongly interested in establishing a long-term relationship with a lover and made some attempts to move into the fourth stage.[19]

According to Troiden, another attribute of commitment is satisfaction with the homosexual identity: the "homosexual should value homosexuality at least as much as, and perhaps more than, the bisexual or heterosexual alternatives and elect to remain homosexual if faced with the opportunity to abandon his homosexuality."[20] Ninety-one percent of Troiden's subjects preferred their own sexual orientation to any conversion to heterosexuality.

In this study, two-thirds of those formally interviewed said that they preferred to remain homosexual even if they "could have pushed a magic button" to become heterosexual—though their degree of enthusiasm varied. A forty-year-old high school teacher remarked that not being homosexual "would make life somewhat easier, but not, necessarily, more enjoyable." In a similar vein, many noted that their heterosexual friends were no happier than their homosexual friends and that they enjoyed the independence and autonomy of the homosexual life-style. A twenty-three-year-old remarked, "I think homosexuals are kind of special. It's hard to say why. It's just that they know who they are. . . . They've made a choice to recognize themselves. . . . You're part of a special community with everyone in the same boat."

On the other hand, the remaining one-third indicated that they might prefer change. "It'd be easier," said Sam Montana. "The world is set up for straight people." His good friend Jack Worthington sounded similar sentiments: "If I had a choice, I would rather not be gay. I'm pretty happy now. But I would have fewer conflicts."

The most telling evidence indicating that respondents were less than enthusiastic about their sexual identity was their reticence to acknowledge such orientation with heterosexual relatives, coworkers, and friends. Except for the bar managers who were interviewed, few had revealed their sexual identities to coworkers. Only one of the three homosexual fathers formally interviewed had informed his children of his homosexuality. Six had informed parents, while about half the rest assumed that their parents suspected. "It's something that's not discussed" was a common refrain.

The perceived need to compartmentalize homosexual and heterosexual worlds prevented the social psychological passage from weekend homosexual to a fully gay identity. Many of the subjects were literally torn between two worlds. In part, this was due to the fact that many of them had grown up, worked, and lived in the same general vicinity. Parents, relatives, and heterosexual friends were all in the area. Yet, as indicated earlier in this study, no one moved closer to the metropolitan core, or gay ghettos, purely for purposes of sexual freedom. Four of those formally interviewed did move away from the study area—one of them to a location near a gay ghetto. Two subjects had once lived in the city, near or in gay ghetto areas. But moves to or from the cities or other locations were for purposes of jobs or housing.

The suburban sociocultural environment of the suburbs seemed to produce a marked ambivalence about moving from the "coming-out" stage to that of "stabilization" (Plummer) or "commitment" (Troiden). After self-identifying as homosexuals, even after some involvement with the homosexual subculture, and even after having taken a lover, many subjects in this study seemed to become "fence sitters" on the boundary between coming out and commitment or stabilization. Such hesitancy and indecision were no doubt due to the middle-class, career orientation of the subjects, but this ambivalence was also the product of the suburban sociocultural environment.

Homosexual Identity, Life-Style, and the Suburban Environment

In the early 1970s, Weinberg and Williams found that subjects from "outlying areas" (populations of 25,000–250,000) were somewhat more circumspect, more fearful of exposure, anticipated more intolerance and discrimination, had fewer homosexual relations, less homosexual sex, less social involvement with homosexuals, and more social involvement with heterosexuals.[21] In terms of the coming-out models of Troiden and Plummer, then, Weinberg and Williams's subjects from outlying areas were less ensconced in the fourth and final stage of coming out: "stabilization" (Plummer's term) or "commitment" (Troiden's). This was definitely true for the suburban homosexuals I observed in the early 1980s. As the observation period lengthened, this remained true, but with some additional qualifications.

Early Years of the Study: Late 1980 to Late 1982

At the time of the 1982 formal interviewing, most of the subjects in the present study were still in the early-to-middle phases of "coming out." They recognized themselves as homosexual and were becoming more involved with homosexual friends and the bar scene. However, only a few seem to have fully entered the commitment/stabilization stage of development. Most of those interviewed or observed were attempting, with varying degrees of success, to enter or build or sustain social networks that could be elaborated to settings outside the bars, seek sexual encounters, and find a lover.

Most of those in Sam's group had known one another before I first met them at the Crossroads in late 1980. With one or two brief exceptions, an "incest taboo" prevented sexual interplay within the group because two couples were part of that group.[22] Members of Sam's group, then, had come to the suburban bars to socialize, "get out of the house," and, for the single members, look for potential sexual partners or lovers. Members of Skip's group had first met one another at the Crossroads, often through sexual encounters. Friendship usually followed such liaisons, and they came to the Crossroads to "hang out" together and seek other sexual encounters. During 1982, Skip met Brad, a person not originally in the group, and he and Brad became lovers and moved in together in the early summer of 1982. One of the single persons interviewed knew members of both Sam's and Skip's group prior to the start of this study. Though he was not a core member, he nevertheless was invited to some of their parties and sometimes went to vacation spots with them. The other single persons interviewed, along with one "independent couple," were usually introduced to the two friendship groups but either chose to remain on their own or were not accepted by the groups. (The others interviewed were the managers of the two suburban bars, the Crossroads and Kings; one manager had a live-in lover and remained so attached throughout the term of the study.)

In Silverstein's terms, the vast majority of the single persons in this study could be characterized as weekend "excitement seekers," most of whom were also interested in becoming "home builders" with a lover.[23] Indeed, jobs/careers/income, a middle-class suburban home or condominium, a lover, and the "suburban good life" were the primary goals of those formally and informally interviewed. Though moderate to liberal in opinions with regard to voting behavior and views on such issues as defense spending, environment, tax cutting, welfare, affirmative action, and so forth, in practice, most of the individuals were quite pragmatic and conservative in placing career and home ownership above all else. (This seemed to have been a common sociocultural trend in the early 1980s, no doubt magnified by the housing crisis and deep recession of that time. About one-third of those formally interviewed and several informally interviewed or observed—some of whom were in their thirties—were forced to live with parents, a situation that was seen as distinctly undesirable both by them and by potential sexual partners.)

The findings of the formal interviewing for this study confirmed Harry and DeVall's observation that a strong middle-class orientation tends to lead individuals to identify with their class rather than with homosexuals and that "such individuals accord their sexual lives a lower priority in their scale of values."[24]

These values, along with the relative lack of sexual opportunities, undoubtedly had much to do with the levels of same-sex sexual contacts reported by the subjects. A wide range of homosexual activities was reported: some had three or four such contacts a year, while a few reported three or four such contacts per month. (These data did not include sexual contacts between couples but did include reported extramarital contacts.) An average frequency was about once a month.

Such data generally reinforced findings on nonurban, middle-class homosexuals in Weinberg and Williams and in Harry and DeVall but contrasted markedly with the data obtained in San Francisco by Bell and Weinberg.[25] Most white homosexual males in Bell and Weinberg's study were more liberal politically and far more sexually active. Two-thirds reported having sex with other men once a week; 30 percent had sex two to three times a week; 13 percent had sex four to six times a week; and 4 percent had sex seven times a week or more.

Conditions at the End of the Study, Mid-1985

By the end of the observation period in mid-1985, three of the five original couples had remained intact, and all but five individuals formally interviewed had entered into either short-term (less than one year), medium-length (one to two years), or long-term love relationships. By taking a lover, then, most subjects qualified for entry into Troiden's fourth stage of homosexual identity formation—"commitment."

For a time, there was a drift toward having more homosexual than heterosexual friends. This trend appeared to level off, though this could have been due to involvement with jobs and occupational mobility and aging or with boredom with homosexual social life, especially the competitive and, for couples, potentially destabilizing bar scenes. Whatever the reasons, continued involvement with career, home, heterosexual relatives, and some heterosexual friends still led to split social worlds and hedging with regard to fuller involvement and commitment to a homosexual life-style and identity.

On the other hand, most of those formally interviewed attended their first Gay Pride Parade in the nearby city in the early 1980s. Most were favorably impressed, and the majority returned as either parade watchers or parade participants the following two years. Three of the subjects were so taken by the positive spirit of the parade and its attendant festivities that they subsequently joined the organization responsible for the event and later became officers of the organization. (This required extensive commuting to the gay urban enclaves, but none of the three gave much serious thought to moving there.)

Generally, most of those interviewed and observed became more relaxed about their homosexual identity and relations with other homosexuals and heterosexuals. Several began to reveal their identity to a few friends. By mid-1985, the second of three homosexual fathers had discussed his sexual identity with his children. He remarked, "It turned out to be no big deal."

Parents, however, remained the stumbling block. After the formal interview phase in 1982, only one more of those so studied informed his parents, friends, or coworkers of his sexual identity. Those who previously had assumed that their parents suspected were more convinced of that than ever; three of those formally interviewed who had previously assumed that their parents did not know now assumed that they did suspect the truth. Interestingly, those who took lovers did not especially try to hide the nature of the relationship from family, but then neither did they openly discuss the issue. Parents who were most easily kept unaware of their son's sexual life-style generally lived some distance away, often in another state.

In many respects, then, individuals formally interviewed in 1982 were generally moving further into the stabilization or commitment phase of homosexual identity. For some, the progression was in a straight-line fashion, but the metaphor that most aptly characterizes this passage is that of "tacking" or a kind of zigzag pattern. Nor was the passage irreversible.

For example, twenty-three-year-old Skip Barrows had moved rapidly into the homosexual subculture after being "clued in" to his homosexual tendencies by the mother of his fiancée when he was twenty. After three years of "playing the field," Skip entered into a two-year love relationship with Brad Smithers, a high school history teacher some five years older than Skip. They both became active in a homosexual civic organization in the city and became much more "openly gay," though neither formally told their parents. But Skip and Brad split up in 1984. Skip, who had changed jobs several times, obtained a well-paid position with a public agency. He resigned his post on the homosexual civic organization, bought a suburban house, entered into another short-lived relationship, then began sharing his house with a female friend and talked of the possibility of marriage and a return to a heterosexual life. He then acquired a second homosexual lover.

An older subject, forty-four-year-old Tom Mahoney, rapidly entered homosexual suburban life, took a lover for six months, and then, after a few years, married a female coworker and withdrew from homosexual life. Another subject in his mid-thirties went through a remarkably fast odyssey during the four-year span of the study. Having become used to having multiple sex partners, Bill abandoned his seven-year relationship with another man in 1983 and entered a relationship with another man that lasted only a few months. The affair ended in violence, followed by a suicide attempt, hospitalization, job loss, reconversion to the fundamentalist religion in which he had been raised, renunciation of homosexuality and alcohol, and then a gradual drift back into the homosexual subculture and the resumption of drinking. Bill then moved to another state to rejoin his former long-term lover, but broke up with him shortly thereafter.

A variety of cultural and social pressures, either unique to or magnified by the suburban environment, seemed to restrain passage into both the coming out and the commitment/stabilization stages of homosexual identity formation and a freer, more open homosexual lifestyle. These factors are discussed below.

Suburban Value and Institutional Matrix

The middle-class suburban settings in which most respondents were raised, lived, or wanted to live strongly reinforced devotion to work, home ownership/maintenance, and continued interaction with heterosexual coworkers, relatives, and friends. Such concerns left little free time for constructing a viable homosexual community. In addition, those subjects who were in their forties and fifties seemed disinclined to be involved with the suburban gay subculture, a "disengagement" process noted by Harry and DeVall.[26]

A "couples culture" as observed by Warren[27] did not emerge in any degree of depth or extensiveness. Again, most subjects claimed they simply did not have the time to construct or engage in extensive social networks. Many seemed content to pursue routine, daily social activities while participating less in gay-oriented activities.

The suburban setting hardly provided institutional support for either homosexual couples or singles. The following passage from Harry and DeVall would appear to apply doubly to the suburban context:

> In contrast to the heterosexual marriage, the enduring homosexual liaison can perhaps best be described in terms of the characteristics it lacks. Aside from its highly disvalued status, the gay relationship is very largely lacking in institutional supports and cultural guidelines. There are neither legal nor religious sanctions helping to maintain the integrity of the gay relationship. With rare exceptions, there are no children about which the parties to the relationship can organize their marital careers. The lack of children in the gay marriage probably also serves to weaken the ties of the gay couple to the community in that the gay couple acquires no obligations to schools, parental associations, or children's associations.[28]

Two of the unions formed by subjects in this study lasted under two years. The explanations for failed or shaky relationships seemed to vary from one couple to another. Jealousy was a factor in the dissolution of some unions,[29] though simple "incompatibility" seemed to be the major reason for split ups. Though the dynamics of homosexual unions could not be a focus of this study, suffice it to say that observations of couples in this context seemed to confirm Letitia Ann Peplau's findings that "our homosexual and heterosexual volunteers are so similar in the satisfactions they derive from their love relationships—and in the issues of commitment, intimacy, and personal freedom that confront them."[30]

As for commercial or other established social settings, the suburban environment lacked the diversity of gay-oriented economic, social, and cultural organizations available in the larger urban centers. There were only two large bar-discos in the area that middle-class subjects in this study would have considered entering, the older Crossroads and Kings, which opened in 1982. A large lesbian-oriented bar was ignored, and two or three smaller establishments were simply dismissed as disreputable.

A branch of the homosexual-oriented Metropolitan Community Church (MCC), a fledgling gay political alliance, two gay-oriented Alcoholics Anonymous groups, and one or two other small civic groups were all struggling along. All but one of those formally interviewed and nearly all informally interviewed and observed rejected such institutions. They had little time for such involvement. Second, those who were at all acquainted with groups such as the MCC or the political coalition were put off by the attributes of those involved, usually their politics, values, or marginal economic status. (Significantly, the one subject in this study who was active in such organizations was also unemployed much of the time.)

The suburban gay organizations reflected a collective, often politically liberal-activist orientation. By contrast, those whom I formally and informally interviewed and observed were devoted to individual enterprises of work, home, and individualism in general. That is, the subjects in this study were intensely individualistic and assimilationist. They wanted to fit into the suburban environment, to be quietly accepted by and live and work among their heterosexual neighbors. Given Dennis Altman's choice between collective identification and action versus individual assimilation,[31] at least 90 percent of those I interviewed and observed opted for the latter. "I would like to think," said Jack Worthington, a close friend of Sam Montana's, "that in the future we will look at people as individuals. I'm not a group-based person."

Though about two-thirds of those formally interviewed were moderate to liberal on many other issues, most were not especially politically aware, and almost no one was politically active. No one interviewed or observed paid heed to the stands of political candidates on gay issues. The vast majority were unaware of or else unconcerned about A.B.1, a bill introduced in the California legislature that would have prohibited discrimination against homosexuals in housing or business practices. As opposed to the findings of David McWhirter and Andrew Mattison,[32] subjects in this study did not become more politically aware with the passage of time.

Nearly all those formally interviewed rejected any comparison of homosexuals with minority groups such as blacks or Latinos. Nor were they interested in group-based coalition politics. Instead, while many respected the gay liberation groups for having won legal rights and limited social acceptance, the suburbanites were put off by the style of gay lib spokespersons.

Marshall Kirk and Hunter Madsen spoke for and to the concerns of many, if not most, of the suburbanites I interviewed. In their book *After the Ball,* they criticized the radical, confrontational, and convention-defying aspects of the gay liberation movement and called for a return to middle-class "respectability" in building relations between the gay and straight worlds.[33] Tim Halston anticipated their arguments for a "respectable" front when he stated, "We've got to focus on respectability and on people cleaning up their act. The suburbs are different. It's more conservative out here. People can't flaunt their gayness, or they'd lose their jobs. We must work behind the scenes."

Nearly all those formally interviewed in 1982 felt confident of continuing progress and increased tolerance for homosexuals. They viewed this change as slow and evolutionary rather than revolutionary. Most simply assumed that prejudice and discrimination against homosexuals would wane through the law of large numbers: as more people came out, it was reasoned, the gay community would become increasingly large, powerful, and visible. Field observation into 1985, however, found that many were clearly becoming worried about the negative effect that the spread of AIDS might have on tolerance toward homosexuals.

Gay Burnout and AIDS

As the study progressed, the effects of the recession and housing crises of the early 1980s eased. More and more of those formally interviewed or observed became more secure in their careers, obtained houses or condominiums, and, at least for a time, coupled up with another male. As these trends developed, participation in the suburban gay subculture, especially in the suburban bars, declined markedly. By the summer of 1985, perhaps only one-third of those formally interviewed in 1982 could be found on a monthly basis at one of the two major suburban establishments. A few had moved out of the area. But most subjects, never pleased with the bar scene anyway, simply seemed to weary of it and suffered a form of "burnout." [34]

Skip Barrows was one who suffered gay burnout:

> Becoming gay is sort of like going through a second childhood. It's like going through high school culture all over again—you know, learning to date and play the various games you play and all that. It's a whole new exciting world. Well, I've *been* through that. . . . Now I've achieved some of the things I've wanted. . . . I'm now and always have been, I suppose, the true, basic, middle-class suburban person. I like to go to work, come home, and unwind. Especially on Fridays, now, I just like to stay home and do things around the house.

Fear of AIDS seemed to have little if anything to do with burnout. Indeed, AIDS appeared to have had little effect at all on the social or sexual behavior of those in this study, at least prior to 1985. Meetings held by local gay community organizations drew little response, and the one community activist interviewed for this study was jeered when he attempted to post a notice on an AIDS seminar inside the Crossroads. Persons who manned tables for AIDS fund raising remarked that interest and contribution levels among suburban patrons were disappointingly low. Lack of concern or awareness of AIDS persisted in the suburbs for at least a year after intense, and apparently widespread, discussion had begun in the urban areas and on local and national television. (In addition to AIDS, nearly all those formally interviewed were unaware of the dangers of hepatitis B among homosexual males, nor were they cognizant of the newly developed vaccine for that disease.)

A number of factors may account for the lack of concern about AIDS and other sexually transmitted diseases. First, most of those studied were coupling up and significantly reducing their participation in the gay subculture, especially interaction in the bars. Thus, reduced participation served to reduce information exchange about AIDS and other matters. Second, while the levels of reported sexual activities varied widely, the overall levels were quite low compared to those reported for urban homosexuals. In terms of probabilities, then, risk factors were somewhat lower. Also, in both interviews and extended observations, the incidence of sexually transmitted disease appeared to have been relatively low. Three persons formally interviewed and a few of their acquaintances acquired hepatitis B, and only one person, an acquaintance of a member of Sam's group and a person not widely known among those formally interviewed, had contracted AIDS by 1985.

Friendship among Suburban Homosexuals

In their study of homosexual couples, McWhirter and Mattison remarked that more studies were needed of the "extended families" that they found in their study of homosexual couples.[35] By "extended families" they meant those persons whom homosexuals chose as "family" for long-term supportive relationships. In a similar vein, Dennis Altman observed:

> Both lack of marriage and exclusion from the heterosexual world of conventional families tend to make friendship all the more important for homosexuals; while sociologists in recent years have shown some interest in gay coupling, they have tended to miss the significance of friendship among both gay women and gay men. Over the years, numbers of people have said to me that they place more importance on their friends than on their lovers and what many gay lives miss in terms of permanent relationships is more than compensated by friendship networks.[36]

Edmund White commented on the breadth and durability of homosexual friendships as friends become lovers and vice versa. He noted that common sexual orientation can bind together friendship groups from diverse backgrounds. White employed the metaphor of the large number of intertwining roots of "banyan trees" to describe the depth and breadth of the multiplicity of homosexual relationships.[37]

In view of the children-school-family values of the suburbs, coupled with the relative lack of social gathering places other than bars, it would seem that friendship groups and "extended families" (to use McWhirter and Mattison's term) would have been something of a necessity in the lives of suburban homosexuals. Clearly, the strongest and longest lasting bonds of support were found in Sam Montana's group. The group had begun to crystallize even before the observation for this study began in the early 1980s. It was in existence beyond the close of this study. Yet changes did occur.

In the fall of 1982, Sam moved in with a partner in the city; this relationship changed from one of love to friendship and back to love again. Sam's former housemate also took a partner in late 1983, and that relationship continues as of this writing. The newly formed union between Frank Orlando and Walt Haines (Frank was the veteran member of the group, Walt the newcomer) lasted only about one and a half years. Walt eventually drifted away from the group when his job took him to another part of the state. Sam's former housemate and his new partner tended to keep to themselves somewhat but still appeared perhaps once every six weeks on a weekend night at one of the two major suburban bars. These developments brought to an end the almost weekly weekend gatherings of the entire group. Still, almost everyone in the group stayed in touch by telephone. Three members, sometimes supplemented by a fourth, interacted with greater frequency, going out to restaurants, the bars, movies, or other spots on a weekly basis. The entire group gathered about two or three times a year to celebrate birthdays and Christmas and New Year's. Conversations among group members could be quite candid and deep. Group members did take one another into confidence. Relationships were close and supportive. Yet, for more serious matters of health or major financial exigencies, heterosexual relatives or homosexual partners were seen as the primary source of support. In terms of Sutherland's classic criteria of "frequency, duration, intensity" of interaction,[38] Sam's group seemed a rather cohesive group.

Sam's group, however, was not as heterogeneous as those portrayed by White.[39] Except for Sam's Argentine roommate, all were white Anglos. (The Latin American acquaintances of Sam's housemate were basically ignored by the group.) Most persons worked in middle- to lower-level white-collar positions with an income of between $13,000 and $30,000. This income range corresponded with an age range of twenty to forty-two, with the older members earning higher incomes. Sam's group had boundaries, and only white middle-class persons were even considered for membership.

Like Sam's group, Skip's was also made up of whites. Though most, with the exception of "Doc" Bonnelli, had lower incomes than those in Sam's group, members of Skip's group seemed less restrained, more capable of having more "good times." Yet, in terms of duration and overall cohesion, Skip's group did not fare as well as Sam's. Members of Skip's group began to drift apart within about two years of the group's initial formation. This was due partly to the dissolution of Skip's love relationship (the split up polarized the other two core members of the group, who had also become partners) and also to the fact that members of Skip's group were younger and less stable financially. As they scrambled for jobs and careers, as Skip put it, "Our lives and our careers simply took us apart in terms of time and distance." By 1985, few members of the group talked to one another even over the telephone. Skip himself was not seen or heard from for months at a time. When I reinterviewed Skip in early 1985, he did not name any members of his former group as current best friends. Another core member of Skip's group, Lance Morrow, bitterly remarked in early 1985, "I miss not having a stable bunch of friends. There are telephones, you know. I haven't heard from any of them."

While the stability of friendship in Skip's group may have come off the worse in comparison with the quality of life in Sam's coterie, it would be interesting to compare such groups with evidence concerning male friendship patterns in the general population. Though there is surprisingly little research on the latter, it appears that males in general do not form many deep friendships with other males.[40]

Paradoxically, then, the development of close, stable bonds of friendship among suburban homosexuals can be considered either unremarkable or, on the other hand, doubly remarkable. With homophobia reduced, it could be argued that friendship develops more easily among homosexuals and that the heterosexual, children-school-family environment of the suburbs promotes the development of a "secret society."[41] On the other hand, building and maintaining friendships among homosexuals can be considered difficult insofar as actual or potential sexual relationships could either unpin or undermine friendship relations. The evidence in either direction in this study is uncertain. While there were no apparent sexually based jealousies in Skip's more sexually open group, it might have been significant that Sam's group, which proved more enduring, maintained an "incest taboo" on sex within the group.

Another barrier to the formation of homosexual friendships may be the shyness and relative lack of interpersonal involvement reported by significant numbers of homosexuals as children and young adults.[42] Somewhat more than a third of the persons in this study indicated that they had been, and sometimes still were, loners or had otherwise felt apart from others. Indeed, nearly one-third of those formally interviewed were currently in the same situation as the majority of men in the friendship studies quoted above: they seemed to be without any close friends and uninvolved in friendship networks. Two of these loners were peripheral members of one or both of the groups discussed above; others remained unattached. While some seemed content with a loner or semiloner status, others were unsatisfied but unsure how to break out of it.

Being a Man

The above discussion of friendship among men, both homosexual and heterosexual, raised the crucial issue of gender: the subjects of this study were males and conditioned accordingly. In combination with their white, middle-class orientation, this variable was crucial in understanding why many of these suburban males remained loners and why it was so difficult to construct gay community organizations.

According to Deborah David and Robert Brannon, there are four themes underlying rules of male behavior: "(1) No Sissy Stuff, anything that even remotely hints of femininity is prohibited, (2) Be a Big Wheel: masculinity is measured by success, power, and the admiration of others . . . (3) Be a Sturdy Oak: manliness requires rationality, toughness, and self-reliance. A man must remain calm in any situation, show no emotion, and almost no weakness; (4) Give 'em Hell: men must exude an aura of daring and aggression, and must be willing to take risks, to "go for it" even when reason and fear suggest otherwise."[43]

Any macho behavior among the suburban subjects I studied was considerably moderated by middle-class upbringing and decorum.

Those formally interviewed were not trying to emulate the rough, silent, leather-clad, working-class "clone" appearance and manner favored by some urban gays. Only a few had black leather jackets. Most wore clean, neat jeans and stylish T-shirts that favored a "California" or "surfer" look. Ragged clothing and torn jeans were viewed as "trashy."

Most of those formally interviewed were politely verbal in social settings. They were able and unafraid of ordinary give-and-take dialogue and banter. Serious conversation about politics or culture was generally avoided. Restrained hugs and kisses were used in exchanging greetings. Other than that, there was little or no toleration of effeminate behavior—though Sam and one of his group eventually dressed in drag for a Halloween party.

There was strong disapproval of public drunkenness. Men were expected to hold their liquor or taper off consumption. Drug use was also disapproved—though one quietly admitted to snorting coke if and when he could afford it.

The male virtue of risk taking and courting danger was *not* seen as admirable as it might endanger career and life-style goals. There was something of an ambivalent outlook toward those subjects who openly sought multiple sexual encounters. It was expected that gay men would be attracted to "hunks" and be tempted to approach such persons for sexual encounters. Occasional conquests of this sort—by single men— were admired. Yet the middle-class standards against "excessive" appetites applied. The few subjects who went to the baths or sought sexual encounters in parks were discreet, even faintly embarrassed. Once AIDS had begun to affect people in the suburban area directly, most of these men became very circumspect and careful.

The traditional male community of the sports world—either participating in or attending sporting events—was not attractive to most. (Only two of those formally interviewed were sports participants.) Practically no one was interested in participating in church, school, or other typical suburban community institutions. Only leisure gatherings or brief vacation getaways could bring the subjects together.

Masculine emphases on self-reliance and individualism, combined with the time and effort needed for work and home building, blocked any perceived need for gay community institutions. Though some men can be effective at building such structures, male sex-role conditioning does not seem conducive to creating and sustaining nonmilitary, non-sports-oriented communities. In suburban, middle-class America, women have been trained as the primary community builders. (However, it should be noted that the increase in two-income heterosexual families has led to complaints by teachers and clergy that they, too, lack people to volunteer for community building.)

Conclusion

The findings of Weinberg and Williams regarding homosexuals in outlying areas away from urban centers were confirmed in the initial phase of this field study.[44] Suburban homosexuals were, indeed, more circumspect, were more fearful of exposure, anticipated more intolerance and discrimination, and had fewer homosexual relations, less homosexual sex, and less social involvement with homosexuals and more social involvement with heterosexuals. The passage of four and a half years, however, moderated some of these tendencies to varying degrees, though the suburban environment and the middle-class orientation of nearly all subjects continued to inhibit greater involvement in homosexual activities.

The formation of homosexual identity was also inhibited in the suburbs, confirming Troiden and Goode's findings on the effect of geographic context. The findings of Dank, Troiden, and others with regard to age or generational cohort were also confirmed in this study: older homosexuals have had a more difficult time "coming out" than younger homosexuals.[45]

Though Weinberg and Williams found that the differences among their urban and outlying-area subjects were small, the data on suburban homosexuals gathered in this study contrasted markedly with those obtained by Bell and Weinberg in their study of urban homosexuals in the late 1960s.[46] However, the extent to which such differences were a product of time or geography, or a combination of both, is problematic.

The findings of this study must be considered a challenge to the thesis that all or most homosexuals, especially middle-class homosexuals, already reside, can reside, or want to reside in large urban areas. Recession, inflation (especially in real estate), and crime or the fear of it have affected homosexuals and heterosexuals alike. Middle-class homosexuals are likely to go where jobs and affordable housing are—just like everyone else. As indicated at the outset of this study, current trends favor the suburbs.

Though the greater institutional diversity and support of large concentrations of homosexuals in the city may continue to hold some allure, it is unlikely that middle-class homosexuals will move there solely for purposes of sexual life-style. Continuing changes in the life-styles of suburban homosexuals, including efforts by some to construct and expand their own support structures or "satellite cultures,"[47] merits attention.

An AIDS Epilogue

"This is the day for which Skip Barrows was born," intoned the Catholic priest. "We are all destined to die. But Skip was not afraid to die. As we are told in the children's story *The Velveteen Rabbit*, when you're loved you become real. And when you're real, you're for all time, forever. Skip was very real. He loved his friends, and his friends loved him."

About forty-five mourners were at the memorial service at Forest Lawn's Church of Our Heritage on a warm August Sunday in 1988. Skip had died two days previously in the arms of his lover, at home, after a two-year struggle with AIDS. The man who had just turned thirty had achieved nearly everything he wanted—a secure, high-paying job, a lover, and a house—only to fall victim to AIDS.

When I began the fieldwork for this study, even when I conducted the interviews in 1982, the spread of AIDS was receiving only sporadic coverage in the media. I did not ask about the disease in the interview schedule. Quietly and steadily, however, word was spreading in the urban gay ghettos of a new and deadly disease. And, as has been well documented, nearly every major institution in society initially neglected the disease. So did many suburban homosexuals.[48]

As the number of AIDS cases began to multiply in the urban centers, the attitude of many suburban homosexuals was somewhat blasé and fatalistic. Many of those formally and informally interviewed desperately tried to neutralize the emerging trend in the national data that probability of contracting AIDS was strongly related to a high number of sexual partners in conjunction with sexual practices.

As the 1980s wore on, nearly everyone had heard of "someone" who was not promiscuous yet had come down with AIDS. Conversely, everyone had heard of promiscuous people who were testing HIV negative. Such incidents reinforced a random "unlucky break" theory of AIDS. "It only takes once," was the common refrain. (The last person interviewed for the study in early 1983 was even more adamant, dismissing the AIDS "scare" as "propaganda.")

Though the suburban subjects of this study were not nearly as sexually active as urban homosexuals, many nonetheless condoned—in fantasy, if not action—having multiple sexual partners. AIDS directly threatened such freedoms. Like the more vocal, gay liberation groups, suburbanites had trouble acknowledging the dangers posed by AIDS with regard to such preferences. Homosexual males were caught in a classic case of cognitive dissonance. Two opposed items of information had been learned: lots of uninhibited sex is wonderful; lots of uninhibited sex can be fatal. One way of trying to balance these two dissonant thoughts was the "random theory" of AIDS discussed above.

As seems to have been the case in the urban centers, personal knowledge of someone who had AIDS or had died of the illness suddenly brought increased awareness. In 1985, a Hispanic acquaintance of Richard Hernandez's died of AIDS. In 1984, Richard had hosted a birthday party for the young man, who worked part time in a local bathhouse. Though few persons interviewed for this study knew the victim directly, word spread.

Early in 1986, George Adams, a friend and one-time date of Sam Montana's, died suddenly of AIDS. Those who had seen George at the local health spa and at the bars thought a slimmed-down George was really getting in shape. Then, suddenly, the recent college graduate and real estate broker was gone. Word of his death moved slowly, allegedly in deference to his family. While the death of Richard Hernandez's friend was neutralized by his bathhouse employment, no such rationale could be applied to George Adams. George had been "out" for only about three years. He had not acquired any reputation for promiscuous behavior.

AIDS and information about it moved slowly and quietly. Most still held fast to the fatalistic "it only takes once" attitude. Activist Al Paulson fumed that the local branch of the county health department did not cooperate in anti-AIDS efforts.

It might be said that AIDS officially came to this suburban area on the last Sunday night of April 1986. On that night, a benefit was held at Kings to raise funds for a popular bartender who had contracted

AIDS. He had limited hospitalization coverage, but the owner of the bar, Joe Sampson, had taken the ill bartender into his home. The fund-raiser was held on the busiest night of the week at Kings and could not be ignored.

Compared to reports from gay centers in New York and San Francisco, the spread of the disease seemed to be quite slow. (By 31 May 1987, there were forty-six reported cases of AIDS in the county health district that contained the Crossroads and Kings. Approximately half these cases were believed to be related to the heavy drug use in minority ghettos in the area. The Hollywood-Wilshire district, on the other hand, had 1,056 AIDS cases.)[49]

The middle-class subjects of this study appeared to become AIDS aware much more rapidly than the younger, more blue-collar clientele of both Kings and the Crossroads. By 1987, most subjects reported that they had begun to restrict sexual activities and that they had been doing so for quite some time. But most were anxious about being tested for the AIDS antibody. Indeed, it was a difficult subject to bring up in casual conversation. To my knowledge, only two of those formally interviewed had been tested for the AIDS antibody by the end of 1986. By mid-1988, two more had been tested.

In 1987, Bill Englander had returned to California from Colorado, where he had tried, unsuccessfully, to rebuild a relationship with his ex-lover. He stayed for a time with his brother and then for a while with Frank Orlando. Bill tested positive for the AIDS antibody and reported to two other subjects that he was beginning to experience symptoms of the disease. He suddenly left California and, presumably, returned to the Midwest to be cared for by relatives. At the time of this writing—mid-1988—no one had heard anything else.

Skip and Bill were two of the most sexually active people formally interviewed. Their cases confirm data from national sources indicating a correlation between level of sexual activity and the probability of acquiring AIDS. On the other hand, another of the most sexually active persons interviewed, Doc Bonnelli, claims to have tested negative. Two other persons informally interviewed who had a history of frequent sexual encounters also tested negative.

Mark Ford and Doug Lucas, a couple who had lived together for five years, were among the first to be AIDS aware. They had a close friend who worked with the Shanti organization, one of the first groups to provide support services to AIDS patients. Doug claimed to have curtailed all "extracurricular activity." In view of Doug's history of sexual adventures, Doug and Mark practiced safe sex within their relationship. They also still occasionally have safe-sex encounters with those whom they feel they know "very well." As of 1988, both had thought about being tested for AIDS, but neither had done so. Doug claimed mistrust of confidentiality rules.

Brad Smithers, still active in urban gay civic organizations, stated that he had cut down on sexual activity a great deal. What few encounters he had recently were strictly safe sex. Brad reported channeling libidinal energies more into organizational activities and friendships.

Both education and occupation appeared to have played a role in AIDS awareness. Among those first alarmed by AIDS whom I observed were those in the health professions and, next, those in other professions. Men who had homosexual friends or acquaintances in urban areas—such as Brad Smithers, Mark Ford, and Doug Lucas—were also AIDS aware early on.

Activity at the local bars dropped off for several years beginning in 1984, according to Crossroads manager Carl Smith. "It really kicked us in the ass for about three years," he said. "But, lately, our crowds have been picking up. Weekends are great—though not as good as they used to be. It's sort of like the herpes epidemic a few years ago. That hit us, too. People stopped going out for a while. Then they came back."

Those subjects who still visited the local taverns periodically—such as Jim Ramos—concurred. Though the crowds were beginning to come back, however, some noticed a difference. "There's a lot more of just looking than there used to be," commented Chuck Reynolds. "People don't go home with one another like they used to." But Carl Smith disagreed. "I don't know about that. There are a lot—no, let's say a core group—of people here who still say 'anything goes.' People still aren't playing safe."

The ability to reign in sexual impulses had a definite effect on those I observed with regard to response to AIDS. Subjects such as Doc Bonnelli, Bill Englander, Skip Barrows, and, more quietly, Walt Haines had formidable sex drives—whether derived from social conditioning or "libido." Bill Englander and Walt Haines frequented bathhouses, and Skip paid only occasional visits. By 1990, all but Doc had contracted AIDS.

Those who were "prudes"—owing to libidinal energies or social conditioning—adjusted far more easily to the necessities of safe sex.

Tim Halston and Jack Worthington were quite ready to abandon what little involvement they had with same-sex contacts and the gay subculture in general. Neither had ever liked the bars. Tim stopped going altogether. "It's so depressing," he said with a shudder. "When you think that all those people standing around are probably diseased—ugh. It's so creepy." Jack Worthington had entered into a long-distance relationship but admitted that he would probably have stopped seeking and going out altogether if he had not found his mate when he did.

AIDS and Heterosexually Married Men

"Most of my married customers are gone," said bar manager Carl Smith in 1988. "I suppose most of them are staying home with the wife and kids. Yeah, that's the group I really don't see much of anymore."

Any sexual counterrevolution wrought by AIDS may have had the greatest effect on heterosexually married homosexuals. Broderick has suggested that up to half of all homosexually oriented males may be married to women.[50] It is reasonable to contend that many of these heterosexually married homosexuals live in the suburbs.

If true, then the decline of middle-class, middle-aged males in suburban gay settings may be largely due to the flight of marginal or married homosexuals from such contexts. The AIDS threat has unquestionably upped the risks of sporadic homosexual extramarital activity, and abandonment of marriage for a more openly gay life-style must be viewed as even more chancy.

Katie Leishman has posed an intriguing possibility regarding those with ambivalent or weak gay identities, especially if they have bisexual impulses. Of these "closet straights," she has written, "The painful dilemma of closet gays has already become a major theme of the epidemic. Less will be heard about another group, who might be described as closet straights. AIDS gives gay men a powerful motive to examine the sources and strength of their commitment to their sexual preference."[51]

Except for Tom Mahoney, who married heterosexually, practically no one in this study "re-converted" to a heterosexual lifestyle or identity. But AIDS considerably hastened other processes propelling disengagement from gay life for many, if not most, of those formally interviewed.

Notes

1. Joseph Harry, "Urbanization and the Gay Life," *Urban Problems* 17 (1974): 13–27; Joseph Harry and William B. DeVall, *The Social Organization of Gay Males* (New York: Praeger, 1978), pp. 134–51.
2. See Carol A. B. Warren, *Identity and Community in the Gay World* (New York: Wiley, 1974); Landon Y. Jones, *Great Expectations* (New York: Ballantine, 1980).
3. See Laud Humphreys and Brian Miller, "Identities in the Emerging Gay Culture," in *Homosexual Behavior,* ed. Judd Marmor (New York: Basic, 1980), pp. 142–56.
4. Charles Silverstein, *Man to Man: Gay Couples in America* (New York: Quill, 1981); David McWhirter and Andrew M. Mattison, *The Male Couple: How Relationships Develop* (Englewood Cliffs, N.J.: Prentice-Hall, 1984). R. R. Troiden, "Becoming Homosexual: A Model of Gay Identity Acquisition," *Psychiatry* 42 (1979): 362–73; R. R. Troiden and Erich Goode, "Variables Related to the Acquisition of a Gay Identity," *Journal of Homosexuality* 4 (1980): 143–56. Harry and DeVall, *Social Organization;* Barry Dank, "Coming Out in the Gay World," *Psychiatry* 34 (1971): 180–98. Laud Humphreys, *Tearoom Trade* (New York: Aldine, 1970); Laud Humphreys, *Out of the Closets,* 2d ed. (Englewood Cliffs, N.J.: Spectrum, 1975).
5. T. S. Weinberg and Colin Williams, *Male Homosexuals: Their Problems and Adaptations* (New York: Oxford University Press, 1974), p. 132. Troiden and Goode, "Variables," p. 385.
6. C. Mack Gilliland, "Lamplighter in the Suburbs," *The Gay Pride Souvenir Program* (Los Angeles: Christopher Street West, 1982).
7. All names of persons and locales in this study are, of course, pseudonyms.
8. Warren, *Identity and Community;* Barbara Ponse, *Identities in the Lesbian World* (Westport, Conn.: Greenwood, 1978); Susan Krieger, *The Mirror Dance: Identity in a Woman's Community* (Philadelphia: Temple University Press, 1984); Alan Bell and Martin S. Weinberg, *Homosexualities* (New York: Simon & Schuster, 1978); Joseph Harry, *Gay Children Grown Up* (New York: Praeger, 1982), and *Gay Couples* (New York: Praeger, 1984).

The strength of the ethnographic approach, of course, is that one can study a small number of persons in depth for a number of months or years. There are, however, two weaknesses of such procedures. The first is lack of quantification and precision. The second has to do with doubts as to how "representative" the key characters in an ethnography are. However, the hidden and stigmatized nature of homosexuality makes the gathering of "representative samples" of such persons extremely difficult, if not impossible. As Bell and Weinberg have written, "Nowhere has a random sample of homosexual men and women ever been obtained, and given the variety of circumstances which discourage homosexuals from participating in research studies, it is unlikely that any investigator will ever be in a position to say that this or that is true of a given percentage of all homosexuals" (*Homosexualities,* p. 22). Even more specifically related to the aims of this study are the comments of Weinberg and Williams (*Male Homosexuals,* p. 96): "However, representative samples are not necessary when the researcher's aim is neither to generalize specific quantitative values nor to generalize beyond a specific group or situation."

9. See Weinberg and Williams, *Male Homosexuals;* and Harry and DeVall, *Social Organization.*
10. Dank, "Coming Out"; Kenneth Plummer, *Sexual Stigma: An Interactionist Account* (London: Routledge & Kegan Paul, 1975); Troiden, "Becoming Homosexual"; Eli Coleman, "Developmental Stages of the Coming Out Process," *Journal of Homosexuality* 7 (1982): 31–43.
11. Troiden, "Becoming Homosexual," p. 363.
12. Warren, *Identity and Community.*
13. Plummer, *Sexual Stigma,* p. 141.
14. Dank, "Coming Out"; Troiden and Goode, "Variables"; Gary McDonald, "Individual Differences in the Coming Out Process for Gay Men: Implications for Theoretical Models," *Journal of Homosexuality* 8 (1982): 47–60; Warren, *Identity and Community.*

The precise definition and nature of these stages and their boundaries seemed clear enough in many cases but problematic in others. For example, the signification and full self-identification or "coming out" stages seemed to merge in the case of forty-year-old Jake, who spent his childhood and adolescence in a rural part of the Midwest. At the age of fourteen, he discovered a book on human sexuality hidden in his parents' home. There was a chapter on homosexuality. "When I read that chapter, I knew immediately that's who I was. I'll never forget it, as it was one of the most traumatic evenings I've ever had in my life. I just knew. I had to go through this entirely alone. There was simply no one to talk to. Oh, I sort of considered briefly discussing it with the family doctor. I just felt very alone. I wondered if there were anyone else like me. After that night, I continued to participate in school activities and to date and all that. But it was all a facade, and I knew it."

As most of the models predict, Jake went through this signification process alone. Yet there was no brief or lingering period of doubt or denial as in most signification events. Instead, Jake simultaneously "defined himself to himself as a homosexual," the definition of coming out as offered by Troiden ("Becoming Homosexual," p. 367). As will be seen in the following section, the boundary between coming out and stabilization of homosexual identity was not always clear, nor was passage necessarily one way.

Another theory of homosexual behavior and identity, that of T. S. Weinberg ("On 'Doing' and 'Being' Gay: Sexual Behavior and Homosexual Male Self-Identity," *Journal of Homosexuality* 4 [1978] 143–56), while generally confirmed, sometimes was difficult to operationalize. Weinberg studied sexual behavior and homosexual male self-identity among thirty male homosexuals in terms of a combination of sequences of *engagement* in sex, the *suspicion* of homosexual orientation, and *labeling* oneself homosexual. Thus, the possible sequences could be "ESL" (engagement-suspicion-labeling), "SEL" (suspicion-engagement-labeling), "SLE" (suspicion-labeling-engagement), and a more direct pattern, "EL" (engagement-labeling). In applying Weinberg's categories to the present study, problems emerged in some individual cases in determining the sequence of orderings, especially "engagement" vs. "suspicion." The two events often occurred simultaneously, and there was some difficulty in determining just which experiences should count as "homosexual" since the subjects themselves might not have viewed them as such. Still, use of these categories generally yielded the same findings for my sample as for Weinberg's. The most common pattern was

"ESL" (eleven cases). The second most common pattern—as in Weinberg's study—was "SEL" (seven cases). There were four cases each in the "EL" and "SLE" sequence categories.

15. The term is Troiden's ("Becoming Homosexual," p. 370).

16. See Harry and DeVall, *Social Organization*.

17. Troiden, "Becoming Homosexual," pp. 368, 369. See also Dank, "Coming Out"; and Harry and DeVall, *Social Organization*.

18. Silverstein, *Man to Man*. Weinberg, "On 'Doing' and 'Being' Gay."

19. Yet one person formally interviewed, and two more informally interviewed, did not adopt homosexual identities even though all three had long-term relationships with other men. Clearly, such a situation strains Dank's definition of "closet queen" as one "who may continue to have homosexual desire and may possibly engage in homosexual relations for many years, but yet . . . not have a homosexual identity" ("Coming Out," p. 192).

    The primary explanation, again, lay in age cohort and sociohistorical factors. Two of the men who had long-term partners were over fifty. They had maintained their homosexual liaisons in the more sexually repressive 1950s, 1960s, and 1970s. Most of their friends were heterosexual, as was their universe of meanings. They lacked information and meaning about homosexuality. "We lived in a world of our own," said one, while another, recalling his relationship, which began in the mid-1950s, said simply, "We knew our relationship was unusual, but we *didn't have a name for it then*." The third person in this situation was thirty-nine when I met him in 1983 and had been heavily involved in a church-school community. Again, his information pertaining to definition and discussion of homosexuality had been severely limited. Ultimately, he and his partner became divided over homosexual self-identification. His partner refused so to acknowledge the situation, ended the relationship, entered psychotherapy, and eventually married a woman.

20. Troiden, "Becoming Homosexual," p. 371.

21. Weinberg and Williams, *Male Homosexuals*.

22. See Warren, *Identity and Community*.

23. Silverstein, *Man to Man*.

24. Harry and DeVall, *Social Organization*, p. 63.

25. Weinberg and Williams, *Male Homosexuals*; Harry and DeVall, *Social Organization*; Bell and Weinberg, *Homosexualities*.

26. Harry and DeVall, *Social Organization*, pp. 25–26. Harry and DeVall also note that increasing involvement with middle- or upper-middle-class occupations tends to diminish involvement in the homosexual milieu and increase the number of heterosexual contacts.

27. Warren, *Identity and Community*.

28. Harry and DeVall, *Social Organization*, p. 80.

29. See Silverstein, *Man to Man*.

30. Letitia Anne Peplau, "What Homosexuals Want in Relationships," *Psychology Today* 15 (March 1985): 28–38.

31. Dennis Altman, *The Homosexualization of America, the Americanization of the Homosexual* (New York: St. Martin's, 1982), p. 190.

32. McWhirter and Mattison, *The Male Couple*.

33. Marshall Kirk and Hunter Madsen, *After the Ball* (New York: Doubleday, 1989).

34. See Harry and DeVall, *Social Organization;* Laud Humphreys, conversation with the author.

35. McWhirter and Mattison, *The Male Couple.*

36. Altman, *The Homosexualization of America.*

37. Edmund White, "Paradise Found," *Mother Jones,* June 1983, pp. 10–16.

38. Edwin H. Sutherland, *Criminology,* 4th ed. (Philadelphia: Lippincott, 1947).

39. White, "Paradise Found."

40. In interviewing over two hundred men and women, Lillian Rubin discovered that "over two-thirds of the single men couldn't name a best friend. Of those who could, it was much more likely to be a woman than a man who held that place in their lives. In contrast, over three-fourths of the single women had no problem in identifying a best friend and that person almost always was a woman" (*Intimate Strangers* [New York: Harper & Row, 1983], p. 129). In buttressing her own findings, Rubin discussed a *Newsweek* article on the paucity of close and nurturing friendships among men ("Of Male Bondage," *Newsweek* 99 [1982]). With regard to the relationship between male friendship (or lack thereof) and homosexuality, one statement quoted in Rubin's work stands out: "Let one male approach another with talk of needing a kindred spirit and the listener will start looking for the closet from which the speaker must have emerged" (*Intimate Strangers,* p. 131).

   In a similar vein, Herb Goldberg wrote that "many men I interviewed admitted to not having one intimate male friend whom they totally trusted and confided in. However, most of them seemed to accept this as being a normal and acceptable condition" (*The Hazards of Being Male* [New York: Signet, 1976], p. 127). Like Rubin, Goldberg noted the perceived sexual threat posed by same-sex friendship: "Getting close to another man, particularly if one does not have an equally close female in one's life, often mobilizes intense sexual anxieties, doubts, and suspiciousness" (p. 132). Marc Fasteau also commented on the stilted, superficial quality of male-to-male friendships and noted that "a major source of these inhibitions is the fear of being, or being thought, homosexual" (*The Male Machine* [New York: McGraw-Hill, 1974], p. 15).

41. Compare Warren, *Identity and Community.*

42. See Harry, *Gay Children.*

43. David and Brannon quoted in Michael S. Kimmel and Martin Levine, "Men and AIDS," in *Men's Lives,* ed. Michael S. Kimmel and Michael A. Messner (New York: Macmillan, 1989), p. 346.

44. Weinberg and Williams, *Male Homosexuals.*

45. Troiden and Goode, "Variables"; Dank, "Coming Out"; Troiden, "Becoming Homosexual."

46. Bell and Weinberg, *Homosexualities.*

47. Humphries and Miller, "Identities in the Emerging Gay Culture."

48. Randy Shilts, *And the Band Played On* (New York: St. Martin's, 1987).

49. Data provided by the Los Angeles County Department of Public Health.

50. Carlfred Broderick appeared on "The Oprah Winfrey Show" on 15 October 1986.

51. Katie Leishman, "Heterosexuals and AIDS," *Atlantic Monthly,* February 1987, p. 52.

SEVEN

Miguel: Sexual Life History of a Gay Mexican American

Joseph Carrier

The following brief sexual life history of an acculturated gay Mexican-American male, born in an east Los Angeles barrio in 1948, illustrates some important cultural and behavioral differences that exist between the Anglo and the Latino gay worlds. Gay liberation in the United States has essentially been a middle-class Anglo phenomenon, a social movement organized and run by middle-class Anglo-American males. Gay neighborhoods and establishments in large American cities are thus predominantly populated by Anglo males. Ethnic minority gay males who move in the mainstream Anglo gay world are generally highly acculturated Latino, black, and Oriental males.

The Latino gay world in the United States is essentially composed of relatively small social networks that utilize "gay Latino bars" and private living spaces as meeting places. To my knowledge, there are no "gay ghettos" in Latino areas of large American cities. Unlike many of the Anglo-American males who populate gay neighborhoods in San Francisco, Los Angeles, Chicago, and New York, many Latino gay males (perhaps a majority) continue the Latino tradition of maintaining very close ties with their families and "straight" friends even when they have moved away from their homes.

The small social networks are made up of overlapping circles of "gay" Latino friends. Group cohesion in gay networks is generally maintained by regularly scheduled weekend parties that include "camping," gossiping, food, and dancing. The parties are also often used to introduce new gay friends into the social networks. An important characteristic of the friendship circles is the inclusion of "straight" friends and relatives in many of their social functions. It is therefore not at all unusual to find "straight" people included in their parties, social outings, and visits to Latino gay bars.

Although Latino gay bars are still relatively small in number compared to Anglo gay bars, there is usually at least one in most cities having a large Latino population. The largest number of exclusively Latino gay bars are in California, the majority (eight at last count) being in the greater Los Angeles area. The major specialities of these bars are "disco dancing" and/or "travesti" (i.e., male transvestite) shows. Like Anglo gay bars, they are used both for socializing with friends and as a marketplace for sexual partners. Unlike Anglo gay bars, however, they are not specialized by particular interest groups. There are, for example, no Latino "leather," "country and western," or S&M bars.

Certain "straight" drinking establishments in Latino barrios—cantinas, bars, and nightclubs—are also utilized by some gay Latinos to socialize and drink and to pick up straight Latino males as sexual partners. By social convention, most of the customers in these targeted places, which are modeled on those found south of the border, are men only, and most are Latino immigrants. It is not at all uncommon occasionally to find Latino "drag queens" (i.e., cross-dressing males) operating out of some of these bars, usually with the tacit approval of the owners.

Latino gay males may choose to relate only to the Anglo gay world, only to the Latino gay world, or to parts they like of both. In general, the choices they make appear to be related to acculturation. The greater their degree of acculturation, the greater the likelihood that they will participate in the Anglo gay world. Given that the AIDS epidemic first appeared in Anglo gay communities, those Latino men most likely to contract AIDS are those most fully acculturated in the Anglo gay world. Donald Wooten and his colleagues found that "a disproportionate number of Hispanic AIDS cases are reported from neighborhoods in which Hispanics are more assimilated. Nearly two-thirds of all Hispanic cases come from the least concentrated half of the Hispanic population. For the largest three risk categories . . . as well as for the case total, the number of AIDS cases decreases as the concentration increases. Since the population denominators for each group are equal, cumulative Hispanic AIDS incidence seems to rise with the degree of assimilation into the non-Hispanic population."[1]

Although Latinos in the United States share a common Latin American heritage, considerable differences in behavior may exist *between* groups depending on the country of their origin. The following sexual life history of an acculturated gay male of Mexican origin in California should thus be considered only suggestive of some of the cultural differences that exist between Anglo and Latino gay males. One should expect sexual life histories of acculturated gay males from other Latino societies to reveal similar differences with Anglo gay males, but they may also reveal important differences with Mexican-American gay male patterns of homosexual behavior.

Considerable behavioral differences may also exist *within* any given Latino group depending on the degree of acculturation to the mainstream Anglo culture. Degree of acculturation is in turn related to such variables as length of time in the United States and where and under what circumstances sexual socialization takes place. Patterns of homosexual behavior of Mexican-origin males in California thus vary from those that closely parallel male homosexual behavior in Mexico to those that closely parallel middle-class Anglo male homosexual behavior.

Miguel's sexual life history must therefore be viewed as an example of only one of the many paths that males of Mexican origin might follow in the development of individual patterns of homosexual behavior. In Miguel's case, it is the pattern of one first-generation U.S.-born Mexican American. It is of interest to note that the largest Latino population is composed of Mexican immigrants and first- and second-generation U.S.-born Mexican Americans. They make up close to two-thirds of the Latino population in the United States. In California, they make up over 85 percent of the total. Recent estimates by Robert Burciaga-Valdez indicate that "35 percent of the Mexican-origin population in California are immigrants and another 42 percent are first generation U.S.-born."[2]

Acculturation and Homosexual Behaviors

Before turning to Miguel's sexual life history, a brief overview will be presented of the ways in which acculturation may have affected his homosexual behaviors. Research findings on Mexican-American ethnicity by Susan Keefe and Amado Padilla suggest that there is "no single continuum of acculturation and assimilation. . . . Native-born Mexican Americans acculturate, but it is selective; and some ethnic traits, especially the maintenance of family ties, are sustained and surprisingly even strengthened from generation to generation." The most significant changes due to acculturation appear to occur between immigrant parents and their U.S.-born children. There is "no gradual, consistent course of sociocultural change, but an initial burst of Americanization followed by a long-term process of settling into an ethnic community of [Mexican Americans], a unique creation of the contact experience that contributes further to the ethnically plural society of the United States."[3]

The available data on sexual behavior indicate that significant differences exist between the homosexual behaviors of Mexican males in Mexico and middle-class Anglo males in California.[4] A major difference also exists in the way in which homosexuality is conceptualized in the United States and in Mexico.

A large majority of Mexican males involved in homosexual behavior appear to have strong preferences for playing either the anal insertive or the anal receptive sexual role, but not both; and, although they may engage in fellatio, anal intercourse provides the ultimate sexual satisfaction. A sizable minority play both sexual roles but may still have a preference for playing one sexual role over the other in anal intercourse. The foreignness of males in Mexico playing both sexual roles, however, is illustrated by the fact that in the Mexican "gay world" they are called "internationals."

Homosexual role playing appears to be the result of the sharp dichotomization of gender roles in Mexico. This dichotomization leads to a widely held belief that feminine males basically prefer to play the female role rather than the male. The link between male effeminacy and homosexuality is the additional belief that as a result of this role preference feminine males are sexually interested only in masculine males with whom they play the passive sexual role.

Although the motivations of males participating in homosexual encounters are without question diverse and complex, the fact remains that in Mexico cultural pressure is brought to bear on feminine males to play the receptive role in anal intercourse, and a kind of de facto cultural approval is given (i.e., no particular stigma is attached) to masculine males who want to play the active insertor role in anal intercourse.

One effect of homosexual role playing in Mexican society is that only the feminine male is labeled a "homosexual." By societal standards, the masculine self-image of Mexican males is not threatened by their homosexual behavior as long as they play the anal insertive role and also have a reputation for having sexual relations with women.

Recent data on the attitudes and sexual behaviors of Mexican males in California who emigrated at the age of puberty or older indicate that as a result of their sexual socialization in Mexico the majority continue to hold the same beliefs about homosexuality as they did before emigrating.[5] Those immigrant males previously involved in homosexual behaviors in Mexico continue to prefer either the anal insertive or the receptive sexual role and to follow cruising patterns similar to those found in their home states in Mexico.

Compared to Mexican males, Anglo males are generally believed not to have as strongly developed preferences for playing one sexual role over the other and not necessarily to look on anal intercourse as the preferred or ultimate sexual technique in homosexual encounters. The prevailing findings in the research literature are that it appears to be unusual for middle-class Anglo males to adhere to a particular sexual role and that fellatio is the most frequently practiced sexual technique.

For example, a survey of the sexual techniques of 575 Anglo homosexual males in San Francisco, conducted in 1969–70 by the Institute for Sex Research, found that "almost all of the homosexual men had used a considerable variety of sexual techniques during the year prior to interview. And almost none of them had exclusively engaged in one particular form of sexual contact. Fellatio was the sexual technique most frequently employed."[6] Previous studies by Evelyn Hooker and by Marcel Saghir and Eli Robins and more recent studies by J. Chmiel and his colleagues (connected with the AIDS epidemic and dealing with middle-class Anglo male homosexual behavior) have also made similar findings.[7]

Another major difference is that in mainstream Anglo culture in the United States the harsh judgment is often made that *all* males involved in homosexual behavior, no matter how infrequent, are "homosexual." Thus, even males with only a few homosexual encounters, regardless of sexual role played, may be given this stigmatizing label. The major effect of this is that "straight" Anglo males in general appear to be far more concerned about being approached by homosexual males than do "straight" Mexican males. "Queer bashing," for example, is an Anglo phenomenon that occurs only rarely in Mexico.

Given the significant differences that exist between the attitudes and behavior of Mexican and Anglo males, one should expect then that, as a result of selective acculturation by individuals of Mexican origin to mainstream Anglo patterns of sexual behavior, there will be considerable behavioral variations among Mexican-American males involved in homosexual encounters.

Recent findings from an ongoing study I am conducting with Raúl Magana support this expectation in that, not only have we found considerable variation in the homosexual behaviors of our Mexican-American respondents, but we have also found that in the evolution of their homosexuality the pathways followed appear to be determined to a large extent by whether their sexual socialization in adolescence was mostly with Mexican or Anglo-American partners. Composition of friendship networks while growing up thus determines to a large extent whether their homosexual behavior tilts toward Anglo-American or Mexican homosexuality.[8]

Sexual life histories of our Mexican-American respondents suggest that, although there are some variations in attitudes toward homosexuality held by persons living in traditional Mexican-American barrios, in general they parallel the belief systems held by the *mestizo* Mexican population in Mexico.[9] Machismo still provides an important guideline for masculine behavior. Little boys are taught to be "tough," not "soft and feminine like," by their older brothers, cousins, and neighbors. And they are made aware of the fact that males not considered tough or masculine run the risk of being labeled "puto" or "joto" (i.e., feminine and homosexual). As one respondent put it, "During junior and senior high school years male classmates could be vicious about kidding anyone not tough. . . . it was not uncommon for them to show their prowess with the challenge: 'I'll show you how tough you are,

I'll punk you . . . if you don't cool it, *me voy a chapetear* [i.e., make a woman of you].'" *Puto* and *joto* are commonly used expletives between young males in their barrios and may "be often used to call friends assholes or to harass someone known or suspected to be gay. . . . it is used relentlessly for any male with feminine traits."[10] As long as a male lives in his barrio, all-male socialization tends to continue, as is the case in Mexico, even after marriage.

Miguel's Sexual Life History

The following sexual life history of Miguel is based on participant observation and interviews conducted by the author over a period of sixteen years, from 1969 to 1985. At the time of our first formal interview, Miguel had just celebrated his twenty-first birthday. Our last formal interview took place a few weeks before he died at the age of thirty-seven. Miguel was my first research subject when I embarked on what has turned out to be a lifelong study of Mexican and Mexican-American male sexual behavior. He was, however, much more than an object of study. He was a close and dear friend who shared his family and friends as well as the most intimate details of his life. He helped me understand the joys and the sorrows of being a gay Mexican American. Miguel did not die as a result of AIDS. He died from a long bout with an equally dread disease that afflicts gay people, alcoholism.

Miguel's Family Background

Miguel was a first-generation *mestizo* Mexican American. His father was born in northern Mexico, his mother in east Los Angeles of Mexican parentage; all his grandparents were born in Mexico. He was the second of five children. He had one older sister and three younger brothers. Along with many aunts, uncles, and cousins, they grew up together in a Mexican-American barrio referred to as "East Los."

Miguel's father spoke to his children only in Spanish; his mother spoke mostly in English but at times in a mixture of English and Spanish. The father wanted his family run according to Mexican traditions. He was a quiet man, who never had much to say to his children. When he did, he usually spoke to them through their mother: "Why don't you tell Miguel not to do that," or, "I don't think he should go there."

Miguel recalled that while growing up he and his brothers and sister were afraid of their authoritarian father. The mother disciplined with words, the father with a strap. He recalled that the relationship between his mother and his father was relatively good. He and his siblings, however, were closer to their mother than to their father. She is remembered as being "more sympathetic with American ways, more reasonable"—a bridge to the Anglo world. The father always wanted them to behave like good Mexican children. And, although they had rather limited financial resources, the children were sent to private Catholic schools that were run mainly by Anglo nuns.

The Barrio

Miguel's barrio, "East Los," is located in an unincorporated area of Los Angeles County, a short distance from the center of downtown Los Angeles. It is populated mainly by low- and moderate-income immigrant Mexican and Mexican-American families who generally live in small houses on narrow and sometimes irregularly shaped lots. As is the custom in Mexico, the barrio contains a central *mercado* (market), many churches, small grocery stores, restaurants, night clubs, and cantina-style bars. The population density is high.

There are no "gay bars" in the barrio, but as noted above males searching for sexual encounters with other males often find partners in some of the "straight" restaurants, nightclubs, and cantina-style bars. Just a short distance outside the barrio, there are two neighborhood-type gay bars; one attracts mainly Anglo males, the other Latino males.

Miguel's Childhood

Miguel remembered his childhood as a very happy time. He and his older sister were very close and played a lot with cousins from both sides of the family who lived nearby. Because of large age differences—the oldest of his brothers was four years younger—he did not feel as close to his brothers. Compared to his male cousins, he remembered himself as a child being more quiet and somewhat aloof. From his early teens onward, he considered himself to be a loner. On looking back, he believed that this personality trait could be related to his being quiet and aloof as a child.

Miguel also recalled that his mother was very religious and that he was active in the Catholic church from a very early age. He said that outside the family the person that influenced his childhood the most was a German Dominican nun. From the third grade up to his first year in high school he spent most Saturday mornings helping her with her chores at the private Catholic school he attended.

Prepubertal Sexual Experiences

Miguel's first remembered sexual experiences were between the ages of four and five. They were with a male cousin one year older and his sister and consisted of games that included touching each other's bodies and sex organs. He remembered feeling that "we shouldn't get caught doing it," which gave their games an aura of secrecy and shame.

The three-way sexual games with his cousin and sister continued once or twice a month for about six years and were played in the nude when possible. Their games were never discovered by either set of parents or other family members. They ceased when Miguel's sister reached puberty at thirteen and no longer wanted to play sexual games with them. The three nevertheless continued to be close friends.

Adolescence

Miguel's first ejaculation occurred in bed a couple of years later at the age of thirteen while lying next to a younger brother who was seven at the time. They had been sleeping together for two years but had not been involved in any sexual games. Miguel said that he did not think his brother was aware of what had happened because they were wearing pajamas. They continued to sleep together, and several years later they occasionally engaged in mutual masturbation.

Miguel's major sexual target at that time, however, was his male cousin. They got together at least once a month for mutual masturbation. When his cousin moved to a different neighborhood, they exchanged letters and used a coded sentence to denote desire for sex: "Do you want your flowers watered?" Their meetings together were almost always for sexual relations and continued for the next ten years.

As their sexual relationship progressed, Miguel began to realize that his desire for sex was much stronger than his cousin's. He wanted to do much more than just mutual masturbation. During his last year of

high school, he finally got his cousin to try something new, anal intercourse. His cousin agreed to play the receptive role. Miguel, however,
always managed, as he put it, "to avoid being used anally." He was able
"to get away with it," he said, "because my cousin enjoyed being
fucked and because I was happy to go down on him and he would go
down on me." Miguel's sexual relationship with his cousin continued
even after the cousin married at age twenty. His cousin would arrange
meetings when his wife and child were away. Their sexual relationship
ended only because Miguel found "other guys" he liked "having sex
with better."

Miguel's reason for not wanting "to be used anally" was clearly revealed in a conversation about his first "one-night stand with a stranger" when he was seventeen: "He wanted to fuck me! I resisted. . . . I
wouldn't let him. I thought it would break my manhood. It's too passive and unmanly." Miguel had grown up knowing that there was one
thing he "didn't want to be, a *puto* or *joto* . . . one of those female-like
guys that take it up the ass."

When asked whether he remembered feeling guilty after having a
homosexual encounter, Miguel replied that he had "no feelings of re-
morse." He said that he had loved to look at the male nude from as far
back as he could remember and had never had any problems about his
choice of male sexual partners. Although religious, he did not believe
that his sexual practices were sinful.

Being a Mestizo Mexican American

Miguel was a trim, good-looking man of average height and build with
large, beautiful dark brown eyes and straight black hair. His demeanor
was masculine but only rarely macho and never feminine. There was
no denying his Indian heritage, however, and he sometimes exhibited
a passivity toward the outside Anglo world, something he disliked in
himself, and wished that his skin color was a lighter brown.

Miguel often said that he could leave his barrio and go to the Anglo
world outside but that he "couldn't get outside his skin." He was resentful of the racial slurs used against him by Anglo classmates in his
Catholic schools: (he was called "beaner," "spic," "brown boy," "indian") and of being chastised for speaking Spanish to school friends
(nuns would rap his knuckles with a ruler when they caught him). He
used to tell me that sometimes he would have liked to slip out of his

skin and become a "paddy." "Paddy" is Mexican-American gay slang for blond, blue-eyed, adolescent Anglo boys.

Miguel was nevertheless proud of his Mexican heritage, proud to be a Mexican American who could speak Spanish as well as English. He hated the bad reputation Chicano gangs gave his barrio and skillfully never became actively involved with them. He was in addition strongly motivated not to be a dependent person. He wanted to support himself and started working when he was thirteen. By the time he turned eighteen and had finished high school, he had held a number of part-time jobs. To establish independence from his family just prior to graduating from high school, he moved into a small house his parents had purchased next door. But within a few months, in response to his religious calling and with the encouragement of his family, he moved to northern California and became a brother in a Catholic monastery.

Young Adulthood

The monastic life, however, did not suit Miguel. He left after six months because he felt he was "missing too much on the outside." He returned to his barrio and moved back into the little house next door to his parents. His mother was very unhappy over his leaving the monastery. His father said little but was also not pleased.

Miguel's coming home turned out to be a major milestone in his life: he came out to himself and accepted that his homosexual feelings were more important than his heterosexual. He said he "had no guilt feelings over giving up the church," that he had been "celibate while living at the monastery." But he realized on returning home that he had never really felt sexually attracted to women. He was a loner in high school and "made no attempt to put up a front by taking out girls." As a part-time janitor's helper in a girls-only school, he remembered that he was "around girls a lot . . . used to notice boys at the school's gate waiting to see girls . . . and there I was right there with them and had no feelings about them." He rationalized his disinterest in women at the time on the grounds that since he worked after school he had no time anyway.

Miguel, at age eighteen, decided to explore the outside Anglo world for male sexual partners. Still concerned about maintaining a masculine appearance to outsiders, he nevertheless accepted that he was sexually attracted to men, not women. He intended to keep his sexual relationship going with his cousin, but he wanted to enlarge his homosexual world.

Shortly after returning from the monastery, he decided to spend a weekend in Ensenada, Mexico, with one of his few high school friends, an Anglo named Fred. Miguel had always been physically attracted to Fred, so even if nothing happened he felt "it would be a fun weekend." But, on the last night of their trip, Miguel said, "I lucked out. We were both drunk when we got back to the motel. . . . we took a piss at the same time. . . . Fred saw me looking down at his cock and started getting a hard on. I followed him back into the bedroom and pushed him onto his back on the bed and went down on him. I jacked off while sucking him. He pretended to be asleep. We never talked about it. . . . it was a one time thing."

Miguel also soon discovered that he could get picked up while walking or waiting for the bus along the streets of nearby downtown Los Angeles. His first experience was with a forty-year-old man who asked him if he "wanted to screw a woman." The second was with a thirty-year-old man who approached him at a bus stop and asked "what [he] was up to." Miguel said he "screwed both of them" at their apartments. He was delighted to find that he could easily maintain his preferred sexual practice, insertive anal intercourse.

After being home only two months, he realized that he was living too close to his family to carry out his new life-style. His mother made comments, and his brothers started harassing him about the "weird friends" he sometimes brought back to his little house. His sister, having difficulty with her father over her independent ways, left the house to live with some friends in another neighborhood. Miguel decided that it was also time for him to move, but into the Anglo world. He got a job with a large downtown department store as a messenger, bought an old car, and moved into an apartment with some newly found friends.

First "Gay" Year Homosexual Encounters

Miguel's sexual life opened up about halfway through his eighteenth year, in part as a result of having his own automobile. Driving along Sunset Boulevard one day in November 1966 near downtown Los Angeles he picked up a twenty-two-year-old effeminate Anglo male hitchhiker named Edward. They went to Edward's apartment, where for the first time Miguel had sex with an uninhibited gay-identified male. Miguel said, "We did everything . . . '69,' I screwed him, got screwed." On recalling the event just three years after it had occurred, he got very excited and said that it changed forever the way he felt about his body and what he could do sexually.

Miguel and Edward continued their sexual relationship for the next three months. During those months, he also had sex with Edward's twenty-two-year-old gay roommate Charlie, but he only "screwed him." As time passed, playing the anal receptive role with Edward left him feeling guilty afterward and somewhat depressed. Miguel also French kissed Edward, but he did not really enjoy it either; it made him feel "kind of stupid, silly, to tongue kiss another guy." He had French kissed girls first—something he had learned from his barrio friends during his early teens—so it was a more acceptable feeling.

A couple of months later, Miguel decided he had to change the way he cruised. He had been arrested by an undercover police officer while cruising along Hollywood Boulevard. It was his first contact with the law as a result of his homosexual behavior, and he was extremely fearful about being sent to jail and having his parents find out the reason for his arrest. Luckily, a female judge dropped the charges to disturbing the peace, and he was fined only fifty dollars. Miguel decided to stop picking up hitchhikers.

Since he was still too young to get into gay bars legally, Miguel decided it would be safer to spend most of his cruising time looking for sexual partners in a predominantly gay teenager's coffeehouse called Geno's, which Edward and Charlie had taken him to near Hollywood. The people Miguel met at Geno's further opened up the Los Angeles Anglo gay world for him.

Geno's served only soft drinks and coffee, so many patrons went there to socialize and cruise and then, through gay friendship networks, get invited to private gay parties after closing time, where they could dance and get drunk if they wanted to. Miguel said that until he was twenty-one he found most of his sexual partners either at Geno's or at after-hours private parties.

During the year following his discovery of Geno's, Miguel was so impressed by his sexual experiences and the gay world he moved in that he said he could clearly remember all his Anglo sexual partners and what they did in bed. There was a total of ten; three he had met at Geno's, the rest at after-hours parties. Half of them were in their late teens (eighteen to nineteen); the other half were in their early twenties (twenty-one to twenty-two). He had insertive anal intercourse with all of them but was receptive anally with only one. He had mutual oral sex ("69") with six. Only one was a one-night stand. Most of the rest (seven of ten) he had sexual relations with about five times; of the remaining two, he had ten sexual encounters in a little over a month with one named George and a sustained relationship (emotional as well as sexual) lasting four months with the other, named Tim.

Miguel further expanded his sexual repertoire during this year of intense homosexual activity. The two partners he was most involved with, George and Tim, introduced him to the pleasures of "rimming" (anal-oral contact). Miguel said that he had always been fascinated by the anus during sexual intercourse and knew that rimming existed. "They call it *beso negro* in Spanish," he said. But it seemed to him to be a disgusting practice, so he had not previously tried it with his cousin. When George first did it to him, Miguel noted that he was willing to let it happen because he was intoxicated not only with alcohol but also with George's looks, his first real blond, blue-eyed "paddy." George did it to him from the "69" position, so Miguel reciprocated by rimming him. Rimming also turned out to be a regular part of his sexual experiences with Tim, another blond, blue-eyed "paddy," and continued to be an important part of his sexual repertoire for the rest of his life with those males that especially "turned him on."

The Next Eleven Years

During the following eleven years, Miguel participated almost exclusively in the Anglo gay world. On reaching twenty-one, he phased out Geno's and turned to drinking and cruising in the gay bars of Hollywood and downtown Los Angeles. He also started having sex in bathhouses and in Griffith Park, a wilderness park adjacent to Hollywood. He said that he found the majority of his sexual partners in bars. Most of the rest he found in bathhouses and the park, a few occasionally while walking along Hollywood Boulevard. Looking back on these years, he estimated that he had on the average at least one or two different sexual partners weekly and that a large majority of them (80–90 percent) were one-night stands.

Most of his sexual partners were Anglo males, whom he loved to dominate as the anal insertor. He usually allowed them to take the lead in the kind of sex carried out, but he preferred to end up "screwing them in the ass." And he liked sleeping curled around them, his "cock against their ass." He was anal receptive only occasionally—with someone with whom he really felt a strong sexual attraction. Even then, being receptive usually left him feeling "grouchy and depressed."

Miguel became a part of the Anglo gay world, but he never lost the feeling drummed into him since early childhood by his male friends and relatives in the barrio that playing the female role in anal intercourse caused a "breaking of manhood . . . was too passive, unmanly." Every time he went to visit his parents in the barrio, he was reminded of it by graffiti on walls that had gang names marked out with asterisks and *putos* written nearby by rival gang members, indicating that the marked-out gang members "took it up the ass."

Miguel did not have male lovers. Instead, he occasionally had what he described as "short-time regulars: guys I can do things with like going to the beach and making trips. We have sex . . . no lovey dovey stuff . . . I don't like kissing and all those mushy things." But he did like to cuddle after sex, so when possible he liked spending nights with his regulars and his one-night stands.

Miguel had only two long-lasting intimate relationships with gay men. Both were with relatively wealthy Anglo gay men about ten years older and were established through sexual contact. He moved in and out of both of their lives during these eleven years. Miguel lived with one of them on and off for several years but always carefully noted to outsiders that he paid his share of expenses and that they no longer had sex and were thus just close friends. He lived with the other, "a Hollywood type" with a luxurious apartment, only on occasional weekends and also always wanted outsiders to know that it was not an exploitative relationship. He often credited himself with providing younger sex partners for the older man. One of the things he shared with both men was a love for travel. Through them he was able to travel places he would not have otherwise been able to afford. These travels helped motivate him to become a flight attendant when he as in his mid-twenties.

Miguel had some homosexual encounters with Mexican males during this period, most taking place in Mexico. He made his first trip south of the border a few months after his twenty-first birthday. He visited me in Guadalajara, where I was living at the time, and then took off on his own to visit Mexico City and Acapulco. He spoke Spanish well but was shy being around Mexicans and felt somewhat embarrassed about his Mexican-American accent. One of the friendship circles I was studying at the time was made up of very young (fifteen to eighteen) effeminate gay males who preferred to play only the receptive role in anal intercourse. On finding Miguel in my apartment, they immediately befriended him, complemented him on how well he spoke Spanish, and took him sight-seeing. When they returned to my apartment, they played their version of "spin the bottle" in which the winner had the option of having sex with Miguel. By the time he left Guadalajara, he had had sex with all but one member of the friendship circle.

On his way back to Los Angeles, Miguel stopped off in Guadalajara and told me about the many homosexual encounters he had had in Acapulco and Mexico City. He was surprised by how easy it was for him to find Mexican sexual partners, the more so since he was sight-seeing most of the time and not cruising. In Acapulco, he was also surprised to find American and European men coming on to him for sex.

Miguel returned to Mexico several times, but he told me that finding sexual partners was never his motive for traveling there; rather it was for the pleasure of being in the country of his origin. He usually took his parents or some of his family members with him. His major sexual interest during this time was still with "paddy."

Family Relationships

For his emotional needs, Miguel maintained close contact with his family and friends in the barrio throughout his life. He visited his parents weekly when living in Los Angeles and participated in most family celebrations. After becoming a flight attendant, he took them on many vacations not only to Mexico but also to other parts of the world served by his airline.

Miguel believed that his mother knew that he was gay, but they never talked openly about it. The only exception was when she was mad; then she would say things like, "I know about your friends." He further believed that his father did not know. He said, "He'd be broken by news about it." Only the oldest of his three younger brothers knew for sure; the other two probably suspected, he thought, since he had never married.

Miguel's relation with his sister was especially close. They had their secret past together, and she knew he was gay because he had told her shortly after returning from the monastery. Also, she had discovered a few months after he had come out to her that she was a lesbian and had divorced her husband. She and Miguel, along with an understanding female cousin, spent a lot of time together. Whenever the Anglo world was too much for him, he would turn to his sister and cousin for support and understanding.

Miguel's sister confirmed that their mother knew he was gay. She told me that on divorcing her husband and returning home she had confided in her mother that she had had a sexual affair with another woman and was a lesbian. Her mother responded to the news with anger and disappointment. She was perplexed as to what she had done wrong that made her two oldest children homosexual. She knew with certainty, however, that their father must never be told. So far as I know, he never has been.

Miguel's major conflict with his parents was related, however, not to his sexual orientation but instead to what he perceived to be their excessive use of alcohol. He was annoyed by finding them on many evening visits "loaded on beer." They were argumentive with him when loaded and invariably "picked on" him about something he had done that displeased them. Many of their quarrels were related to family finances. From Miguel's perspective, they took advantage of his generosity. In particular, he was annoyed by their not naming him sole heir of some property that they had jointly invested in.

Despite the drinking and quarrels, Miguel nevertheless loved his parents, siblings, and extended family and continued to spend lots of his spare time socializing with them. He went to mass with them, attended family fiestas, baptisms, and weddings, and was always there when needed because of illness or some other family crisis.

Heterosexual Relationships

One result of Miguel's becoming a flight attendant was a series of close relationships with some female coworkers. When first interviewed at age twenty-one, he said that he had never felt sexually attracted to women and so had never developed any close heterosexual relationships. He tried to change his feelings as he grew older, however, because he feared loneliness in old age and believed that one hedge against it would be the companionship of a wife and children. Age heightened his fear of rejection. "Age is a disturbing thing," he said. "I feel I'm not good looking. . . . Getting older isn't helping me. . . . The older I get, the less people are bound to approach me."

In his early twenties, Miguel started "taking some girls out from work" and would go "as far as French kissing, fondling their breasts, and getting an erection," but he never tried to have sexual intercourse with them. When asked how he thought his girlfriends felt when he did not try to take them to bed, he replied that it made him "all the more desirable in their eyes."

Miguel's first major heterosexual affair was with an Anglo flight attendant named Susan. They worked the same flights to Hawaii and the Far East for almost a year. During turn-around time, they spent many days together at the same hotel, enjoyed each other's company, became very close friends, and then lovers. According to Miguel, Susan really believed that they would eventually get married. He said that he had also hoped that they would get married and have children, but he was uneasy about his ability to maintain a marriage and cope with his homosexual desires at the same time. Their relationship was terminated close to a year after it started, but prior to marriage, when Susan discovered that he was having a sexual relationship with another (male) flight attendant as well as with her.

Miguel's second major heterosexual affair, which started a few months after he broke up with Susan and got on a different route, was with a Mexican-American flight attendant named Lupita. He and Lupita did not work the same flights but were on the same route, so they were able to be together often during turn-around time. Once again, Miguel hoped that he would eventually feel comfortable enough with Lupita and she with him to get married and have children. While their relationship was relatively good, it was never as close as the one he had had with Susan. Miguel attributed this to the fact that Lupita was probably suspicious from the beginning that he was also having sexual relations with men as well as with her. Although they talked openly about homosexuality and about male flight attendants known to be gay, something he never did with Susan, he still did not have the courage to tell her about his bisexuality and thus directly find out whether she would consider marriage knowing about this aspect of his life.

Fearing rejection once again, Miguel terminated the relationship after he and Lupita had been going together about six months and got himself transferred to another route.

Following his breakup with Lupita, Miguel became preoccupied with the notion that he was losing his reputation as a macho heterosexual flight attendant, a reputation that he had carefully built to counter the belief held by many in the industry that most male flight attendants are gay. He was very disturbed by this probable change in his image but felt powerless to do anything to prevent it from happening. He was convinced that Susan and Lupita were spreading rumors among his colleagues in the airline that he was gay.

With the realization that his interest in men was so strong that he would never be able to give up having homosexual relations and would never be able to find a woman interested in marrying a bisexual man, Miguel decided that he must accept the fact that he would never get married and never have a family. He also decided that, while he would continue to present himself as macho and straight, he had to accept the fact that behind his back people at work would continue their gossip that he was gay.

Miguel's Drinking Problem

It was about this point in time that Miguel's excessive consumption of alcohol began to interfere with his work. Though his dilemmas at the time about aging, loneliness, marriage, and self-image probably contributed to his drinking problem, they were not the only factors since he had been drinking excessively for several years and had been previously arrested for drunk driving.

Sociocultural as well as family factors also contributed to Miguel's pattern of excessive drinking. Recent research on the drinking practices of Mexican Americans has documented the fact that at both low and high frequencies of alcohol consumption Mexican-American males have patterns of higher consumption per drinking occasion than do males in the U.S. general population and that their patterns of high-intoxication-level drinking extend into and beyond middle age.[11]

Additionally, Miguel's gay life-style and access to alcohol as a flight attendant reinforced a compulsive drinking pattern that probably started when he worked as a salesman for a liquor distributor in Los Angeles, his job for a couple of years prior to joining the airline.

While working for the distributor of alcoholic beverages, he changed from drinking only beer to drinking liquor as well. One result of this was that, during an evening out with friends or at a bar, he would get drunk faster and consume larger amounts of alcohol than in his beer-drinking days. He also developed the tendency to finish a bottle of liquor once it was opened.

Miguel's Final Years

On turning thirty, Miguel changed his gay life-style. He was beginning to have to deal with the fact that he was an alcoholic. He also began to feel acutely the effects of the agist Anglo gay world, which penalizes its members for growing old. He found it more and more difficult to find "paddy" sex partners in gay bars and elsewhere. This in turn led to longer drinking bouts in bars. When he was put on medical disability by the airline for stress-related alcoholism, he decided to move back to his barrio.

During his final seven years, Miguel reestablished to himself and to others his Mexican-American identity. He grew a mustache, bought a motorcycle, and got a couple of tatoos. He lived in a rented house on the edge of his old barrio and continued his close relationship with his family. He did not give up all his Anglo friends, but he spent most of his time socializing with a small circle of gay Mexican-American friends at his house and at local Latino gay bars.

Miguel fought for a monetary settlement with the airline over his stress-related medical leave for alcoholism. He maintained that he could no longer effectively work as a flight attendant because the stress of flying would not allow him to recover from his alcoholism. He also declined to accept lower-paying jobs offered by the airline. He did accept medical services in the form of psychotherapy.

After close to a year on medical leave, the airline refused to make a monetary settlement, terminated the medical leave, and offered to reinstate Miguel as a flight attendant. Miguel accepted the offer. He was not happy to be back at his old job, but he was not able to face the alternative prospect of having to find a new job and the possibility of having to train himself for another profession.

Throughout what were his final years, Miguel had a rich and varied sex life. He told me that he had no difficulty in finding interested neighborhood boys as sexual partners; in fact, many came knocking on his door as the word got out about the availability of "sex and pot." But he had to be discreet and not let the barrio know about the sexual nature of their visits to his house.

Miguel shared his house and rent—and also sexual partners—with a relatively younger Mexican-American gay friend. He also established ongoing sexual relationships with several teenage boys in the barrio, two of them brothers. Though Miguel still enjoyed fellatio, he always ended up his sexual sessions playing the anal insertive role.

In addition, Miguel cruised the local Latino gay bars for sexual partners. Two of his best "Chicano" gay friends worked at one of them, and he would often stay there until closing time, when they would return to his house with selected "tricks" for a party. From time to time, he would return to the Anglo gay world in search of "paddy" sexual partners, but with little success.

Miguel tried to deal with his drinking problem through psychological counseling and Alcoholics Anonymous, but neither worked for him. He also tried to use marijuana as a substitute for alcohol, but that did not work either. Nothing seemed to help. He continued to drink as heavily at home as he did in gay bars.

Miguel developed pancreatitis and was warned that he must severely limit his consumption of alcohol or face a life-threatening coma. For about a year after the diagnosis, he went on and off the "antabuse" drug as a means of controlling his consumption of alcohol. He then stopped using it and slipped back into uncontrolled drinking. After a week of sustained heavy drinking, he became comatose and was hospitalized for about one week. His physician told him on leaving the hospital that his next coma might be his last one.

Miguel went back on the antabuse drug program, but on recovering his health once again discontinued it and resumed his old drinking practices. I remember going into his favorite Latino gay bar late one evening during this period and being told by his bartender friend that he had started drinking again and had just left. Six months later, on a Sunday morning, he died in a coma after a weekend of unabated heavy drinking.

Conclusion

Miguel's brief life had a tragic ending that is not unique to Mexican-American gay men. Alcoholism is an endemic disease in the gay world, one facilitated by the oppression of society at large, by gay cruising patterns that utilize drinking establishments as primary locations for meeting potential sexual partners, and by gay social events and parties that often include extensive alcohol consumption by participants as part of socialization.

Gay Mexican-American men may in addition have to deal with a cultural drinking pattern that leads many Mexicans and Mexican Americans to alcoholism.[12] Miguel often complained about finding his father and sometimes his mother inebriated. Although he never blamed his parents for his alcoholism, Miguel knew that his pattern of drinking was affected by their behavior.

Miguel's sex life was obviously influenced by both Mexican and Anglo cultural patterns of sexual behavior. He believed that he had had the best of both worlds and reflected happily many times about his good luck in having had access to both of them. Although he had enjoyed the Anglo gay world while he was in it, he felt fortunate about being able also to be sexually excited by men of Mexican origin.

During his final year, Miguel occasionally talked about the possibility of dying young. He looked at the possibility fatalistically. He had lived a good life by his reckoning and was happy about having moved back to his barrio and maintaining close relationships with his family and old friends.

Not too long before he died, Miguel told me about one of his many flying dreams. He said he had looked down and saw a line of people filing past a young man in a coffin. He was upset over the possibility that people would look down at him when he was dead and feel pity. He did not want that to happen and told his family that, should he die as a result of his disease, they should make sure that his coffin was closed at the rosary and the funeral. His family respected his wishes.

Notes

1. Donald Wooten et al., "AIDS among Hispanics in California," *California AIDS Update* (Sacramento Office of AIDS) 1, no. 6 (1988): 10.
2. Robert Burciaga-Valdez, "A Framework for Policy Development for the Latino Population: Testimony before the California Hispanic Legislative Conference," Paper no. 7207 (Santa Monica, Calif.: Rand Corp., 1986), p. 1.
3. Susan E. Keefe and Amado M. Padilla, *Chicano Ethnicity* (Albuquerque: University of New Mexico Press, 1987), pp. 189, 8.
4. For *mestizo* Mexican behavior patterns, see Joseph M. Carrier, "Cultural Factors Affecting Urban Mexican Male Homosexual Behavior," *Archives of Sexual Behavior*

5 (1976): 103–24, and "Mexican Male Bisexuality," in *Bisexualities: Theory and Research,* ed. F. Klein and T. Wolf (New York: Haworth, 1985). For Anglo patterns, see Alan P. Bell and Martin S. Weinberg, *Homosexualities: A Study of Diversity among Men and Women* (New York: Simon and Schuster, 1978). See also n. 9 below.

5. See Raul Magana and Joseph M. Carrier, "Mexican and Mexican American Male Sexual Behavior and Spread of AIDS in California," *Journal of Sex Research* (in press).

6. See Bell and Weinberg, *Homosexualities.*

7. See Evelyn Hooker, "An Empirical Study of Some Relations between Sexual Patterns and Gender Identity in Male Homosexuals," in *Sex Research: New Developments,* ed. J. Money (New York: Holt, 1965); Marcel T. Saghir and Eli Robins, *Male and Female Homosexuality: A Comprehensive Investigation* (Baltimore: Williams & Wilkins, 1973); and J. Chmiel et al., "Prevention of HIV Infection through Modification of Sexual Practices" (paper presented at the International Conference on AIDS, Paris, June 1986).

8. See Magana and Carrier, "Mexican and Mexican American Male Sexual Behavior."

9. The majority population in Mexico is *mestizo,* i.e., people of mixed Spanish and American Indian ancestry.

10. The quote is from a Mexican-American interviewer.

11. See M. Jean Gilbert, "Mexican Americans in California: Intracultural Variation in Attitudes and Behavior Related to Alcohol," in *The American Experience with Alcohol,* ed. L. Bennett and G. Ames (New York: Plenum, 1985); and Raul Caetano, "Alcohol Use among Mexican Americans and in the U.S. Population," in *Alcohol Consumption among Mexicans and Mexican Americans: A Binational Perspective,* ed. M. Jean Gilbert (Los Angeles: University of California, Los Angeles, Spanish Speaking Mental Health Research Center, 1988), pp. 53–84.

12. See Gilbert, ed., *Alcohol Consumption among Mexicans and Mexican Americans.*

EIGHT

The Symbolic Strategies of Chicago's Gay and Lesbian Pride Day Parade

Richard K. Herrell

The *Chicago* magazine listings of things to do for June 1988 contained the following item: "Neighborhood Festivals: Chicago is a city of neighborhoods, and these local festivals are a reflection of that ethnic diversity. All during the summer you can eat brats, tacos, pierogis, krumkake, and other ethnic foods, and then dance it off doing the marengue or the polka. For specifics call the Mayor's Office of Special Events."[1] This advertising copy is a sunny paraphrase of Chicago's rhetoric about itself, a city richly provided with colorful, tuneful, tasty differences. As for the inequalities, racism, and constant political warfare that deeply divide the city, well, that doesn't make for good rhetoric or ad copy.

In the last ten years, as the number of Chicago's parades and neighborhood festivals has grown dramatically, the Gay and Lesbian Pride Week activities, including the Pride Day Parade, are now routinely listed in city publications and newspapers. A few years ago, former mayor Jane Byrne, out of office and in her endless search to get back in, popped up out of a black Mustang convertible during the parade lineup and coyly announced to reporters that she was there that day because "this is one of our summer neighborhood festivals."

This chapter examines Chicago's Gay and Lesbian Pride Day Parade specifically in the context of Chicago's parades and festivals; an analysis of the gay and lesbian parades in New York, San Francisco, Los Angeles, or Europe might be quite different. The gay and lesbian parade in Chicago has adopted and transformed the parades of "ethnic groups"—the city's Irish, Polish, Mexicans, Italians, and so forth. "Ethnicity" has become a model for gays and lesbians, who now think of their community as one like other communities in Chicago, like them in having a space and a special parade to claim that space symbolically one day each summer, to express their relative cultural autonomy in the city, and to speak as a community with interests to legislators and other policymakers, but critically different from them in their historical exclusion from normative society.

I am considering strategies here not as utilitarian behavior but as elements in understanding creative acts that, in Kenneth Burke's words, "size up . . . situations, name their structure and outstanding ingredients, and name them in a way that contains an attitude towards them." In Burke's now-famous formulation, poetry "adopts various strategies for the encompassing of situations." Situations are "real," and the "strategies for handling them have public content." Naming is done "strategically"; it "embodies attitudes." Furthermore, implicit in poetic organization is the "assertion of an identity."[2] This self-understanding and representation of all kinds of culturally constituted units, including roles, statuses, groups, categories, etc., are constantly constituted, negotiated, and contested.

Burke was, of course, writing about poetic organization, and parades are not poems but organized social activities. Nevertheless, like all social actions, parades are goal directed, communicative, purposive activities, and all communicative behavior entails creativity. Burke's fundamental categories of *situation* and *strategy* focus our attention on critical aspects necessary to describe any creative act in a world of public cultural symbols.

The parade is a cultural routine in which strategic (for Burke, symbolic, creative) responses are made to the facts of being gay or lesbian in American society. The situation of gays and lesbians, including the parade's organizers, participants, and onlookers, has focused on two issues: first, invisibility, the assumption of universal heterosexuality—assumed unless there is some reason to believe otherwise—and, second, the stigma and entailed oppression of homosexuality, which is seen as sin by the religious establishment, sickness by the medical establishment, and crime by the state. These three institutional voices of homophobia have phrased their representations of gay men in part as the malfunctioning or malformation or maladjustment of gay men as *men,* men whose masculinity is in some way flawed, damaged, or abused. The more general cultural expressions of homophobia typically represent male homosexuals either as dangerous hypermen given to sex unbridled by the domestication of women or as men who are women (as traditionally seen), that is, as weak and thereby traitors to manhood in their (sexual) submission to other men and their failure to dominate women sexually. In either view, male homosexuals are thus seen as men whose inappropriate gender characteristics violate the correct power relationship between men and women.[3] The annual parade is, in part, a strategic response to the situation of being gay in a homophobic society.

An ethnographic account of complex activities such as parades must account for the speech and nonspeech acts that communicate (or fail to communicate) to others who share the same means of communication. "Symbolic strategies" in Burke must not be limited to consideration of aesthetic "symbols" or the sign type "symbol" of linguistic analysis but must encompass the pragmatic, purposeful, communicative behavior among people in the same society, implying a social theory of the use of signs, including speech and nonspeech acts. Thus, in Michael Silverstein's words, "a cultural description [is a] pragmatic description of how the social categories of groups of people are constituted in a . . . set of pragmatic meanings in many kinds of behavior."[4]

To consider the semiotic devices at work in parades, we cannot be limited to the purely linguistic realm of semantics but must think about the vast complex of linguistic and nonlinguistic signs known as indexes.[5] Anything in a communicative event that focuses the receivers' attention on a component of the social situation is an index.[6] Indexes signal the "presence of some entity" in the context of communication in which they are used. Purely indexical signs "signal some particular value of one or more contextual variables," the meaning of which is purely pragmatic.[7] Most important, they signal the structure of the context in which the index is used.

Parades in Chicago communicate to the city at large largely through nonlinguistic indexes that identify the parade as an event, as a particular, known category of organized activity, and that distinguish one parade from another by indexing "community." Communication is achieved through mostly nonlinguistic (but often audible) indexes. A parade is distinguished from other nonparade events (i.e., is indexed as a parade) by color guards, bands, floats, and "marching units" or contingents. The media and participants judge the relative importance of a parade by the number of participants, the number of contingents, the number of watchers, the length of time it take the parade to pass the reviewing stand, who attends, the extent of media coverage, and so forth.

What distinguishes one parade from other parades is its distinctive colors, flags, music, and other indexes of "community." Parades in Chicago are typically characterized by participants and commentators as representing or exemplifying a "culture" in the American folk sense of Irish or Mexican or Italian culture, typically characterized as including "cuisines, sights and sounds," "heritage and creativity," and "language, mores, and customs." Bystanders and organizers speak of a parade or festival as a way to "learn" about a culture.[8] A woman who had brought her young children to the Columbus Day Parade said she "wanted to teach them something about Italian Americans."[9] Likewise, "community" has come to mean virtually any group or even category of socially defined persons. (Witness the common and somewhat ludicrous expression "heterosexual community" that has gained currency during the AIDS crisis.) The unmarked "greater" or "mainstream community" is composed of specific, marked "communities."[10]

In order to understand the Gay and Lesbian Pride Day Parade, I consider what and how it communicates specifically as a Chicago parade and how it uses the means of communication found in other parades in the city. Along with other parades, it indexes a "community," naming it in a particular—in a strategic—way. I examine how indexical, mostly nonspeech elements used by the organizers, marchers, and onlookers at these parades both presuppose and, especially, create "community," "ethnicity," and "culture."

Current trends in ethnographic writing call our attention to the multivocality of all cultures as our experience of cultures at hand forbids the abstract reification typical of much "cultural" and "social constructivist" analysis of exotic "others."[11] In his classic ethnography of a New England town, W. Lloyd Warner characterizes Yankee City's tricentennial procession as "the citizens of Yankee City collectively stat[ing] what they believe themselves to be." Paraphrasing Warner, James Fernandez writes of a kayak festival and parade in Spain that "the citizens of Arriandas and Asturias collectively state what they do not really believe themselves to be and thus leave open what they can become." [12] To develop further these understandings of ways we can understand the meaning of processions, in the annual gay and lesbian parades I find a contested, historically relative field of possible ways of casting "community" in which parade organizers, participants, and on-lookers all take part in arguing about what the "gay community" is or can be or should be.

To interpret some of these overall meanings of the Gay and Lesbian Pride Day Parade, I outline two sets of contrasts: first, the difference in symbolic strategy between Chicago's Pride Day parades in 1979 and in 1987 and, second, the difference between the 1987 Pride parade and other, nongay parades in Chicago, in particular, Chicago's parade par excellence, the St. Patrick's Day Parade. [13]

Chicago's Gay and Lesbian Pride Day Parades

Chicago's Gay and Lesbian Pride Day Parade is one of several held annually on the last Sunday in June across the United States to com-memorate the Stonewall Rebellion—the spontaneous, violent reaction by gay men and lesbians in New York City in 1969 to one of the arbitrary bar raids common at that time. These riots mark the emblem-atic beginning of the contemporary gay and lesbian rights movement, and those who came of age during the 1970s in its wake are sometimes called the "Stonewall generation." The parades have been held every year (with slightly different names in different cities) through the heady years of the birth and maturation of the gay liberation move-ment into the current full realization of the AIDS crisis.

Chicago's Gay and Lesbian Pride Day Parade and rally are planned and coordinated every year by the Pride Week Committee. On the day of the parade, participants assemble during the two hours beforehand along a three-quarter-mile stretch of Halsted Street while parade watchers gather along the parade route. Virtually an event in itself, the lineup takes on a party atmosphere as public address systems on floats and in apartment windows blare dance music and Sousa marches. After the step off, the parade moves south down Broadway, a narrow, two-lane business street, for about a mile. After the parade, a rally in

Lincoln Park features speeches, presentation of awards for best floats and contingents, and music performed by the gay and lesbian choruses and guest performers.

Although attendance has grown substantially in recent years, participants who have seen the huge parades in New York and San Francisco find Chicago's event a small-town affair. The parade proceeds through Newtown—the social, organizational, entertainment, and residential focus of the city's gay scene—not down State Street or North Michigan Avenue, as though New York's and San Francisco's Gay and Lesbian parades were held in the gay neighborhoods there, on Christopher Street in the Village instead of Fifth Avenue or on Castro Street instead of Market Street.

As a gay neighborhood, Newtown had been established as a residential and to a lesser extent as an entertainment area by the early 1970s, but few of the organizations, bars, and businesses that anchor the community today date back to that time. Located along Chicago's north side lakefront, Newtown consists of three or four north-south corridors separated and crosscut by business streets, bounded roughly by Diversey in the south, Irving Park in the north, Sheffield in the west, and Lake Michigan in the east. It encompasses several entertainment strips, including a three-quarter-mile stretch along one of the thoroughfares in which there are fourteen gay bars. Residential properties near the lake and to the south are expensive, and rents are high. The population is largely white, single (gay and straight), and professional. To the north and west, the neighborhood abuts Uptown, whose population is generally poorer and more working class. The demographics of streets and blocks change rapidly as real estate developers rehabilitate old properties, driving less affluent residents of all races and sexual orientations away to less expensive neighborhoods.

Newtown is also the center of the gay community's social and community life, centering on the gay and lesbian community center and on the many gay and lesbian organizations headquartered in the neighborhood that meet in rental space provided by the center or in several small churches (mainline Protestant and one Catholic).

The neighborhood itself has become a complex symbol of the gay community—its place in the city and in the life of Chicago's gay men and lesbians. When I interviewed gay men and lesbians about Newtown, they typically called it the gay "turf" or "territory." They defined the neighborhood in terms both of a space bounded by certain streets and Lake Michigan and of anchors, important places—such as bars, organizations, buildings, etc.—that focus the community's life there.

In my interviewing, I asked what makes Newtown a gay neighborhood. A long-time resident thought for a moment and said, "What makes that neighborhood gay for me is just that gay people live there. The Jewel is gay and the Dominick's is gay and the Treasure Island is gay [large neighborhood supermarkets] because gay people shop there."

More generally, most of the men and women I interviewed (residents of this neighborhood as well as others) see Newtown as a "place to be gay"—not to engage in homosexual acts (in fact, most of the establishments offering easily accessible sexual contacts are elsewhere) but to be safe from abuse, meet with other gay friends, attend meetings of gay organizations, patronize gay-owned businesses, and meet new friends. For most, Newtown is simply the place where they can be with other gays and lesbians: "It is where I feel most comfortable walking down the street. Like I belong. Most of the people I see are just like I am."

In the 1970s, the parade aimed to establish the presence of gay people, to try to overcome invisibility. "We are everywhere!" became one of the movement's most common slogans, and the parade visually emphasizd two of the gay world's most notorious indexes: drag and leather. These two controversial images of male homosexuality—dangerous hypermasculinity and abandonment of manhood altogether—became the two visible and visually aggressive ways for gay men to assert themselves as gay in public, to be not invisible.

In 1979, the color guard was led by three leathermen. Although in the minority, leather and drag and beefcake were everywhere. "We *are* different from you," the parade said. "We have sex with each other. Kinky sex, too." The parade deliberately called attention to the elaborate sexual semiotica of the leather world. Keys, bandanas, and pieces of leather worn by men and also some women—many more than the leather crowd itself at that time—publicly announced and advertised for the kinds of sex acts the wearer sought. Drag queens, female impersonators, and the guerilla theater of "gender fuck" seemed to say, "Yes, we dress up as women, and we're going to rub your noses in it." Less flamboyantly—one could say antiflamboyantly—lesbians refused to "dress up like ladies," as one woman put it. Men displayed the sexual polarity of their stereotypic representations, while women deemphasized presenting themselves with gender-specific expectations at all.

The strategy of the early gay liberation movement was confrontation, its issue visibility, and its means for demonstrating difference drag, leather, and "zaps" (street demonstrations, sit-ins, guerrilla theater, etc.). The Stonewall uprising became a creation myth of the new gay community, of a new way to be gay. Sex *was* the revolution. The private was aggressively identified as public, and the parade celebrated precisely the sexual difference between gay and nongay.

By 1987, the parade exhibited the changed context of a Chicago that had elected its first woman and first black mayors, encouraging all minorities to renew demands for a progressive agenda at city hall. For the third time, the mayor proclaimed the week Gay and Lesbian Pride Week and June 28 the Gay and Lesbian Pride Parade Day in Chicago. In the 1987 parade, there were 126 entries, including bars, social service and community organizations, political organizations, beer distributors, gay and lesbian religious congregations, several aldermen and other local political figures, professional associations, service providers for people with AIDS, sports leagues, student and academic associations, and performing arts organizations. Thirty of the entries—nearly a fourth—were not self-identified as lesbian or gay. Estimates of the parade participants, including spectators, ranged up to eighty thousand.

As in the last several years, the color guard of the 1987 Chicago parade was led by the gay and lesbian social service organization's youth group for gay and lesbian teenagers. While the parade seemed no less celebratory than the earlier ones (although some observers claimed it was more somber), there was much less drag and leather. But, more important, what was being said by the parade and rally had changed. Gay politics has become mainstream, and so have the messages of the parade. Civil rights legislation is advocated so that "we can be just like the rest of you, because we are just like the rest of you." Not zaps but lobbying is the tactic of choice. As AIDS has come to dominate all gay politics, activists argue that AIDS is not a "gay disease"—it affects everyone. The goals are not confrontation but assimilation. Today, the parade aims to establish that "gay"—the community of gay men and lesbians—is *not* simply "homosexuality," sex acts performed by two people of the same sex. It is all the things gay people are and have done. It is the gay and lesbian community itself. Said one participant of the first time she saw the parade, "What I took pride in at the first one was all the gay churches, all the gay organizations and businesses, because I was unaware of it. It was a real enlightening experience for me."

The parade was not less "party" and more "political," but what is being said and what semiotic means are employed have changed. In 1987, the parade specifically challenged the ways homosexuals have been defined as sinners, sick people, and criminals. Gay politics (along with American politics generally since the 1960s) has changed. Confrontation has given way to assimilationist discourse.

Although the official theme of the parade was "Proud, Strong, United," during the lineup, members of a political organization passed out signs that read, simply, "Veto Senate Bill 651 House Bill 2682." The signs were added to every float, contingent, car, and motorcycle. Unlike their usual focus on the flamboyant, the media in Chicago noticed that every entry carried signs urging Illinois's governor James Thompson to veto these bills on his desk that would establish the tracing of sexual contacts for people who are infected with HIV, institute mandatory testing, and allow quarantine of those infected. The *Chicago Tribune* reported the parade as "subdued in comparison to years past. The few drag queens and skimpily clad young men were outnumbered by sedate marchers representing various church groups, singing ensembles and associations somehow connected with AIDS."[14]

Whereas in the 1960s and 1970s sex itself was foregrounded as the revolutionary act (and indeed the gay liberation movement was part of the political and sexual revolution of the 1960s), sex and "gendered" aspects of representing gay man are now "automatized" (left in the background rhetorically).[15] At the rally following the parade in 1987, the crowd responded with thunderous applause as the major speaker called out, "Make our opponents talk about our love, not our sex. Our love is the same as theirs." Presenting the gay community as composed of families, of churches and sports leagues, of clubs and professional associations, of everything about normative society except simply sexual behavior, has become the new strategy. The political agenda as frequently calls for the right to a conventional family life as for sexual freedom. In the era of AIDS, the personal script and collective myth for "coming out" (i.e., "coming out of the closet," telling others that one is gay) is based no longer on the sexual revolution of Stonewall but on a community of individuals and organizations involved in fund-raising for research, taking care of people with AIDS, offering networks of support, and defending the rights of the infected: in short, not on acts of sex but on acts of love.[16] As the politics has become less radical and more assimilationist, participation in the parade has steadily increased.

Parades in Chicago

Chicago's gay and lesbian parade takes place in a city of parades. In the early 1950s, Mayor Richard J. Daley brought the St. Patrick's Day Parade downtown from the Irish neighborhoods and made it a public demonstration of his constituency and his coalition. The Chicago Irish had created the Democratic machine in the early decades of the twentieth century, when they were the abused and despised working and under class of Chicago. Moving the St. Patrick's Day Parade downtown signaled the arrival of Irish influence at City Hall.[17] Under Daley, the Irish, Polish, and other "white ethnics" (as they are now known) ran Chicago's political machine. As black Chicagoans, including Harold Washington, were brought (in a highly qualified role) into the system, they learned the business of city government. Chicago's black leadership used their new-found knowledge to gain power under Washington's leadership.

Neighborhood events—and especially neighborhood events that move downtown—are a correlate to ethnic identity and political maturity in Chicago. The "neighborhood" is the home turf of the "ethnic community" in Chicago's political lexicon. Virtually every neighborhood has a summer street festival of some sort, featuring a parade or procession, entertainment, and food from the local eateries, as an expression of its cultural and neighborhood autonomy, typically celebrating an immigrant identity and "cultural awareness." Having a parade for one's neighborhood, community, or ethnic group is critical for having a political presence in the social consciousness of the city.

The summer calendar for these events is extensive; there are as many as three and four a weekend. The *Chicago Tribune* listed ninety-six festivals and parades for the 1988 season, including a series of "Ethnic Festivals" held at Navy Pier downtown: the Festival Polonaise, the Irish Festival, the Pan American Festival, the Festa Italiana, and the

Rhythm and Blues Festival. Many other festivals in Chicago are modest neighborhood events, organized by and for local merchants as a venue for their food and wares. Others among Chicago's ethnic minorities—which are usually not called "ethnics"—also have fairs and festivals: the Chinatown Moon Festival, the Fiesta Del Sol (Mexican) in Pilsen, and the Bud Billiken Day Parade (African American) on the South Side.

Ward organizations, neighborhood events, and the relation between neighborhoods and downtown are all imbued with the "ethnic algebra" of Chicago politics. Being "ethnic" and having an "ethnic identity" is a critical part of Chicago's political map and idiom. "Ethnic communities" are seen to have interests as such and are expected to demand representation. These parades and festivals have become tightly linked with influence real and perceived: Who comes? Who speaks? Who marches? Harold Washington was the first mayor who spoke at a Gay and Lesbian Pride Day rally. After his appearance, mass media reports for the first time treated the parade as something other than flamboyantly dressed homosexuals having a party in the street. After Washington's death, the articles reporting the 1988 parade in the gay and lesbian newspapers focused on who among the candidates for mayor attended or failed to attend the rally and parade: the acting mayor, Eugene Sawyer, failed to appear for a scheduled speech at the rally, while his archrival, Alderman Tim Evans, alone among the mayoral candidates (all of whom supported passage of the pending "gay rights" ordinance) made a surprise showing, riding in a convertible with a fellow alderman.

St. Patrick's and Others' Days

Chicago's parade par excellence is the St. Patrick's Day Parade. The banner of St. Patrick carried at the front of the parade is the only reminder that this parade has its origin in the feast-day procession of the Irish saint. In 1988, there were approximately 40,000 marchers in the three-hour parade, whose theme was "Saluting Chicago's Outstanding Irish." An official organizer said there were 170 units, 58 floats, and 62 marching units and bands. The national television networks covered the parade. An estimated 450,000 onlookers lined the route down Dearborn Street in Chicago's Loop.[18]

Everything in sight is colored green for the parade. The Chicago River and the Civic Center fountain are dyed green. Faces, hair, and beards are painted green. There are leprechauns, shamrocks, and shillelaghs, traditional Irish music and dance. Participants and onlookers wave Irish flags. Buttons read, "Kiss me, I'm Irish," or ask for a more intimate sexual encounter because the wearer is Irish.

The joke about St. Patrick's Day in Chicago is that everybody is Irish for the day. There are the African Irish and the Polish Irish and the Italian Irish. Participants take an "O'" for a "Mac" to the front of their names. Alderman Roman Pucinski of the Forty-first Ward marched with a stenciled "O'Pucinski" on his green coat. What they really say is that everybody who is involved in city politics is "Irish" on St. Patrick's Day. Chicago's black mayor Eugene "O'Sawyer" and Illinois's Scandinavian governor James "O'Thompson" wore green hats and carried shillelaghs as they marched at the head of the parade in a media crush with the grand marshall and the other important politicians, part of the huge contingent called the "green line," all wearing green sashes reading "Sons of St. Patrick." One of the city's most enduring images is that of Richard J. Daley's smiling, thickly jowled face at the center of the line of politicians, marching shoulder to shoulder and all carrying shillelaghs, at the head of the parade. Said one alderman of the 1988 parade, "It's a lot more fun when you've got an election coming. You see all the candidates maneuvering for the front line. You see some real good pulling and elbowing and kneeing." An immigrant who left Ireland for Chicago twenty-five years ago said that nothing remotely resembling this "silly pageantry" goes on in Ireland: "There, it is a religious holiday. They started a parade in Dublin for all of the Americans in Ireland."[19]

Until twenty years ago, the St. Patrick's Day procession in Dublin was a small event—a true feast-day procession. Then the national tourism bureau took it over and remade the procession on the model of an American parade. Yet without the context of, for example, Chicago's politics, it is curiously empty of rhetorical force, more like the Macy's Thanksgiving Day Parade than Chicago's St. Patrick's.

Most of the floats in a recent Dublin parade (as in the Macy's parade) were corporate advertisements: Coca-Cola, distilleries, breweries, department stores, airlines, a supermarket chain, and a bakery with a crew of singing and dancing bakers. There were no social or political organizations, only one shillelagh in the hands of one leprechaun, few shamrocks, and relatively little kelly green. The one historical or political element enacted in the parade was the invasion of Ireland by Vikings and their expulsion by Brian Boru in 1014 A.D. There were many—more than fifty—high school bands from the United States, Canada, and the United Kingdom, with baton twirlers, drill teams, and cheerleaders. Many more participants performed Irish dances and music in Chicago than in Dublin.

Without its American political context, the parade in Dublin is meaningless, except as public, especially corporate display. "Being Irish" in Dublin is meaningless in the way "being Irish" in Chicago is in its specific Chicago political sense: the Irish who first came over to dig the Illinois-Michigan canal, who came later during the potato famine, rose from the bottom of Chicago class structure to rule the city. Both parades have more to do with being Irish in America than with "Irish culture" in any sense.

As all ethnic and racial minorities in Chicago have grown in size and organizational skill, the two large Hispanic communities—Mexican and Puerto Rican—have gained a place of increasing importance in the city's politics. Their downtown parades reflect this importance. Chicago's 1988 Mexican Independence Day Parade, sponsored the Sociedad Civica Mexicana, was led by the band of Juarez High, the high school in the heavily Mexican neighborhood, Pilsen. Grand Marshal Alderman Jesus Garcia followed with the "line of important people." Mayor Sawyer, waving a Mexican flag, took his place with the other honorary grand marshals. There were 120 contingents, and police estimated that about 250,000 people watched the parade.[20] Countless participants and onlookers waved Mexican flags.

Behind the dignitaries were a mariachi band and the queen of the parade, Teressa I. The queen and her court, runners-up for the title of queen, were decked out in Aztec regalia. At her coronation at the Banquete Azteca before the parade, a dance troupe performed elaborately choreographed Aztec pieces to music said to be Aztec with themes representing the pageantry of Aztec festival occasions. The queen was carried to her coronation on the shoulders of four men in Aztec costumes. She was solemnly crowned with a feathered headdress and a cloak while the men danced around a fire in front of the new queen.

Also at the head of the parade were men dressed in the manner of the character Charro wearing sombreros, twirling lassos, and riding horses. Groups of schoolgirls dressed like Charro's partner China Poblana marched along flouncing their long skirts. In the Illinois State Lottery float, actors dressed to represent the numbers in the lottery number selection process wore sombreros and waved Mexican flags. Coca-Cola sponsored a float full of participants in Aztec costumes.

In the Eighth Puerto Rican Parade, the equestrian police and color guard, carrying the American and Puerto Rican flags, were followed by the "Puerto Rican Parade Committee—Knowing its people." The honorary grand marshals, including such important politicians as Alderman Luis Gutierrez and Mayor Sawyer, wore sashes as in the St. Patrick's Day and the Mexican Independence Day parades.

Chicago's Puerto Rican political leadership marched behind a banner reading, "Pueblo estos son tus representantes . . . *Este es tu poder!*" ("People, these are your representatives . . . This is your power!"). The honorary grand marshals and important politicians, including Puerto Rican aldermen and Mayor Sawyer, marched at the front, and throughout the parade participants and onlookers wore *pavas,* the straw hats of *jivaros* ("hillbillies"), and waved the red, white, and blue Puerto Rican flag. The guest Mexican contingents in the parade were immediately identifiable by their sombreros and Mexican flags. A group of young Japanese-American women from the United Ethnic Neighborhoods Council wore kimonos.

Floats and school bands featured salsa (the popular music innovated by Puerto Ricans in New York and wildly popularized in Puerto Rico, identified by the Spanish-language media commentary as *musica typica Puertorriquenas,* "typical Puerto Rican music"), while cheerleaders and other marchers carried their banners marching with *marengue* steps (the dance originally from the Dominican Republic, now identified by Puerto Ricans as their own).

As Chicago's electorate has become increasingly divided between the traditional machine voter and the black voter, a second parade has emerged as the biggest parade in Cook County, having surpassed even the St. Patrick's Day Parade: the Bud Billiken Day Parade, held every August since 1929 (Bud Billiken is a fictional character from Chinese myth). The most important parade for black Chicagoans and the largest black-sponsored parade in the nation, it draws a crowd ranging from 200,000 to 700,000. In 1988, the 230-unit parade took four hours to make its way down Martin Luther King Drive to Washington Park on Chicago's South Side, making it the second longest parade in the United States after the Rose Bowl Parade.[21] The parade has grown in size and significance in tandem with the ascendency of black politics, culminating in recent years in the election of Harold Washington.

The Bud Billiken Day Parade, in spite of its size and importance, has remained in its original neighborhood, "Bronzeville," the old name for the oldest and for many years the only black neighborhood in the city.[22] In 1989, the parade attracted most of the candidates for state and national office as well as musical and entertainment celebrities. A perceptive reporter noted the significance of person and place in this parade: "Film director Spike Lee walked arm in arm with the Rev. Jesse Jackson, down Martin Luther King Drive, crossing [blues great] Muddy Waters Drive. It was a street-corner convergence of four distinguished black Americans at the 60th annual Bud Billiken Parade, and it symbolized the enormous parade's intent—to celebrate black accomplishment and pride."[23] Bystanders remembered for television reporters that they had come to the parade with their mothers and grandmothers every year since they were children. Floats and high school bands featured the many forms of black American music: blues, rhythm and blues, rap, house, and soul as well as music and choreography owing their spirit to the generation of Cab Calloway. Budweiser sponsored a blues band, and the Illinois State Lottery models were lotto balls in black tie and top hats like dancers in a Cotton Club production number. One contingent featured African clothing, hairstyles, and drumming. Above all, the parade celebrated black empowerment, visible in the frequently displayed portrait of Harold Washington.

Parades and the Indexes of "Community"

Formally, all these parades are similar: they all have mostly self-organized contingents that walk or ride on floats down the street; signs and banners; singing and chanting; participants and watchers wearing distinctive clothing and carrying distinctive flags; musicians or speaker systems playing distinctive music; and so forth. They structure space—whether a neighborhood or the Loop—by moving through it. Community, neighborhood, and influence in City Hall are all demonstrated or sought. Participants aim to establish a relationship to the city—the city built by Richard J. Daley and transformed by the mayorships of Jane Byrne and especially Harold Washington.

The context of all this declaration of community is a Chicago parade, an event of a certain type that employs a predictable pattern of indexing. Focus is placed on "community" indexed by a small number of signs: flags (Irish or Puerto Rican or Rainbow) and colors (green or lavender); music (salsa or traditional Irish or house) and dance (*marengue* or jig or Aztec); hats (*pavas* or sombreros or green fedoras) and "folk costumes" (Charro and China or leather and drag); the *use* of a particular language itself (Spanish or ersatz Gaelic); the location of the parade (Pilsen or Newtown or the Loop); and countless miscellaneous emblems such as the omnipresent shillelaghs and shamrocks or lassos. These indexes are not, of course, linguistic, although formulaic chants, slogans, and shouted words may also serve to index community ("Viva Mexico!" "Run, Jesse, Run!" "Two! four! six! eight! what makes you think your doctor's straight?" (etc.).

The indexes used in any one parade typically are few, often superficial, even trivial as expressions of culture, but highly visible, audible, and (at the festivals) gustatory—easily identifiable in a city full of immigrants. The items that function as indexes are not "symbols" of (do not "mean") Irishness or Africanness. They index (point to, focus attention on) but do not define "being Irish" or "being African" in Chicago. Parades assert identity and position in Chicago, and the indexical items carried, worn, shouted, or played reference particular communities. While the indexes themselves may have other significances and even great emotional force for individuals and within the communities that use them (wearing leather to a leatherman or maintaining the knowledge of traditional music to an Irishman), their use in the context of the parade functions semiotically to reference a "community" different from other "communities." In Mexico, Charro and Poblana represent regional characters, but, in Chicago, they index the Mexican-American community. A *pava* in Puerto Rico may be a hillbilly hat, but in a Chicago parade it indexes the Puerto Rican community. How do you make an Illinois State Lottery float Mexican or African American? Put sombreros or top hats and tails on the actors playing the number balls. How do you make Budweiser beer Irish? Put a green sweater on Spuds McKenzie. The pragmatic strategies of marchers, onlookers, planning committees, marshalls, contingents, advertisers, and other participants display their skill at more or less successfully calling attention to their communities.

To use a parade in Chicago to create community is to use an ethnic model. "Ethnic" parades operate from groups where the features that identified them as a community are today less stigmatized than those associated with the gay community. Chicago's Irish are no longer stereotyped as stupid, lazy, alcoholic, "papist," and so forth. Ethnic parades typically emphasize emblems that index internal homogeneity, dwelling on "folk," "cultural," and "national" elements.

Inexorable changes in Chicago's demography and politics have put shillelaghs in non-Irish hands. The 1989 mayoral contest depended on a candidate winning support outside the two large blocs, the traditional white and black voting blocs. Richard M. Daley won the support of the city's Hispanic population, helping give him the critical majority. At the Puerto Rican Parade after his election, the new Mayor Daley announced on the Spanish-language television station, giving the familiar syntax a paradigmatic twist, "Today everybody is Puerto Rican in Chicago!"

Established political forces, operating benignly from such institutional bases as the Mayor's Office of Special Events, which publishes annual calendars of these events, are in a position to validate and legitimize these "ethnic" definitions, which largely background issues of race, class, and discrimination; "ethnicity" as used in these parades tends to exclude race and class as issues. Tacos and pierogi and soda bread may be equals gastronomically but not politically. When he called on America to refer to its black citizens as African American, Jesse Jackson problematically shifted attention from a racial to an ethnic model of community. Yet virtually all Chicago's "communities" increasingly participate in collective city rituals on these terms. The ethnic model has a rhetorical leveling effect, blurring and hiding race and class in a Wilsonian world of separate, equal "nations." (The struggle of the Bureau of the Census to develop a method of recording Hispanic Americans [Spanish surnamed] as a category of persons exhibits the difficulty in handling the discontinuity in the American cultural construction of race and culture.) Because ethnicity has so little positive content (food, costumes, music, dance, and a vague fifth term often left implicit like a trailing ellipsis), the ambiguities of race and ethnicity are obviated and the potential for the "safe," nonthreatening representation of "identity" and difference maximized.

The Gay and Lesbian Pride Day Parade as a Chicago Parade

Thus far I have written of the indexes of community in Chicago parades as though they were uniform in value and impact. There is, however, a creative quality to the use of pure indexes that, to a greater or lesser degree, can affect the structure of an event, not by changing it, but by making certain aspects of that event more explicit and thereby leaving others in the background. Indeed, in the most creative case, a proposition about the social situation is asserted as true "because of the occurrence of the signal token." The index does not reference already existing socially defined entities; the aim of its use is to transform them, creating "those 'facts' in the very context in which they are uttered."[24] Indexes thus vary from an extreme of presupposition to the opposite extreme of creativity. Herein lies their strategic potential.

In their use of indexes of community, ethnicity, culture, and power, parades presuppose and create relationships with the city, with neighborhoods, with the mayor, and with the City Council. They are part of the communicative activities of the city as a whole, and having a parade at all can create community. The strategy of any particular parade depends on shared understandings of the norms for having parades. The recipients of the messages are both the community itself and the city at large, which witnesses the parade by watching from the sidewalk or by seeing the pictures and stories on television and in the newspapers.

The gay parade creates community precisely to the extent that it has become a Chicago parade on an ethnic model, not a political protest march. In the usual ethnic parades, while the indexes in and of themselves have only trivially to do with a culture, they nevertheless presuppose its existence. Two things distinguish the Gay and Lesbian Pride Day Parade from others in the city. First, the ratio of creative to presupposed indexing in it is higher than it is in the established "ethnic parades": the gay parade operates with an especially high ratio of creative indexing because it is creating community as it goes along. Second, following closely from this high ratio—actually the cause of it—is the controversy over how the community should present itself in the face of stigma.

Wearing a sombrero or carrying a shillelagh is not controversial within the Mexican and Irish communities of Chicago. Except for the limited and self-limiting case of first-generation immigrants, the cultures celebrated in these parades and festivals are largely outside the personal experience of the celebrants. The daily experience of most "ethnics" has little to do with a "culture" of origin (although it may have a great deal to do with class and race, even though there is little to distinguish many ethnicities except for ideology).[25] Even then, the culture evoked is that of a romantic past, not the leveled experience of a common Americanness: public and Catholic schools, the Cubs and the Sox, Madonna and Michael Jackson, "Miami Vice" and "Dynasty," Democratic party politics and fights for City Hall influence. It is not dangerous to emphasize difference if you are not really different.

The sombrero and jig presuppose the Mexican-American and Irish communities, but a gay and lesbian church creates a definition of community in the face of historical prejudice and activist oppression from the church. The parade creates community where none is perceived by society at large to exist. What it is to be gay itself is being argued about—is contested—in the mix of ways and discourse about how the gay community defines itself in a Chicago parade. How the community should "index"—should create—itself is the controversy. Watchers and marchers alike do not agree about—indeed fight about—how to define the community in the parade. The two modalities I describe as assimilationist and confrontationist are both present and unresolved in the parade today. When I interviewed participants about their experiences of and feelings about the parade, they expressed violently opposing attitudes about what the parade should be. Should the parade rid itself of drag and leather in order to hide stigmatizing stereotypes? Should it emphasize assimilationist goals and means, such as using the Gay and Lesbian Rainbow Flag, the color lavender, and contingents of community organizations? How should the community present itself in front of television cameras?

Some parade participants report angry arguments in meetings of gay organizations over whether the club should march in the parade. Members said they felt embarrassed, even humiliated by what they saw.[26] Another emphatically rejected the need to "cater to straight people at all," as he put it: "I love our silliness. Being gay is fun. The humor in our movement is important. It's joyous, it's fabulous. We're forced to look at ourselves in a way they'll never understand. We're sensitive to who we are, to what our strengths are." More typically, when I asked in interviews how people respond to the parade's flamboyant side, most defended drag and leather in the parade but wanted to temper its presentation: "It's always seemed a party to me. How do we *present* ourselves to the public? We have an obligation to present all kinds of our people to the world and in a constructive way. Stonewall wouldn't have happened without drag queens. There should be drag queens and leather people on that street, but I've seen people on that street who don't present drag and leather in productive ways. I think it depends on what people want to accomplish with the parade. If you want to make it a political statement, I don't think there's a place for drag and leather. If it's just to have fun, be yourself, then fine."

In interviews and conversation, gay men and women frequently speak of the gay community as "my people" and "my family." Whether or not it is appropriate to use the notion of ethnicity here as it is used in social science, the notion is well established in Chicago—a critical native category and a critical concept in Chicago's political culture. The Pride Day Parade has thus found its place not as a citywide statement for gay and lesbian Chicagoans but as one more of Chicago's neighborhood celebrations. It is held in the gay neighborhood, not downtown—the neighborhood itself an index, as Humboldt Park, Pilsen, and Bridgeport index the Puerto Rican, Mexican, and Irish communities, respectively. Political debate in the gay community reflects the ambiguity of achieving this status. Is this desired normality or simply a trivialization of the purpose of the event? Is it a parade or a march? Is it a party or politics? Is this for ourselves or for others?

The very notion of a "gay and lesbian" community (or a gay and lesbian "community") is surprising to, even contested by many outside it, as well as by some within. In the view of the hegemonic culture, the homosexual (the pervert, the sodomite, the arrested personality, the "fag," the "dyke") is an *individual* to be cured, prosecuted, or saved—not a *social person*—in the constructed views of Western medicine, law, and religion. For the fag-bashing street-gang member, the homosexual is a subhuman deserving beating, a legitimate victim. Because gay people have been denied the institutions and routines of ordinary life, they self-consciously create a community built on these emblems of ordinary, normative American life.

In most of the downtown and neighborhood parades and festivals that have a single or multiethnic focus, people wear costumes they wear at no other time, perform ethnic music otherwise played only at weddings, and eat food that no one eats everyday. The festivals of the "white ethnics"—especially the Irish, Polish, and Italians—establish difference where sameness among them is perceived. The parades create a system of difference using emblems of the (mostly European) origins of white Americans, items used rarely except on occasions such as these, to assert dissimilarity where very little exists. If one is an Italian or Irish or German American, the difference implied by a parade is safe. Parades in Chicago provide a context in which an ethnicity is contrasted with other ethnicities, not tied to the country of origin of the participants; Dublin's St. Patrick's Day Parade is modeled on Chicago's, not the other way around. The indexes function to establish an unreal cultural difference, often concealing the underlying, actual, political one.[27]

In the gay parade, everyday sameness is asserted where difference is perceived: we are Methodists and lawyers and doctors and athletes and sing in choruses and bowl in sports leagues. It is, as journalist Richard Goldstein put it, a "ritual of normalcy," as though the normal is exotic here, what outsiders do not expect.[28] The long-standing chair of Illinois's leading gay and lesbian rights advocacy organization said much the same thing to a suburban newspaper reporter when he said that the "gay rights movement is a movement towards banality." Here everyday life of everyday Americans, not ethnic particularity, goes on parade. The presence of the congregation from St. Patrick's Catholic Church in the context of the St. Patrick's Day Parade presupposes the relationship between Irish-Americans and the Catholic church. By contrast, the presence of Dignity, the gay Catholic congregation, in the context of the gay parade foregrounds the problematic relationship between gay people and the Catholic church and contributes in part to the creation of a definition of gay community as its context.

Unlike its predecessors of ten years ago, the gay and lesbian parade today uses a society-wide system of heterogeneity in religion, politics, sports teams, musical organizations, and other interests to claim an essential similarity. It says to Chicago, "We as gay people are fundamentally different among ourselves and that's why—and how—we're just like you." It is a victory for those who see the cost to group identity of letting stigmatizing stereotypes be seen as too high.

As responses to the situation of homophobia, the confrontationist strategy of gay men in the 1970s foregrounded gendered representations of homosexuality, while lesbians challenged conventional gendered representation of themselves as women, in both cases inverting the cultural prescription that women adorn themselves as women and men refrain from exhibiting their gender. In 1987, the assimilationist strategy left these gendered representations in the background: gay men as males different from other men or as persons different from lesbians. The roles and institutions both in AIDS work and in conventional associational life are not similarly gendered.

AIDS has profoundly affected nearly everything in the gay community, and the parade—including the discourse about the way the community should present itself—is no exception. AIDS has unquestionably shifted the emphasis from foregrounding sex as the distinctive feature of being gay to foregrounding everything else about being gay—which is to say, the things that gay people share with everyone else. The particular political focus of the 1987 parade emphasized the civil rights issues facing gay people, and men with no previous interest or involvement in politics at all, now faced with the threat of mandatory testing, contact tracing, and a recently passed law allowing doctors to test patients for HIV infection without the patient's knowledge or permission, are participating in the many organizations and services that have sprung up to raise funds, lobby politicians, and care for people with AIDS. These AIDS-related laws have shifted the issue from gay liberation's establishing visibility to losing control over visibility.

Postscript

I am revising this paper on the twentieth anniversary of the Stonewall Rebellion. Since I first wrote this analysis, there has been a marked increase in activism nationally, including civil disobedience and demonstrations courting arrest at the Supreme Court in Washington, D.C., and near Chicago at a pharmaceutical firm that manufactures a drug used in the treatment of AIDS. The zap has been reborn. The AIDS Coalition to Unleash Power (Act Up), a national network of street activists involved with AIDS issues, regularly organizes demonstrations on a variety of issues. Outrageous camp humor also returned to the Chicago parade in 1988 with a visit from San Francisco of the Sisters of Perpetual Indulgence, a group of self-styled "gay male nuns" whose wild antics and costumes satirize the norms of America's moral order. For the first time in many years, a leather bar had a large contingent in the 1988 parade, displaying men in leather and the message "Leather Sex [is] the Original Safe Sex."

Yet, even in its activism, today's strategy is not that of the 1970s. Act Up's "favorite form of legal public disruption" at its zaps is a same-sex "kiss-in." [29] As in the speeches at recent Chicago Pride Day rallies, it is not "homosexual acts"—not sex—but romantic love in the vehicle of kissing, the purest icon of love in our literary and cinematic culture, that becomes the symbolic strategy.

The 1989 parade took as its theme "Stonewall 20—a Generation of Pride" amid the increase of both social acceptance and homophobic violence, legislative gains in civil rights, and established Reaganism in the nation's courts. In December 1988, Chicago's City Council had passed a highly controversial amendment (first introduced in another form in 1973) to the city's human rights ordinance that prohibits discrimination in housing, employment, education, and accommodations based on sexual orientation as well as race, sex, age, religion, and other categories of persons. Greeted with wildly enthusiastic cheers, newly elected mayor Richard M. Daley rode at the front in a turquoise vintage Thunderbird convertible—the first Chicago mayor ever to ride in the parade. Halfway through the parade, Daley got out of his car and walked the remaining distance, flanked by gay and nongay political leaders, as the mayor leads every important political parade in the "line of important people." Daley, who is facing a reelection battle in 1991, announced to reporters that "it is important for me to take part in this parade to show my support of the gay community, which I believe has contributed to a better quality of life in this city. I represent all the people and that even means the gays." [30] Close behind, Sheriff James O'Grady's parade unit—including a color guard, equestrian police, and a marching drill team—astounded onlookers old enough to remember the notorious bar raids known as "fruit patrols" carried out by the police department during the elder Daley's tenure. The parade committee's chair appeared on the evening news announcing that Chicago now knows the gay and lesbian community is one to be reckoned with like "all the other communities in the city." Nearly every contingent and countless onlookers in the crowd of ninety thousand waved the rainbow flag. The leather bar's float resembled the other bar floats in every respect but the participants' clothing. An extravagant bar float visually quoted by each of the local television news reports to show the flamboyant side of the parade featured men in bikinis who nevertheless appeared no more flamboyant than a floor show production number on television.

Yet, in spite of the apparent respectability of the "community on parade," euphoria over the gay rights ordinance, and attention by an incumbent mayor in need of voter commitment, a community-based political agenda is unfinished business for gays and lesbians. AIDS has unleashed unprecedented public hostility toward gay men, and new studies reveal high levels of hate-inspired violence directed at lesbians and gay men. I have watched and listened to utter exasperation and outright anger expressed between radical or progressive and conservative Republican gay men, between lesbian feminists and working-class "gay women," between gay activists for low-income housing for the poor and gay developers. Conflict in strategy—indeed, in the presentation of self through presentation of everyday, ordinary diversity— would seem to undermine a goal of one community at all.

It is precisely because so little is settled about who and what gay and lesbian people are—as people, as citizens, as congregants, etc.—and so much is contested that such wide-ranging creative communicative behavior is possible in an event such as a parade. In the past few years, a controversy has arisen over the admissibility of nongay men on teams in the gay sports leagues. If being gay no longer primarily means being a "homosexual" person, then what does it mean to speak of a gay team, or gay league, or a gay national championship? Other than in tautological terms, what is a gay community?

Even among activists, what to make of the notion of "gay community" provokes controversial, extreme positions, from putting the word "gay" in quotes as a naive, "insidious" misnomer and dismissing the "misty-eyed myths about community" among persons who share "nothing but the repression of same-sex sex and same-sex love"[31] to crediting the "miracle" of community building during the past twenty years for making life with "integrity" in a "rational world" possible.[32] Far more important than the opinions of leaders such as these, however, is the experience of the generation of young gays and lesbians who have just come of age and who take the existence of a community of gay and lesbian people and organizations for granted as critical to their adult lives, unlike the fear expressed by their elders, who often view the community as fragile, divided, and threatened.[33]

The difference between the gay and other American "subcultural" communities is that, for gays and lesbians, the experience of community derives, not from parents and peers during childhood, but from adult participation in a network of institutions and from shared responses to the pervasive denial of social personality itself. In the face of that denial, building (certainly not simply asserting) community is political activity, however insufficient it may be in and of itself to bring about the ends of a radical gay agenda.

Until American society at large accepts homosexuals as part of itself, the Gay and Lesbian Pride Day Parade will exhibit the community's own unsettled and conflicting social definitions and the struggle of gays and lesbians to find a place of equality in the polity and respect in the society. What—if any—community will ultimately emerge remains equally unsettled.

Notes

I owe a special debt to Bonnie Urciuoli for her careful reading of an early draft of this chapter and her thoughtful suggestions. In discussions about the theoretical issues raised here, Gloria Goodwin helped me clarify my arguments about strategy and index-icality in parades. I also want to thank Gilbert Herdt and Andrew Boxer for their helpful comments on earlier versions of this material and James C. Darby, whose passion for videotaping the life of Chicago made an invaluable contribution to this analysis.

1. *Chicago,* June 1988, p. 38.
2. Kenneth Burke, *The Philosophy of Literary Form* (Baton Rouge: Louisiana State University Press, 1941), pp. 1–3, 39.
3. These two sides of the popular representations of gay men are captured in two controversial films, both directed by William Friedken: *The Boys in the Band* (1970), which portrays gay men as pathetic, silly, and weak, and *Cruising* (1980), in which they are homocidal and sex obsessed.
4. Michael Silverstein, "Shifters, Linguistic Categories, and Cultural Description," in *Meaning in Anthropology,* ed. Keith H. Basso and Henry A. Selby (Albuquerque: University of New Mexico Press, 1976), p. 54.
5. On the concept of indexing in linguistic and anthropological analysis, see Michael Silverstein, "Cultural Prerequisites to Grammatical Analysis," in *Linguistics and Anthropology,* ed. Muriel Sevilla-Troike (Washington, D.C.: Georgetown University Press, 1977), pp. 139–51, "The Three Faces of 'Function': Preliminaries to a Psychology of Language," in *Social and Functional Approaches to Language and Thought,* ed. Maya Hickman (Orlando, Fla.: Academic, 1987), and "Shifters, Linguistic Categories, and Cultural Description."
6. Charles Sanders Pierce, *Philosophical Writings of Pierce,* ed. Justus Buchler (New York: Dover, 1955), p. 108; Silverstein, "Three Faces of 'Function,'" p. 32.
7. Silverstein, "Shifters, Linguistic Categories, and Cultural Description," p. 29.
8. For a typical example of these representations, see the souvenir book from Asian Fest 1989, Chicago, produced by Asian Festival Inc.
9. *Chicago Sun-Times,* 11 October 1988, p. 5.
10. The souvenir book from Asian Fest 1989, Chicago.
11. See esp. James Clifford and George E. Marcus, eds., *Writing Culture* (Berkeley and Los Angeles: University of California Press, 1986); George E. Marcus and

Michael M. J. Fischer, *Anthropology as Cultural Critique* (Chicago: University of Chicago Press, 1986); and Renato Rosaldo, *Culture and Truth: The Remaking of Social Analysis* (Boston: Beacon, 1989).

12. W. Lloyd Warner, *The Family of God* (New Haven, Conn.: Yale University Press, 1961), p. 89. James W. Fernandez, "Convivial (and Ironic) Attitudes: A Northern Spanish Kayak Festival in Its Historical Moment," in *Persuasions and Performances: The Play of Tropes in Culture* (Bloomington: Indiana University Press, 1986), p. 265.

13. For my analysis, I have relied on personal photographs, observation, press reports, and videotapes of the parades and interviews with participants in the parades and onlookers.

14. *Chicago Tribune,* 29 June 1987, sec. 2, p. 3.

15. I intend my use of "foregrounding" and "automatization" to be consistent with Havránek: "By *automatization* we thus mean such a use of the devices of the language, in isolation or in combination with each other, as is usual for a certain expressive purpose, that is, such a use that the expression itself does not attract any attention, the communication occurs, and is received, as conventional in linguistic form, and is to be 'understood' by virtue of the linguistic system, without first being supplemented, in the concrete utterance, by additional understanding derived from the situation and the context. . . . We can speak of automatization only in those cases where the speaker's intent does not fail to obtain the desired effect, where the link between intent and effect is not broken, unless there is a change in the environment to which the utterance was addressed. . . . By *foregrounding,* on the other hand, we mean the use of the devices of the language in such a way that this use itself attracts attention and is perceived as uncommon, as deprived of automatization, as deautomatized, such as a live poetic metaphor" (see Bohuslav Havránek, "The Functional Differentiation of the Standard Language," in *A Prague School Reader on Esthetics, Literary Structure, and Style,* selected and translated from the original Czech by Paul L. Garvin [Washington, D.C.: Washington Linguistic Club, 1955], pp. 9–12).

16. Martin Levine makes much the same point about change in the nature of friendships among New York "clones" during the era of AIDS (see chapter 2).

17. On the history of the Irish in Chicago, see Lawrence McCaffrey, ed., *The Irish in Chicago* (Urbana: University of Illinois Press, 1987).

18. *Chicago Sun-Times,* 18 March 1988, p. 14.

19. Ibid., pp. 5, 14.

20. *Chicago Sun-Times,* 18 September 1988, p. 9.

21. *Chicago Tribune,* 12 August 1988, sec. 4, p. 24.

22. On the importance of the Bronzeville neighborhood in the history of African Americans in Chicago and in the solidification of the Democratic machine, see Roger Biles, "Big Red in Bronzeville: Mayor Kelly Reels in the Black Vote," *Chicago History* 10, no. 2 (1981): 99–111.

23. *Chicago Sun-Times,* 13 August 1989, p. 4.

24. Silverstein, "Cultural Prerequisites to Grammatical Analysis," pp. 142–43.

25. On the greater importance of class than culture in understanding ethnicity in the United States, see David M. Schneider and Raymond T. Smith, *Class Differences and Sex Roles in American Kinship and Family Structure* (Englewood Cliffs, N.J.: Prentice-Hall, 1973).

26. The controversy over the gains and costs of the parade rages on. Kirk and Madsen renewed their embarrassment over the presentation of community in the parade and their belief in the damage it causes. Although it is ten years after such sentiments were commonly expressed, their book and its reception are testimony to the heat these issues still raise. See Marshall Kirk and Madsen Hunter, *After the Ball: How America Will Conquer Its Fear and Hatred of Gays in the '90's* (New York: Doubleday, 1989).

27. I also do not want to argue that ethnic identities are fixed and unchanging after a period of adaptation in the United States. Recent research documents the rich and subtle ways in which the representations of ethnicity are constantly and variably negotiated and renegotiated. (See esp. Michael M. J. Fischer, "Ethnicity and the Post-modern Arts of Memory," in Clifford and Marcus, eds., *Writing Culture*, pp. 194–233; and Renato Rosaldo, "Changing Chicano Narratives," in *Culture and Truth*, pp. 147–67. See also the remarkable essay on the complexities of representation among Italian Americans in response to the *Godfather* movies by Barbara Grizzuti Harrison, "*Godfather II:* OF Families AND Families," in *Off Center* [New York: Playboy Paperbacks, 1981], pp. 138–44.) Nevertheless, the context of participation in "ethnic parades" places all Chicago communities in regular, predictable relationships of difference brought out only on special days.

28. Quoted in "The Talk of the Town," *New Yorker*, 13 July 1987, pp. 17–18. This remarkable commentary suggests that New York's parade may be much like Chicago's in its creation of community through the parade.

29. Act Up responds to writer and activist Darrell Yates Rist's "The Deadly Costs of an Obsession" (*Nation*, 13 February 1989, pp. 195–200, reprinted in *Christopher Street*, no. 132 [1989]: 16).

30. *Chicago Sun-Times*, 26 June 1989, p. 3.

31. Yates Rist's "The Deadly Costs of an Obsession" unleashed a furious controversy over the place of AIDS on the gay agenda, the notion of the homosexual person, and the reality of the community itself. I address here only his conclusions about the gay community, not his discussion of AIDS: "We 'gays' share nothing but the amorphous consequences of the repression of same-sex sex and same-sex love; . . . a discrete homosexual 'nature' is an insidious political fantasy; . . . what presents itself as 'gay sensibility' is really no more than a series of baroque turns on the history of urban manners, which 'gays' outside New York and San Francisco find as provincial and effete as the greater part of the 'non-gay' population does. The right response to the culture's tyranny over sexual and romantic expression is defiant politics, not misty-eyed myths about community" (Darrell Yates Rist, reply to responses, *Christopher Street*, no. 132 [1989]: 20).

Among the many respondents was Gore Vidal: "Hence, gay ghettoes, gay sensibility (what in God's name do Eleanor Roosevelt and Roy Cohn have in common?) and gay life-style as promoted by those cynical hustlers at the *Advocate* in the 1970s and early 1980s" (ibid., p. 14).

While Vidal questions the *sense* of "gay community," Yates Rist questions its reality, or even possible reality. One need not posit a homosexual "nature" to understand the sources and *social* (non-"mythical") reality of the gay community, any more than the idea of Irish community or Mexican community in Chicago, which contain within themselves the same range of "natures" as does the total gay population, posits a discrete Irish or Mexican "nature." Yates Rist simply attributes a romanticized (mythical in the folk American sense) substance to other communities, which he then finds absent among gay people. Yates Rist (like Vidal) justifiably dismisses the weak underpinnings of essentialist conceptions of homosexuality, but he also dismisses the social constructionists' position while offering no epistemological alternative for understanding anything about homosexual persons at all.

32. "In terms of homophobia in the larger society, I don't think much has changed [in the twenty years since Stonewall]. But the gay liberation movement has meant that I can have integrity, that I'm not hiding anything. I can live in a rational world. Before Stonewall, we were mostly isolated individuals. Since then, a community has developed—gay churches, gay choruses, gay athletic events. All that had started before AIDS, but dealing with AIDS—having to educate ourselves about it, raise money for treatment, set up buddy programs, and care for the sick and dying—that has solidified it. We did a very fast job of growing up. That has been the miracle of the past twenty years" (Al Wardell, board member for ten years and cochair for six years of the Illinois Gay and Lesbian Task Force, quoted in the *Chicago Tribune,* 26 June 1989, sec. 5, p. 2).

33. Teenagers were interviewed in the context of the Horizons youth project (see chapter 1).

Contributors

ANDREW BOXER is director of the Center for Adolescent Research at Humana/Michael Reese Hospital and Medical Center, Chicago. He is also assistant professor of psychology in psychiatry at the University of Illinois, Chicago. And he is the author of over twenty articles, including "The Life Course of Gay and Lesbian Youth: An Immodest Proposal for the Study of Lives" in *Gay and Lesbian Youth,* ed. G. Herdt, 1989.

JOSEPH CARRIER received his Ph.D. in social sciences at the University of California, Irvine. His research on the sexual behavior of Mexican and Mexican-American men in northwestern Mexico and southern California has been ongoing since 1969. He is currently a consultant to the AIDS Community Education Project, Orange County (Calif.) Health Care Agency.

E. MICHAEL GORMAN is a social anthropologist and an epidemiologist who has long-term interests in gay identity and community, health and behavior, social epidemiology, and health policy. The primary focus of his work since 1982 has been the HIV epidemic. He has worked at the U.S. Centers for Disease Control, Atlanta, and the Health Sciences Program of the Rand Corporation, Santa Monica, California; he is currently program director of the California HIV Planning Project at the Western Consortium for Public Health, Berkeley. He also holds an appointment as lecturer in the School of Public Health, University of California, Berkeley.

GILBERT HERDT was educated at the University of Washington and the Australian National University, from which he received his Ph.D.

253

in 1978 for the study of initiation rites and masculinity among the Sambia of Papua New Guinea. He is currently chairman of the Committee on Human Development and professor of human development and psychology and in the College at the University of Chicago. His interests center on the study of culture, sexuality, and gender, as reflected in his *Guardians of the Flutes* (1981), *The Sambia: Ritual and Gender in New Guinea* (1987), and (with Robert J. Stoller) *Intimate Communications: Erotics and the Study of Culture* (1990), as well as many edited collections, including *Rituals of Manhood* (1982), *Ritualized Homosexuality in Melanesia* (1984), and *Gay and Lesbian Youth* (1989). He is currently completing a book that examines the culture and development of gay and lesbian youths in Chicago.

RICHARD K. HERRELL received his B.A. in political science from Pomona College and M.A. in anthropology from the University of Chicago. He has conducted research on domestic ritual and occupational culture in Western India and on the gay and lesbian community of Chicago. He is currently completing his dissertation and working for a private research company.

MARTIN P. LEVINE is associate professor of sociology at Florida Atlantic University and a research associate at Memorial Sloan Kettering Cancer Center. He helped found and led both the Sociologists AIDS Network and the Lesbian and Gay Caucus and was an adviser to the Presidential Commission on the Human Immunodeficiency Virus Epidemic and the National Academic of Sciences' Panel on Monitoring the Social Impact of the AIDS Epidemic. He edited the anthology *Gay Men: The Sociology of Male Homosexuality* (1979) and has published widely on the sociology of AIDS, sexuality, and homosexuality. In addition, he volunteered at the Body Positive of New York and Gay Men's Health Crisis.

FREDERICK R. LYNCH received his Ph.D. in 1982 from the University of California, Los Angeles. He is assistant professor of sociology at California State University, Los Angeles.

STEPHEN O. MURRAY received his Ph.D. in 1979 from the University of Toronto. He is the author of thirty articles and four books, including *Sociological Theory, Homosexual Realities,* and *Sexual Diversity and Homosexualities* (in press).

JOHN L. PETERSON is an assistant research psychologist in the Department of Medicine at the University of California, San Francisco, and at the Center for AIDS Prevention Studies. His recent major publications include chapters in *Bisexuality and HIV/AIDS* and *Preventing AIDS in Drug Users and Their Sexual Partners* and articles in the *American Psychologist* and the *Journal of Drug Issues*.